WORLD DIRECTORS

Film re___ __ __ ___ capacity to beguile, entertain and open up windows onto other cu_____ __ __ other medium. Nurtured by the growth of film festivals worldwi___ __ __ _____ _____ from all continents, a new generation of directors has eme___ __ __ environment over the last few decades.

This new ___ __ _____ o present and discuss the work of the leading directors fro__ __ _____ world on whom little has been written and whose exciting work __ __ _____ ussion in an increasingly globalised film culture. Many of these __ __ have proved to be ambassadors for their national film cultures as __ ____ _ties of the societies they represent, dramatising in their work ___ __ _____ __ s of art that are both national and international, of local relevance __ __ _____ sal appeal.

Written by ____ __ _____ 'm critics and scholars, each book contains an analysis of the _____ __ orks, filmography, bibliography and illustrations. The series w___ _____ ___ lm-makers from all continents (including North America), asses_ing __ _ impact on the art form and their contribution to film culture.

Other Titles in the Series

BAZ LUHRMANN

Pam Cook

A BFI book published by Palgrave Macmillan

First published in 2010 by
PALGRAVE MACMILLAN

on behalf of the

BRITISH FILM INSTITUTE
21 Stephen Street, London W1T 1LN
www.bfi.org.uk

There's more to discover about film and television through the BFI. Our world-renowned archive, cinemas, festivals, films, publications and learning resources are here to inspire you.

Palgrave Macmillan in the UK is an imprint of Macmillan Publishers Limited, registered in England, company number 785998, of Houndmills, Basingstoke, Hampshire RG21 6XS. Palgrave Macmillan in the US is a division of St Martin's Press LLC, 175 Fifth Avenue, New York, NY 10010. Palgrave Macmillan is the global academic imprint of the above companies and has companies and representatives throughout the world. Palgrave® and Macmillan® are registered trademarks in the United States, the United Kingdom, Europe and other countries.

Cover image: *Australia* (Baz Luhrmann, 2008), © Twentieth Century-Fox Film Corporation/Dune Entertainment III LLC/TCF Hungary Film Rights Exploitation Ltd
Images from *Australia*, © Twentieth Century-Fox Film Corporation/Dune Entertainment III LLC/TCF Hungary Film Rights Exploitation Ltd; *Moulin Rouge!*, © Twentieth Century-Fox Film Corporation; *Strictly Ballroom*, M&A Film Corporation/Australian Film Finance Corporation; *William Shakespeare's Romeo + Juliet*, Twentieth Century-Fox Film Corporation; *No. 5 The Film*, Revolver Film/Bazmark.

Printed in China

This book is printed on paper suitable for recycling and made from fully managed and sustained forest sources. Logging, pulping and manufacturing processes are expected to conform to the environmental regulations of the country of origin.

British Library Cataloguing-in-Publication Data
A catalogue record for this book is available from the British Library

ISBN 978-1-84457-158-1 (pbk)
ISBN 978-1-84457-157-4 (hbk)

CONTENTS

ACKNOWLEDGMENTS

First and foremost, warm thanks to Baz Luhrmann and Catherine Martin, who took the time in June 2005 to give me in-depth interviews at the House of Iona, Sydney, just as baby William Alexander appeared on the scene. Everyone at Bazmark was very helpful, especially Amanda Luhrmann and Schuyler Weiss, who ensured that everything went smoothly, and Alex McClements, who introduced me to the Luhrmann personal archive. Many Australian friends and colleagues helped to bring this book to fruition: Mark Nicholls, who arranged my first visit to the University of Melbourne on an International Scholar award in April–June 2005 and provided generous hospitality; the students and staff there who welcomed me; Barbara Creed and Jeanette Hoorn, who organised my second trip to the University of Melbourne in November 2006 on a Macgeorge fellowship and took very good care of me; Wendy Haslem and Angela Ndalianis, who gave me advice on Australian cinema and many other matters; Adrian Danks, Con Verevis, Deb Verhoeven and Deane Williams, the organisers of the 2006 Film and History Association of Australia and New Zealand conference at RMIT, Melbourne, who invited me to deliver a plenary paper on Baz Luhrmann; and Deb Verhoeven, Alexander Gionfriddo and Sarah Sanderson at the AFI Research Collection in Melbourne, who were exceptionally helpful in guiding me through this invaluable resource and its extensive materials on Australian cinema.

I'm also indebted to the following people: Rob White; Sophia Contento and Rebecca Barden at BFI Publishing/Palgrave; Janet Hawken; and colleagues in Film at the University of Southampton, especially Tim Bergfelder and Sally Keenan. My research benefited from funding from the University of Melbourne, the University of Southampton and the Arts and Humanities Research Council (www.ahrc.ac.uk), who granted me a Research Leave award in 2005. Thanks to all those who offered me their thoughts about Baz Luhrmann; to Mark Nicholls, who shared his expertise on Italian cinema and other subjects; Brian and Gerie McFarlane, who contributed more than they know; Wendy Haslem, who helped me to clarify some important issues; Faye Ginsburg and colleagues at the Cinema at the Periphery conference held at the University of St Andrews in June 2006. Very special thanks go to those loved ones whose day-to-day support carried me through the research and writing process: Sam Cook, Greg Ward and Sylvia Paskin. This was a rewarding project that changed my life in some respects, not least in introducing me to a vibrant Australian film culture and the people who contribute to and sustain it. I have many happy memories of time well spent in Melbourne and Sydney, the Great Ocean Road and two puppies called Fred and Ginger.

INTRODUCTION

Baz Luhrmann's fourth feature, the epic historical drama *Australia*, opened in November 2008 in Australia and the USA, and on 26 December the same year in the UK. Its release was highly anticipated; it had been seven years since Luhrmann's last film *Moulin Rouge!*, and *Australia* had been touted by its makers as a departure from the studio aesthetic of the celebrated Red Curtain Trilogy (*Strictly Ballroom*, 1992; *William Shakespeare's Romeo + Juliet*, 1996; and *Moulin Rouge!*, 2001). Luhrmann had intended to kick off a new cycle of historical epics with the story of Alexander the Great, starring Leonardo DiCaprio and Nicole Kidman; preparations were well under way,[1] until Oliver Stone's *Alexander* opened in 2004 to lacklustre reviews and poor box office. The Australian project was moved to the top of the list, which at that stage included a European-themed subject as well as the Alexander the Great biopic.[2] Luhrmann is known for his perfectionism, and for the length of time his projects take to complete. *Australia*, his most ambitious and expensive venture yet, was no exception.[3] In its final stages, the film's backers, 20th Century-Fox, delayed the planned release date amid media reports that Luhrmann was still editing the movie and would deliver it to the studio one reel at a time.[4] There were also rumours that Luhrmann was under pressure from Fox to change the tragic ending after negative responses at preview screenings – a story that Luhrmann strenuously denied, asserting that he was in total control of the film.[5] The hype surrounding *Australia* was characteristic of *Romeo + Juliet* and *Moulin Rouge!* too. The production of both was accompanied by press stories of dramas and difficulties dogging the shoot, and their release provoked an extraordinary amount of excitement and conflicting reactions from critics. Those films and *Australia* were high-profile events attracting an unusual level of media attention.[6]

One of the interesting aspects of Luhrmann's work is its relationship to the event movies that have become a significant feature of contemporary

Hollywood and of global media production generally. His films do not exactly fit the high-concept blockbuster category described by Justin Wyatt and others,[7] though they have elements of such phenomena. For example, they rely on honed-down classical storytelling and simplified characters; they rework the boundaries of genre; they emphasise image and music; they abound with knowing references to other movies and media; they are design-led, tying in their distinctive visual and aural style to channels of communication spanning television, video games, DVD, CDs, the press, publishing and the Internet; and they feature big-name stars and spectacular display — all of which is geared to maximising box-office returns and ancillary revenues. High-concept movies are often contrasted with more modestly budgeted independent productions with 'serious' intent, which are perceived as possessing depth in contrast to the 'surface' aesthetic of the high-concept blockbuster. However, with the emergence of the major independents, or 'mini-majors', in Hollywood during the 1990s,[8] the increase in the DVD market and the rise of multiplex cinemas showing both mainstream and art movies, to some extent the distinction between independent and blockbuster production has become blurred, along with their supposed aesthetic differences. The science-fiction franchise the *Matrix* trilogy (1999–2003), with its high production values, innovative visual effects and foundations in philosophy and mythology, is a case in point. The trilogy's reliance on surface style was also one of its thematic strands, and its intellectual pretensions were the subject of academic treatises.

Another feature of contemporary event movies is the slipperiness of their national origins. Luhrmann's last three films, because of their relatively big budgets and the fact that he has a first-look agreement with 20th Century-Fox, are often regarded as Hollywood productions; only *Strictly Ballroom* is defined and perceived as Australian. Such instability of national identity is compounded in Luhrmann's case by the fact that, on an aesthetic level, all his films conjure up their settings as imaginary dreamscapes that transcend time and place. As Wyatt points out,[9] in the fluid context of what is called New Hollywood (although through successive waves of globalisation 'Hollywood' as a centre hardly exists any more), many different industrial structures and working practices prevail. In the context of the

Australian film industry, Luhrmann's production set-up is unusual, if not unique. Bazmark Inq., the company set up in 1997 by Luhrmann with his wife and chief collaborator, designer Catherine Martin, is an independent production company primarily based in the Sydney house where Luhrmann, Martin and their children also live. Bazmark's agreement with 20th Century-Fox dates from around 1993 and has gone through many transformations in the intervening years. This arrangement, which has become increasingly complex, allows Bazmark, among other things, to use the Fox Studio Australia facilities in Sydney while retaining a high degree of creative and operational autonomy. The fact that the deal has lasted so long suggests that it is mutually beneficial, despite occasional differences between the partners. However, to some observers, the contract with a major Hollywood studio inevitably has negative impact on the nature of Luhrmann's output.

Luhrmann's association with Fox is one of the ways in which his work crosses cultural boundaries. Indeed, crossing boundaries is a major creative preoccupation and provides the basic structure for all his films to date. It also defines his career, which spans theatre, opera, fashion and music production as well as film-making. There is something of the *agent provocateur* in Luhrmann's approach to his artistic endeavours, and he has said many times that his primary aim is to engage audiences by creating something unexpected from the familiar. In this respect he is a modernist who identifies with 'the shock of the new'. In so far as he recognises that the new is crafted from what already exists, he could be called a postmodernist (a label that has been applied to his films), but his work tends to escape categorisation, with the result that critics find it difficult to place. Luhrmann uses classical story construction, in which the outcome is often already known. The shocking and the new lie in the way the story is told, in broad strokes using cartoon-like imagery, clashing genre conventions and a histrionic acting style that do not chime with cinematic realism. The 'look' of the films is similarly overheated, with a dramatic use of colour design that complements the fast editing pace and overtly mobile camera. This aesthetic of artifice borders on travesty and can be alienating, causing some to describe it as 'flashy'. Luhrmann exploits the exhibitionist nature of cinema, putting all the elements of the medium on display. In that sense, he can be seen as a new kind of showman-auteur, a mixture of entrepreneur, performer and artist whose work harks back to the early 'cinema of attractions' identified by Tom Gunning.[10] Luhrmann and Martin compare their personal and working lives to that of a circus family travelling the globe, and the circus analogy is appropriate to their work and to their working methods.

Luhrmann sets out to inspire a sense of wonder akin to the astonishment experienced by the spectators of early cinema.[11] Wonderment is engendered by dazzling displays of technical virtuosity as much as by visual and aural artistry. The skill and craftsmanship involved are made visible through a painterly technique that draws attention to technological processes rather than naturalising them in the interests of realism. Not all viewers respond to this project positively, and the reaction of critics veers between admiration, embarrassment and derision. The reception of *Australia* echoed that of *William Shakespeare's Romeo + Juliet* and *Moulin Rouge!*, with wildly conflicting press reviews contrasting with the audience response, which built gradually and fed into and sustained the lucrative DVD markets. In light of the fact that *Australia* was released in a climate of worldwide economic crisis, it performed well at the Australian and international box office, despite widespread predictions of its failure.[12] The mixed press response, which ignited lively debate on Internet discussion boards, added to the controversy surrounding Luhrmann's films, consolidating their status as media events. Such controversy plays an important role in the branding of his work.

Cinema is an industry in which branding has always been significant, from the early use of onscreen logos to assign ownership, to tie-in arrangements and product placement in films themselves. In the market-driven context of contemporary global media production, branding has become increasingly important in constructing a recognisable identity for a film or group of films, which is then used to promote the work across multiple channels of communication. Because of its association with commerce, branding is often viewed with suspicion as incompatible with cultural or artistic concerns. While some independent film-makers may find themselves marginalised or excluded as a result of market-led policies, Luhrmann has embraced the branding process and has actively contributed to establishing an identity for his work through the Red Curtain label. This

Baz Luhrmann:
visionary identity

process has been crucial to the films' longer-term success, and to consolidating Luhrmann's artistic credibility; it also helped to maintain his visibility during the seven years between *Moulin Rouge!* and *Australia*. Luhrmann is best known for the Red Curtain style, and though subsequent films may be presented as a departure, the Red Curtain cycle remains the benchmark against which other work is defined and evaluated.

Luhrmann's persona (understood as a constructed identity that circulates in multiple media sites)[13] is central to the branding operation. He projects himself as a buccaneering adventurer – a risk-taker in a high-risk industry – who pushes himself and those he works with to the limit, which implies a certain ruthlessness. He is often referred to by co-workers and collaborators as a visionary and placed in the tradition of European film-makers such as David Lean, albeit in more hyperbolic mode. His life story – that of a young boy who grew up in rural New South Wales then ran away to the city (Sydney) and became an internationally renowned film director – participates in building a picture of a talented innovator at the forefront of contemporary cinema. At the same time, Luhrmann acknowledges the part played by collaborators in producing his oeuvre, summoning up the image of a dedicated group working towards common artistic goals.[14] He asserts that there is no distinction between his life and his work and that each feeds into the other. Every project is presented as intensely personal, an episode in Luhrmann's creative journey. This strategy provides an overall sense of continuity between different media artefacts and reaffirms his status as an auteur.

Branding holds together a number of contradictory elements in Luhrmann's work and career. When it comes to the films' mixed national origins, branding has a vital role to play. Luhrmann has always asserted the significance of his Australian roots and stressed the contribution of a group of highly skilled, home-grown film-makers. The Australian media for its part claims Luhrmann and his movies as Australian, even when they receive a hostile response.[15] However, as already noted, in the wider arena of global film culture, the work has often been perceived as Hollywood fare. This perception is strengthened by the use of international cast members and an aesthetic that borrows freely from classic Hollywood and world cinema, and by the 20th Century-Fox studio logo that dominates the screen at the beginning. The Bazmark company logo also appears on the front titles; in the case of *Australia*, it flickered onscreen in a new, enhanced animated form as a reminder of the film's national provenance. This gesture defined the work as Australian even though Fox, as principal backers, retained copyright. *Australia* put its national identity on display: the locations, cast and crew were Australian, and the focus was on little-known episodes in the country's history such as the bombing of Darwin by the Japanese during World War II. The production was aimed at putting Australia on the map, not least in its tie-in with the government agency Tourism Australia, for whom Luhrmann directed two commercials promoting the country as a life-changing experience to potential overseas visitors.

Yet, as usual with Luhrmann's films, there was a sting in the tail. At the heart of the story, narrated by the young Aboriginal boy played by the unknown Brandon Walters, was the government's policy of removing mixed-race indigenous children from their families and raising them as white – hardly Australia's finest hour, and the subject of bitter controversy.[16] In addition, the strategy of presenting the nation's history through the filter of homage to classic Hollywood cinema produced an arch self-consciousness in the depiction of the white characters that contrasted with the heightened, romanticised naturalism of the landscape and indigenous characters. Nicole Kidman's deliberately exaggerated performance as the English aristocrat and Hugh Jackman's equally over-the-top rendition of the rugged Australian drover recalled the improbable attraction between Katharine Hepburn and Humphrey Bogart in John Huston's *The African Queen* (1951), while the reprise of 'Somewhere Over the Rainbow' throughout *Australia* harked back to *The Wizard of Oz* (1939). These nods and winks to the audience, together with the evocation of a mysterious, unassimilable indigenous culture, projected Australia as a magical, exotic land outside the realms of historical realism. At the same time, this was a vision of a country whose sublime landscapes were scarred by unresolved conflicts and trauma. The idea of a faraway place defined by seductive and dangerous liminal spaces in which it is possible to lose oneself entirely is characteristic of the challenge Luhrmann offers to audiences. The offer contains its own risk: that it might not be accepted by viewers.

Luhrmann's work traverses tensions that are both specific to his Australian context and typical of contemporary media production: between national and transnational; local and global; mainstream studio and small-scale independent production; individual authorship and collaboration; authenticity and artifice; blockbuster and art cinema; classical and avant-garde; and theatre and cinema. In the following pages I explore the way his negotiation of such tensions impacts on the films he chooses to make, and the ways in which they are received. My intention is to illuminate the experience of a particular group of independent film-makers who engage with the complexities of modern global media production from a specific context, and who redefine national cinema in the process. Over the last two decades, film scholars and historians have struggled with the concept of national cinema. The difficulties of containing an international enterprise such as cinema (and every local cinema is also international) within national criteria that are universally or even widely acceptable have preoccupied cultural practitioners at all levels, from government and other funding agencies to film-makers, critics and academics — and, indeed, those audiences who recognise distinctions between national cinemas and the cultural and/or entertainment value attached to them. The terms of debate have typically circulated around topics such as economic and cultural infrastructures; aesthetic and formal strategies; audience address and expectations; relationships between economically powerful global media industries and medium- and small-sized national cinemas; and, inevitably, the efforts of non-Hollywood cinemas to compete effectively in domestic and world markets with what is perceived as Hollywood fare, even when it is financed and distributed by multinational conglomerates. To those concerned with national cinema as a manifestation of cultural diversity and difference, the debate has sometimes been tinged with desperation, as the protective strategies designed to nurture and support the home-grown cinemas are often inconsistent, dependent on the vagaries of different agencies with shifting priorities.

In this scenario, smaller national cinemas are generally positioned as weaker — that is, less visible and less viable economically and culturally, though they may be artistically superior — than the American movies that continue to dominate the global arena. When a smaller national cinema produces an international popular hit, challenging the global hegemony of 'Hollywood', it is sometimes greeted with ambivalence; on one hand its box-office success is desired, on the other it is attained at the expense of national specificity and authenticity. Its achievement is perceived as compromised by its willingness to reach out beyond the niche audiences for national cinemas to mass popularity. Underlying such mixed feelings is the preconception that smaller local cinemas are unequal partners in the process of cultural exchange and circulation of national images, victims of the all-powerful global Hollywood machine. This pessimistic perception of national cinemas is infused with what some have called the 'romance of the margins', in which cultures perceived as minor are forever doomed to occupy a disenfranchised space.[17] To nuance this conception, which, as many have noted, tends to reify both centre and margins, I offer the idea of 'nostalgia for the periphery'. In the context of transnational flow, such nostalgia, recognising the dynamic and fluid relationship between centre and periphery, yearns for a space of creative possibility outside the mainstream that will destabilise and displace the hegemony of the centre. It is this nostalgia, I suggest, that motivates the transnational utopianism at the heart of Baz Luhrmann's films, which strive to be both local and global, and to reach popular international audiences.

The historical context for debates about national cinema can be traced back to developments in the late 1940s, when, in the wake of World War II and in response to internal pressures, the Hollywood studio system was reorganised, and the American industry set its sights on re-establishing control of its strongest foreign markets, especially those in western Europe, and on conquering new territories around the world. As Hollywood expanded its holdings, it also opened its doors to other national cinemas, importing foreign films that were marketed to niche audiences on the burgeoning art-film circuits in America, at the same time as funding foreign films through international co-production deals and runaway productions that took advantage of local subsidies and incentives.[18] As many have recognised, this period saw a renewed expansion of the art-film market and the establishment of a practice whereby smaller national cinemas could disseminate their product in the form of modestly budgeted art films produced by talented auteurs, which would be exhibited at international festivals and attract the interest of major investors. Such films were distinguished by their difference in institutional, formal and aesthetic terms from mainstream Hollywood entertainment: art cinema became a brand. National film movements emerged as a form of opposition to and cooperation with the Hollywood industry, an art cinema distinct from the popular, commercial output of either Hollywood or the smaller national cinemas, and exhibited via alternative circuits to niche audiences. This oppositional stance, with its emphasis on artistic innovation and cultural difference, continues to inform many critical responses to films produced by smaller national cinemas.

However, the art-cinema brand has diversified in the meantime. As already noted, multiplexes and the video and DVD markets have contributed to the re-emergence of the popular art film. The contemporary popular art film is characterised by a disregard for traditional boundaries between art and entertainment; it mixes classical forms with modernist strategies, and crosses over between popular and minority audiences. While it may have discernible national characteristics, it is transnational in approach and realisation, and its national/transnational status is often debated via contextual discourses such as press and other critical response. It has a hybrid, mobile quality, evident in a slipperiness of location (aided by digital technology), the presence of international stars and creative and technical personnel, and the dependence on mixed funding arrangements.[19] The popular art film aims to escape the niche ghetto of the traditional art film, though it appears on the festival circuits and is just as dependent for its success on awards and word-of-mouth interest. Its rise is in some measure due to the expansion of art-film production and distribution by independent companies operating with and at the borders of the major Hollywood studios. It has been aided by the accessibility of new technologies enabling innovative visual effects and the ability to achieve high production values in locations at a distance from the traditional centres of production. It has also allowed certain directors associated with art cinema, such as Ridley Scott, Martin Scorsese, Spike Lee, Jane Campion, Peter Jackson and Baz Luhrmann to move into mainstream territory.[20] In Luhrmann's case, it has provided the means to realise increasingly ambitious and high-concept projects.

The contemporary Hollywood industry has evolved into networks of relationships between independent production companies, the mini-majors and large media conglomerates. Arguably, these networks have facilitated the growth of different kinds of independence operating at varying degrees from the mainstream. Rather than being swallowed up by global conglomerates, some independent production companies have negotiated a position of relative autonomy in cooperation with them, which allows them to benefit from high-quality facilities and sophisticated promotion and distribution resources. The institutional relationship between Luhrmann and

Martin's company Bazmark and News Corporation's 20th Century-Fox can be described in these terms. It is an international relationship, in the sense that it is a formal arrangement between organisations with different national bases.[21] Bazmark's ethos, working practices and output, on the other hand, can be characterised as transnational, epitomising the more fluid relationships of creative and other forms of exchange between people from diverse backgrounds who engage in collaborative cultural activities. The link between transnationalism and cosmopolitanism, understood as a belief in the underlying connections between people, or citizens of the world, informs these practices, which have an ethical dimension, in that they presuppose mutual respect and trust between like-minded people and groups. The cosmopolitan aspects of the transnational and its impact on local cultures are often viewed as rendering the local and regional invisible.[22] It is clear that the obliteration of national, local and regional specificity in the contemporary global era is an important issue. However, the debate tends to polarise between advocates of cosmopolitan transnationalism and those who condemn its perceived erasure of national difference in the interests of global capitalism. Historically grounded case studies of specific transnational operations and their negotiation of local and global demands have appeared that feed into and inflect the terms of discussion.

This book offers such micro-level analysis. In Chapter 1, drawing on my in-depth interviews with Luhrmann and Martin and archive research, I explore the interaction between personal biography and the work that has informed the branding process and contributed to the development of Luhrmann's international persona. His story is distinctively Australian, and is intimately linked to his working practices, production set-up and aesthetic, which are examined in detail. I trace the roots of his collaborative methods in his training in theatre and opera, which played a significant part in the development of the signature Red Curtain style. This local background also defines the relationship of Bazmark to 20th Century-Fox, which in turn affects operational and artistic strategies. The process of close analysis reveals that Luhrmann's brand of cinematic authorship, which he contributes to constructing, emerges from a dialectic between his particular circumstances and the demands of global production. Each film also has

a singular story, which unfolds in relation to life changes and the fluid technological and institutional networks of the contemporary media industries.
In chapters devoted to the preparation, decision-making processes, production, promotion and reception of the individual movies, the wider issues
they raise are discussed at the macro level. Chapter 2 tells the story of *Strictly
Ballroom*, interpolating an analysis of the depiction of time and place and
introducing the notion of travesty as an aesthetic strategy. In Chapter 3, the
production history of *William Shakespeare's Romeo + Juliet* makes way for
reflections on the struggles over authorship involved in literary adaptations
and the use of a hyperbolic language emanating from the context of
Australian postcolonial culture.

Chapter 4 on *Moulin Rouge!* unpicks the strategy of grouping the first three
films under the umbrella of Red Curtain cinema, and develops an argument
about the significance of performance in consolidating the works' national
identity and Luhrmann's status as international auteur. The concept of the
neo-baroque is used to illuminate *Moulin Rouge!*'s heightened visual style
and investment in spectacle. In Chapter 5, the Chanel commercial *No. 5 The
Film* is considered as a transitional work forming a bridge between the Red
Curtain Trilogy and the historical epic *Australia*. Close analysis of the latter
uncovers the complexity of its conception and realisation, explores its controversial treatment of national history and identifies the reasons for the
mixed critical response. Situated within the frameworks of memory and
trauma, *Australia* is viewed as a symptomatic response to the country's
fraught colonial and postcolonial past. The final chapter shifts gear in order
to investigate the impact of technological advances such as DVD and the
Internet on Luhrmann's creative activities, and the role of new technologies
in affirming the value of local production contexts. After delineating
Luhrmann's interaction with new media and his deployment of 'reflective
nostalgia', I close by arguing that the experience of independent film-
makers such as Luhrmann and Martin operating within the contemporary
media industries demands flexible models of cultural production that recognise the contradictions they face and the necessity of strategic thinking.

As the events contributing to Luhrmann's current position as a leading
figure in world cinema are revealed and broader issues open up, some

themes recur and reverberate across the chapters. In reconstructing Luhrmann's life and work, my perspective is that of a sympathetic outsider who admires both, but who also maintains a critical distance. This approach informs my encounter with Australian film culture, which I perceive as communicating across national borders from a local situation. As far as possible, I take Luhrmann and his oeuvre on their own terms, rather than impose a set of judgmental criteria. I use a non-prescriptive method similar to that called for by Tom O'Regan in his conclusion to *Australian National Cinema*, one that acknowledges diversity and competing aspirations and standards of value in national conditions of production.[23] This spirit of radical pluralism inspires my study of Baz Luhrmann as a representative of independent film-making practice that may not always cohere into an ideal, and for that very reason can shed light on contemporary global film culture and its shifting power relations.

* * *

A great deal has been written about Baz Luhrmann, particularly in the press. This is both a blessing and a curse for the researcher, who is faced with a prolific amount of original material that offers contradictory and inaccurate information. Every effort has been made to clear up inconsistencies and inaccuracies. Where this was not possible, conflicting accounts have been presented as such.

One
Once Upon a Time in Australia

Baz Luhrmann is a natural showman. He delights in entertaining others with tales of film-making adventures and misadventures, and in telling his own life story, which he views as inseparable from his creative journey.[1] The idea of a journey (whether actual, emotional or psychological) is a central thread in his artistic output and fundamental to his identity. It also provides a narrative structure for many of the myths on which stories are based. Luhrmann is fascinated by myth, which he sees as a form capable of communicating with people from different contexts and cultures. He talks about his drive to mythologise, or to manufacture high drama from everyday events. At the heart of his work, as with myth, lies a core belief in notions such as fate, destiny, the power of love and the inevitability of death. As he relates it, Luhrmann's life takes on the aura of national myth. It has become part of the brand, or persona that he has built for himself over the past fifteen or so years. It is a fable that captures the ideals on which Australia was built, as a land of immigrants, a new country offering to its settlers the possibility of advancement denied to them elsewhere. While this national myth may not have the power of the American Dream, it does inspire a certain sense of adventure, and a lack of respect for official boundaries. It is no accident that the logo for Bazmark,[2] the company set up by Luhrmann with his wife and chief collaborator, designer Catherine Martin, is a customised version of the Australian national coat of arms that carries the banner 'A life lived in fear is a life half lived'.[3] As a nation, Australia is comparatively young,[4] and it is postcolonial, a legacy that has significant impact on its ethnically diverse culture. This context of postcolonial struggle for an independent identity informs Luhrmann's work, and much Australian cinema. Other influences are Australia's remote geographical position as an island continent in the southern hemisphere, its perceived lack of cultural visibility on the global stage,[5] and the fact that it has a relatively small population for such a large land mass.[6]

Bazmark company logo

Luhrmann's story has a fairy-tale ring: a young boy growing up in rural New South Wales moves to Sydney and goes on to become a celebrated international theatre and film director. Born Mark Anthony Luhrmann on 17 September 1962 in Sydney, he moved to the countryside with his family after his father returned from the Vietnam war. He grew up in the small town of Herons Creek close to the Pacific Highway, a major transport route that runs along the coast linking Sydney to Brisbane in Queensland to the north. His parents owned a gas station, a pig farm and shops, one of which – a dress shop – was run by his mother Barbara. Luhrmann describes the place as isolated, but at the same time there was a steady stream of assorted passers-through, some of them celebrities, some travelling artists. His father Leonard was a keen photographer and diver who had been involved in underwater research on the Great Barrier Reef, and he taught Baz how to use a Box Brownie camera and how to process and print photographs. He was also the proud owner of Bolex Straight 8 and Leica cameras. At one time he took over the running of the local cinema when the owner died. He appears to have been an energetic entrepreneur and educator who encouraged his sons[7] to be physically adventurous, inventive, resourceful and to push themselves to the limit. His belief that 'anything is possible' spurred Baz to try out many different activities, from horse-riding, football, water skiing and diving to playing guitar in a band and ballroom dancing (dressed up in Elvis-style jump suit). Baz and his brothers staged magic shows and plays, and set up an amateur radio station. Amid this relentless round of creative pursuits, Baz made home movies on the Bolex in which he experimented with primitive trick effects.

His father's exceptionally high standards could have contributed to Luhrmann's legendary perfectionism, and he may well have inherited his mother's love of glamour. It is difficult not to attribute elements of the style and themes of his adult work to the bohemian setting and incessant industry of his childhood. His drive to innovate and love of classic Hollywood, his entrepreneurial skills and the epic scale of his ambition can all be traced back to the experiences of those formative years. Having developed so many interests, Luhrmann had a number of different avenues available to him. The most compelling of these was acting, which offered the possibility of reinvention of identity through role-play in different stories. Luhrmann was drawn to cinema as illusion, and the construction of imaginary worlds into which one could escape without being incarcerated. His parents divorced in 1974 and when his father remarried, Luhrmann left Herons Creek in 1977 and joined his mother in Sydney, where he became involved in amateur theatre and film groups. He attended a Catholic boys' school, and Narrabeen Sports High School, where he met Craig Pearce, who later became a key collaborator. In 1979 they appeared together in a school production of *Guys and Dolls*, with Luhrmann as Sky Masterson and Pearce playing Nathan Detroit.[8] That year Luhrmann officially adopted Bazmark as his own name and in 1980, after graduating from high school, he applied to Sydney's premier acting academy the National Institute of Dramatic Art (NIDA), but was rejected as too young. Undeterred, Luhrmann set out to build a career as a performer in film and television. In the next two years he took a minor role in John Duigan's *Winter of Our Dreams* (1981); appeared in six episodes of the popular Australian television series *A Country Practice* (1981–94); formed a theatre company (The Bond); co-directed and acted in a controversial drama-documentary *Kids of the Cross* (1981); and had a small part in Paul Harmon's thriller *The Dark Room* (1982).[9]

Despite growing success as a working actor, Luhrmann applied again to NIDA in 1982 and was accepted. The experience was mixed; over-anxious to impress, Luhrmann acted out being an intense artist by engaging in some wild stunts, which did not go down well with some tutors and fellow students. At the same time, he made his mark as one to watch, and he learned about the history of theatre. Shakespeare and Molière made a significant, long-lasting impression, and Luhrmann began the practice of going to extreme lengths to research every project in depth. Although not enrolled on the directors programme, he was able to stage his own shows featuring other NIDA students. Visiting film and theatre director Jim Sharman (*The Rocky Horror Picture Show*, 1975) was impressed by Luhrmann's production of August Strindberg's *The Ghost Sonata* and mentioned his name to the Australian Opera. Luhrmann became passionate about Brecht and Artaud, but began to realise that rather than follow the style and methods of theatre's great names, he needed to develop his own language. His interest in Joseph Campbell's writings about comparative mythology and in Shakespeare's use of familiar stories situated in magical settings fed into his desire to find a form that would speak to audiences across social and cultural divides.

The first version of *Strictly Ballroom* — a thirty-minute play — emerged from this context of trying out ideas and working methods at NIDA. Luhrmann put together a group of fellow students and, using a collaborative process, part of which involved individual group members occupying a 'hot seat' and having to answer searching questions from the rest of the group, they devised a piece set in the glitzy world of ballroom dancing and drawing on the David and Goliath myth and the Hans Christian Andersen fairy-tale *The Ugly Duckling*. The method of devised theatre, in which the finished work is the result of improvisational 'workshopping' and role-play between group participants, all of whom are active creative contributors, is one that Luhrmann employs to this day. Towards the end of his time at NIDA he was selected to assist on the adaptation of *The Mahabharata* by Peter Brook, one of the principal exponents of devised theatre. Brook's celebrated interpretation of the Hindu story sought to give it universal relevance. Despite his mixed feelings about NIDA, Luhrmann's experiences there crystallised and gave substance and shape to his evolving world-view and modus operandi. The devised stage play *Strictly Ballroom* went through several transformations. It was performed at NIDA and at the World Youth Theatre festival in Bratislava in former Czechoslovakia, where it was warmly received by audiences and won awards for Best Production and Best Direction.[10]

The collaborative ethos of devised theatre is fundamental to Luhrmann's stage and screen work, which cannot fully be understood without reference to it. He likens his function to that of a ship's captain, responsible for initiating the journey or project. Once the other participants come on board, then each of them has a vital part to play in bringing the ship home, but it is up to the captain to keep it on course and not to lose sight of the initial purpose. The project begins with Luhrmann's personal conception, which is tested and transformed via the interpersonal activity of everyone involved, so that the end result is both personal and impersonal. Workshops, in which playing around with ideas and different kinds of performance is encouraged, are a crucial element in the process, and the actors are required to attend these sessions at an early stage prior to the start of production.[11] The ship's captain metaphor is suitably swashbuckling, for Luhrmann and his crew evidently treat each project as an adventure. It is also useful in nuancing traditional notions of authorship in cinema and the cherished idea of a single source (the director) for a film's meaning, style and world-view. Despite sustained critical assault on this notion over decades, it stubbornly refuses to go away. Luhrmann's example offers a more democratic model for the cinematic auteur in which the director's signature is not the only one visible in the finished product, even though he or she is in control of its final shape. While collaborative methods are not unusual in independent film-making, in Luhrmann's case the level of recognition given to creative contributors and the visibility of the crew's working practices in promotional and other material is exceptional, and can partly be put down to his background in theatre, as well as to his production set-up. The emphasis on collaboration is also important in establishing a brand for Luhrmann's output. His name provides the fixative that binds together a fluid entity whose origins cannot be determined with precision. Nevertheless, Luhrmann takes final responsibility for all aspects of the finished product, and every detail is subject to his approval.

The play *Strictly Ballroom* was an ambitious multimedia event even in its simplest form. Shortly after its performance in Bratislava and his graduation from NIDA, Luhrmann was offered the opportunity to direct a musical called *Crocodile Creek* in Rockhampton in Queensland, where he met the composer Felix Meagher, with whom he would go on to collaborate. *Crocodile Creek* was set in the time of the race riots that occurred during the town's gold-mining period and was a large-scale community production featuring local indigenous and Chinese people as well as Anglo-Celtic Australians. In 1986, Luhrmann formed the Six Years Old theatre company with himself as artistic director. One of their productions, *Haircut*, was a reworking of the controversial 1960s rock-musical *Hair*, which had been made into a film, directed by Milos Forman, in 1979. Luhrmann tried his hand at a number of projects, including a revival of the play *Strictly Ballroom* in an extended version that had successful runs at Sydney's Wharf Theatre and the 1988 World Expo in Brisbane. This version was co-written with childhood friend Craig Pearce and began their long-term writing partnership. Another significant venture for Luhrmann in 1988 was the experimental opera *Lake Lost*, devised with Felix Meagher for the Australian Opera's bicentennial RA project. It was while looking for a designer for the production that Luhrmann first met Catherine Martin, then in her final year at NIDA, who co-designed the sets with friend and fellow-student Angus Strathie. They won the Victorian Green Room award for Best Opera Design, while Luhrmann won the Victorian Green Room award for Best Director. Luhrmann and Martin went on to work together on several theatre productions: in 1989 they presented a 1940s-themed event *Dance Hall* at Sydney Town Hall for the Sydney Festival, in which the audience was invited to relive the end of World War II celebrations; in 1990 Luhrmann staged at the Sydney Opera House the acclaimed Australian Opera production of Puccini's *La Bohème*, set in the 1950s, for which Martin co-designed the sets and costumes with Bill Marron;[12] then in 1992 Luhrmann, Martin and Craig Pearce worked together on the film version of *Strictly Ballroom*, which had been optioned by Australian music producer Ted Albert and Tristram Miall for their production company M&A.

Of all the collaborators who have crossed Baz Luhrmann's path, none features more prominently than Catherine Martin (known affectionately as CM), his wife and business partner.[13] Theirs is an alliance in which each

Catherine Martin:
equal partner and chief
collaborator

complements the other. Martin insists that it is a partnership of equals in which Luhrmann has the vision, while she has practical craft skills of making things and problem-solving. Their long-standing artistic and personal coalition is so successful that the title of this book – were it not part of a series about directors – might have been 'Baz Luhrmann and Catherine Martin'. Martin was born in Sydney on 26 January 1965. Her father Angus is an academic (now retired) specialising in French literature, and a movie buff; her mother Claude is French,[14] and she has one brother. During her childhood, the family travelled abroad a lot and spent time in museums and art galleries, which piqued her interest in painting, and she inherited her father's enthusiasm for cinema. She describes herself as a rebel who did not shine academically until her final year at school, when she excelled in the practical section of her art exam. On leaving school she enrolled on a Fine Arts degree programme at Sydney College of the Arts, where she discovered that her leanings were towards applied arts. She dropped out after a year and became an apprentice machinist for one of Sydney's independent fashion designers. After variety of temporary positions in the fashion industry, where she picked up invaluable practical skills, she got a job designing a theatre production and decided to apply to NIDA, where she took the theatre design course. At NIDA she met and bonded with classmate Angus Strathie, with whom she shared an interest in fashion, and they worked together on a number of projects. At the end of their second year, they were recommended by NIDA to Baz Luhrmann, who was looking for a designer for *Lake Lost*, and he came to see their exhibitions. This meeting would turn out to be the beginning of a remarkable relationship.

NIDA was a positive experience for Martin. She studied costume and set design and was trained in research methods, practical expertise and theatre history. The teaching was rigorous and helped to provide a focus for the design aptitude she already possessed. She had always been interested in craft and was taught to sew at age six by her mother, who had a natural instinct for style. One of her tutors at NIDA praised her high level of visual literacy, an essential attribute for a costume and set designer.[15] But she was also fascinated by fashion and as a teenager had dreamed of becoming a fashion designer. This predilection may have chimed with Luhrmann's innovative approach to theatre and cinema. By its very nature, fashion flouts conventional notions of time and place, plundering history for themes and styles that are then cross-bred to create a hybrid concoction. Haute couture played out on the catwalk is flamboyantly theatrical, staging clothing as high drama through spectacular display. Fashion also requires total attention to detail, with each fold of fabric, stitch, hem and seam of utmost importance to the final result – a concern that Luhrmann and Martin share. The influence of fashion on their careers is extensive. Luhrmann, Martin and Bill Marron were responsible for designing the signature issue of Australian *Vogue* in January 1994. Martin stage-managed fashion shows to help fund her studies at NIDA, and in 1998 she directed leading Australian fashion designer Collette Dinnigan's Autumn/Winter collection at the Louvre in Paris for Bazmark. In 2004 Luhrmann directed a three-minute Chanel No. 5 commercial starring Nicole Kidman and Brazilian actor Rodrigo Santoro, featuring costumes designed by Karl Lagerfeld.

The impact of fashion extends to their working methods. When doing preparatory research for their films, once the broad outline of the scenario is unveiled, Martin and the art department begin by raiding fashion magazines and online picture resources for visual material that resonates with or crystallises the story ideas and archive images that Luhrmann has presented to the team. Some of this visual material is interpretive, from a different period than the film's setting, chosen because it evokes the spirit of that time. All the images are then discussed at meetings and selections are made. The visual material is collected into folders that are regularly updated and provide Luhrmann with a supply of artwork.[16] From this collection they work out with him which pictures are suitable and which are not, the order that they will follow and how the story will be told in images. Concept books, elaborate storyboards that are works of art in themselves, emerge from this process. These include sketches, Photoshop material and images from widely varied times and places put into sequence, with the actors pasted in.[17] This material then feeds back into the script, helping to refine and support the story structure. The initial historical research, carried out with fastidious care and attention to documented facts about the relevant period, provides the basis for a reinterpretation and dramatisation of the past that collapses time and place, creating a consciously artificial world through a collage of different styles. From research stage to the final product, Luhrmann and Martin's work is grounded in pastiche. Pastiche, understood as an aesthetic that mixes styles from various sources through quotation, is one of the strategies associated with postmodernism, and it has been taken to task for its lack of originality and authenticity. However, it can also be interpreted as a method that produces complex, multilayered works whose power lies in their challenge to the very notion of origin viewed as a single source of creative activity or meaning.[18]

Pastiche is related to travesty, which in its theatrical form is a device that mimics a particular style or artwork to render it grotesque or absurd. In both cases, the style or styles in question are transformed through the process of mimicry and new associations, which can be critical, humorous, intellectual, emotional, or a combination of all these, come to the surface. The initial object of pastiche or travesty forms part of a new idea or commentary on its familiar status. Travesty is less common in cinema than in theatre, partly because mainstream cinema has developed a language that favours naturalism. It appears most often in forms that rely on the subversion of accepted rules of representation, such as gross-out comedy and animation, or in fantasy genres such as the musical. Travesty is often associated with cross-dressing, which in itself can be seen as a theatrical gesture in the way it dramatises and undermines conventional gender roles. Theatre is a form in which cross-dressing is common, either with the purpose of disguising the identity of the performer, or, as in music hall or burlesque, allowing players overtly to inhabit different personas. Shakespeare's theatre, which has had a profound influence on Luhrmann's work, made frequent use of travesty, cross-dressing and role-play.

From their first collaboration on *Lake Lost* Martin had an affinity with the scale and ambition of Luhrmann's ideas, and his drive to stage a magical theatrical experience. They clicked on an intellectual level and she felt herself involved in a romantic artistic adventure. She admired his discipline and his way of pushing people to achieve their best work. At NIDA she was interested in minimalist set design and in the value placed on period accuracy in British film costume dramas such as Peter Greenaway's *The Draughtsman's Contract* (1982). She found many of her preconceptions about the right and wrong way to approach visual design overturned as her partnership with Luhrmann developed and he encouraged her to adapt the rules to the demands of storytelling. She also had to revise her inclinations to minimalism in order to translate Luhrmann's baroque imagination to stage and screen. Nevertheless, their way of working has always enabled her to contribute her own ideas and style to their projects and to stamp them with her signature. Her contribution has been critically acclaimed and has received numerous awards, including Oscars for Best Art Direction and Set Decoration (shared with Brigitte Broch) and Best Costume Design (shared with Angus Strathie) for *Moulin Rouge!* (2001).[19] Perhaps because of these

public accolades, she has always fully acknowledged Luhrmann's pivotal
function as initiator, decision-maker, creative leader and supervisor. For
his part, Luhrmann has also won multiple awards for his film work,
although the Oscar has so far eluded him.[20]

The convergence of Luhrmann and Martin's interests, experience and
talent was evident in the theatre work they did after *Lake Lost*, and in their
first movie collaboration *Strictly Ballroom*. After talks with M&A, the company that optioned the extended version of the play, Luhrmann eventually
established that he would direct and co-write the script with Craig Pearce,
and settled on Martin and Bill Marron as production designers with Angus
Strathie as costume designer. *Strictly Ballroom* presented a challenge, as
Luhrmann's ideas about the Six Years Old production had to be translated
into cinematic form. At this point, Luhrmann's professional film directing
credits consisted of the 1987 zero-budget music video of Ignatius Jones's
version of The Andrews Sisters' hit 'Beat Me Daddy, Eight to the Bar'.[21]
Strictly Ballroom's script went through several transformations, as
Luhrmann developed his ideas about a theatrical cinematic language. The
production was small scale and inexpensive,[22] but it had a distinctive style
and an appealing brashness. Although not as overtly political as the stage
version, its theme of resistance to stultifying institutional hierarchies and
the social inclusiveness of its utopian ending were inspirational. The budget constraints were turned into an advantage as the tacky glamour of the
Australian ballroom dancing world was visualised through colour-saturated
sets and costumes and camp performances that were deliberately artificial.
The film was not properly speaking a musical, but the score by David
Hirschfelder celebrated classic dance music and the soundtrack featured an
upbeat rendition of 'Love Is in the Air' by John Paul Young that was released
in 1992 as a music video, directed by Luhrmann.[23]

Somewhat to the surprise of the film-makers, *Strictly Ballroom* became a
runaway hit, grossing around six times its budget.[24] It was selected by Pierre
Rissient for a special late-night screening at the 1992 Cannes Film Festival,
where it was a triumphant success. It was an ideal festival film, a quirky,
modestly budgeted art movie that put on display the talents of its Australian
creative team, and it has been credited with kick-starting the Australian

film-making revival of the 1990s. Following *Strictly Ballroom*'s success at Cannes, the film received a vast amount of media attention and Luhrmann was pursued by several Hollywood studios to sign up with them. It was 20th Century-Fox, owned by Australian expatriate Rupert Murdoch's News Corporation, which offered the best arrangement. Luhrmann signed a first-look agreement with Fox that allowed him to proceed with his next production, *William Shakespeare's Romeo + Juliet*. Under the terms of the deal, Luhrmann had to pitch the idea of an updated version of the play that would use Shakespeare's original language to sceptical studio executives who were not convinced that such a film would get an audience. They were persuaded to go ahead after seeing footage of the workshop process with Leonardo DiCaprio and Natalie Portman, who was an early choice for the part of Juliet.

Immediately after *Strictly Ballroom*, Luhrmann and Martin were involved in several non-film projects. In 1993 Luhrmann devised and staged for the Australian Opera a Hindu version of Benjamin Britten's opera *A Midsummer Night's Dream*, set in colonial India, for which Martin designed sets and costumes. The production had successful seasons in Sydney and Melbourne before going to the 1994 Edinburgh Festival, where it won the Critics' Prize. Luhrmann's encounter with Indian culture while researching this production had a long-lasting effect on him.[25] The same year he, Martin and Bill Marron were guest editors on the signature issue of Australian *Vogue*, published in January 1994, which featured Nicole Kidman and Kylie Minogue in the guise of classic Hollywood movie stars and had three pages devoted to *Strictly Ballroom*. The influence of the theatrical Red Curtain style is evident in the issue cover.[26] Also in 1993, Luhrmann and Martin worked with the Australian Labor Party on the televised launch of the Keating government's successful re-election campaign. At this stage, Luhrmann and Martin were working in a number of media besides film, including design, music and live events. *William Shakespeare's Romeo + Juliet* was funded by Fox on an estimated budget eight times that of *Strictly Ballroom*[27] and shot mainly in Mexico, where the production was beset with problems. Despite the difficulties, when *Romeo + Juliet* was released in 1996 it was a critical and box-office success and went on to garner many awards, including the British Academy of Film and Television Arts (BAFTA) prestigious David Lean

award for Direction for Luhrmann.[28] On the back of the film's success, in
1996 a new, two-year, first-look agreement was signed with Fox that
allowed Luhrmann a production base in Australia.[29]

With the international tenor of *Romeo + Juliet*, Luhrmann seemed to have
moved away from the assertively Australian pizzazz of *Strictly Ballroom*. Yet if
his work is viewed as a whole, *Romeo + Juliet* was entirely consistent with the
style and subject matter of his other projects. The updating of a classic text,
the heightened imaginary world of 'Verona Beach', the 'operatic' performances, the emphasis on visual design and music, the use of travesty, the
references to classic movies, and the theme of resistance to the established
order, all displayed the Luhrmann trademark. However, with *Romeo + Juliet*
there was a shift towards transnational production and a global rather than
local national identity for both the film and Luhrmann himself. The change
might be seen as one of the consequences of signing up with Fox and setting
his sights firmly on the American and global markets. It could be concluded
that Luhrmann had taken a familiar route from low-budget festival success
to bigger-budget mainstream production, with a resulting diminution of an
identifiable national and artistic voice. However, Luhrmann's complex
connections to the global media industry do not entirely conform to established patterns. The deals with Fox had certain repercussions, and distinct
advantages. They formed part of a strategic progression for Luhrmann,
Martin and their team, which involved the conscious accumulation of 'creative capital' akin to the cultural capital defined by Pierre Bourdieu, which
gave them bargaining power with the studio.[30]

Romeo + Juliet inaugurated a new stage for Luhrmann and Martin. They
were married on 26 January 1997, Martin's birthday and Australia Day, in a
Sydney registry office, then celebrated the following day with an extrava-
gantly mounted reception at the Sydney Opera House. The same year they
co-founded their production company Bazmark Inq. The company is based
in Darlinghurst, Sydney, in a colonial-style mansion, the House of Iona,
where Luhrmann and Martin also live. The House of Iona was previously
owned by the second wealthiest man in Britain, the Duke of Westminster,
who had extensive property holdings in Australia and across the globe.[31] The
house and gardens have a suitably fairy-tale atmosphere, due to the Duke's

habit of importing exotic and eccentric sculptures and other artefacts and displaying them in the grounds. Luhrmann and Martin have added their own touches of memorabilia and exotica to the interior, which has two wings on the first floor comprising their personal living areas. The ground floor houses Bazmark offices, screening and rehearsal rooms, music production and computer design facilities and Luhrmann's office. The multipurpose 'red room' accommodates a collection of memorabilia, including award trophies and family photographs. The ambience of this workplace is distinctly personal, and the House of Iona has been reconstructed as an arena where life and work, life and art are inseparable. The colonial building has been redesigned by Luhrmann and Martin as a location for postcolonial cultural activity and business, and as a statement about an unconventional, quasi-bohemian lifestyle.[32] The set-up resembles an artist's workshop or a music production studio and is best described as artisanal, housing small groups of technically skilled craftspeople.

The first soundtrack album for *Romeo + Juliet*, consisting of a compilation of songs by various artists, came out in 1996 and was followed in 1997 by a second album of the film's orchestral score by Nellee Hooper, Craig Armstrong and Marius De Vries, both produced by Bazmark. In 1997 Bazmark produced an album, *Something for Everybody*, featuring new recordings and remixes of music from Luhrmann's film and theatre productions, which was released in 1998. The first track was a fifteen-second 'Bazmark Fanfare' that celebrated the new company. The album demonstrated that Luhrmann's approach to music employed a collage technique similar to that of his other work, sampling, updating and remixing music from different sources. A music video of one of the tracks, 'Now Until the Break of Day', a reinterpretation of Benjamin Britten's song from his *A Midsummer Night's Dream* opera featuring indigenous singer and actress Christine Anu and Australian tenor David Hobson, directed by Luhrmann, came out in 1997 and won an Aria Music Award for best Australian video.[33] Hobson had played Rodolpho in Luhrmann's 1990 production of *La Bohème*, and Anu was later cast as Arabia in *Moulin Rouge!*. In 1999, Bazmark Music produced a remix of another of the tracks on the album, the spoken-word 'Everybody's Free (To Wear Sunscreen)', as a single with 'Love Is in the Air' on the B-side. The record, which set an essay by journalist Mary Schmich published in the *Chicago Tribune* to a choral version of 'Everybody's Free (To Feel Good)' by rave singer Rozalla, was a worldwide hit, reaching number one in the UK and Ireland charts.[34]

During this prolific period, Luhrmann was heavily involved in getting the new Fox studio development in Sydney under way. Australia's reputation as a viable offshore production base had risen with the successful establishment of the Warner Roadshow Studios on Queensland's Gold Coast in 1991. In 1996 Fox applied to the New South Wales government for permission to develop the Sydney Showground, which would expand the existing studio facilities and build a family entertainment and education precinct, creating 1,600 new jobs and boosting the New South Wales media industry. The entertainment and education precinct, modelled on the Universal studios theme park but without the rides, would offer the public an opportunity to watch film-makers at work via studio tours.[35] On 2 May 1998, Fox announced a revised deal with Bazmark that would allow Luhrmann and Martin to develop projects in different media, including film, music, theatre and live events.[36] The public announcement of the deal was made during an entertainment spectacle celebrating the opening of the new studio development, packaged by Bazmark Live.[37] The Bazmark Live team followed this up by designing the streetscape for the studio backlot, featuring a show 'Lights Camera Chaos' directed by renowned Australian theatre director Barrie Kosky.[38] The new arrangement meant that Fox owned the rights to all Bazmark's projects. The company's commitment to Fox was such that it could appear that it had now become a subsidiary of a major Hollywood studio.

First-look deals between studios and small independent companies are not unusual in contemporary Hollywood – James Schamus and Ted Hope of the successful US independent company Good Machine had one with Fox, for example.[39] Good Machine was subsequently acquired by Universal and transformed into the subsidiary Focus Features. Despite the advantages offered to small companies, such as increased funding and better resources and distribution, deals of this kind are often perceived to have a negative impact on their artistic independence and output, resulting in a sacrifice of low-budget radical or innovative work.[40] However, each situation is different, and specific to context. In the case of Bazmark, Luhrmann does not view their business relationship with Fox as having necessitated loss of artistic freedom. As he describes it, in broad terms the studio funds their creativity in the sense that it pays for Bazmark staff and the company's overheads, and whatever needs to be done to develop projects. In return, the studio is the first to say yes or no to every project. Luhrmann does not owe the studio any films, and although Fox owns the copyright on all the work, they do not have the right to interfere in creative decision-making. Luhrmann insisted on artistic autonomy from the beginning, and has retained it ever since. According to him, the studio acts as curator, protecting his interests and ensuring that the work is marketed and distributed effectively in different media forms and locations. This allows him to focus on projects without having to worry about finance.

Luhrmann characterises Bazmark's association with Fox Studios Australia in the early stages as one of collaboration, an extension of the company's working ethos. They knew personally many of the people who worked at the Sydney site. Luhrmann has never felt antagonistic or defensive towards Hollywood, and set out to make the best of the relationship. He claims that he and Martin could have become far more financially wealthy had they chosen the route of making multimillion-dollar-grossing blockbusters, but they valued their artistic independence, which they consider to be real wealth, more highly. The extent of that independence might be gauged by the fact that, due partly to life events, in the seven years between the release of *Moulin Rouge!* (2001) and *Australia* (2008), Bazmark produced few projects.[41] In December 2002, Luhrmann revived his production of *La Bohème* in San Francisco and on Broadway. The DVD boxed set of the Red Curtain Trilogy with extensive supplementary material came out in 2002 in regions 1 and 4. One major film venture, *Alexander the Great*, was abandoned in 2004 after a considerable amount of preparation had been done. In 2004, they released the three-minute Chanel No. 5 film, which took over a year to complete. A special music edition DVD of *Romeo + Juliet* was issued in 2007. *Australia* took four years to bring to fruition. Through all this, Fox remained solidly behind Luhrmann and his team.

It would be naive to assume that Bazmark's deal with Fox did not involve sacrifices. However, it has enabled the team to achieve bigger budgets for their work and to gain international recognition with ambitious art movies that preserve the Luhrmann style and identity. Luhrmann sees the global success of their brand as more significant than the films' box-office performance, which has always been stronger worldwide than in the domestic US market. Paradoxically, Bazmark's roots in Sydney and its geographical distance from Los Angeles may have contributed to the level of independence that Luhrmann has been able to retain. Other factors are Luhrmann's entrepreneurial skill, his willingness to engage in the business of showcasing his work, his ability to transmit his ideas with enthusiasm to different audiences and his enduring identification with Australian culture. In the contemporary global media industry, many different kinds and degrees of independence co-exist. In Bazmark's case, a combination of personal attributes, cultural circumstances, economic determinants and technological developments have generated an unusual production set-up and a body of work that demand to be approached on their own terms, rather than subsumed within a pre-existing model.

Luhrmann's third film, *Moulin Rouge!*, a musical starring Nicole Kidman and Ewan McGregor set in late-nineteenth-century Paris, was shot at Fox Studios Australia with an estimated budget of $52,500,000.[42] Preparations began in 1997, and shooting commenced in 1999. One of the primary influences on its conception was Luhrmann and Martin's experiences in India during their research for the opera *A Midsummer Night's Dream*, when they went to see a Bollywood movie and decided to translate its exuberant, eclectic style into western musical form.[43] The story was loosely based on the myth of Orpheus and Eurydice, with overtones of *La Bohème*. The film was the culmination of the Red Curtain cycle, flamboyantly mixing styles and themes to produce a multilayered work that featured dazzling visual effects, spectacular sets and costumes and a hybrid soundtrack. All of Luhrmann's ideas and many of the elements of his other works came together in this busy, show-stopping reinvention of the American musical, which was not in vogue at the time. *Moulin Rouge!* premiered at Cannes in 2001, where it divided critics. It went on to receive mixed reviews from the press, and the

US box office was disappointing. However, it did well in the UK and Australia[44] and gradually grew in popularity, grossing an estimated $179,213,196 worldwide.[45] It also garnered a plethora of awards, including two Oscars for costume design and set design.[46] It was with the release of *Moulin Rouge!* that the parameters for Red Curtain cinema were stated publicly, and retrospectively, setting the seal on the trilogy's brand as part of the Luhrmann oeuvre, and on Luhrmann's status as an auteur.[47] The elements of the Red Curtain brand shift depending on the source, but the key features are a theatricalised cinema set in heightened created worlds, relying on primary mythology and demanding audience participation.

Although it eventually became a major success, *Moulin Rouge!* and its extensive promotional campaign[48] were an exhausting experience for Luhrmann, who moved on to his next project, the revival of *La Bohème* for Broadway, with some trepidation, wondering whether there would be an audience for the production in the immediate aftermath of 9/11. As it turned out, it was deemed a triumph by both critics and audiences and had a successful run on Broadway from 8 December 2002 to 29 June 2003, attracting several awards.[49] For Luhrmann, this seemed to mark a watershed, and he announced his intention of moving away from the studio-based Red Curtain aesthetic with a new phase of historical epics. He began thinking about making the Alexander the Great biopic in 2001 while working on *La Bohème*. Initial preparations began in 2002, when Luhrmann joined forces with producer Dino De Laurentiis, who had long wanted to make a film about Alexander. At this early stage, it was rumoured that Martin Scorsese would be a co-producer and that Universal and Fox would be co-funders, with a budget of around $150 million. The production was to be shot in Morocco, where King Mohammed VI agreed to supply thousands of extras in exchange for the financing and building of a small studio in Ouarzazate, already the home of one of the largest film studios in the world. But as the US invasion of Iraq loomed, the Morocco location became less likely, and there was talk of shooting the film elsewhere, possibly in Australia. Leonardo DiCaprio was tipped to star as the bi-sexual Alexander, with Nicole Kidman a possibility to play his mother Olympias. Then Fox pulled out as funders, to be replaced by Steven Spielberg's DreamWorks. As reports about Oliver

Stone's *Alexander* production for Warner Bros. gathered momentum, with shooting set to begin in mid-2003, Luhrmann's film was put on hold for at least two years.[50] Meanwhile, Luhrmann and Martin had their first child, Lillian Amanda, in October 2003, and Luhrmann began work on a new project, the Chanel No. 5 mini-film starring Nicole Kidman. When Stone's movie premiered in November 2004 to poor reviews, Luhrmann's Alexander project was abandoned, and the Australian-themed epic moved into first place.[51]

The Chanel No. 5 project was a three-minute advertising film funded by Chanel, set in a mythical New York and shot in four days at Fox Studios Australia. Despite its apparently modest scale, it was in full-blown Red Curtain mode and presented as an event movie, the focus of intense media scrutiny. Nicole Kidman was paid the highest fee ever for an actress in an advertising film, and the budget has been estimated at $42 million.[52] Luhrmann envisaged the project as a self-contained short film, or a trailer for a film that might have been. The simple love story drew on Kidman's character Satine from *Moulin Rouge!*, and her image resonated with other celebrated women who had been identified with the perfume, such as Marilyn Monroe and Catherine Deneuve. In a modern twist, the scenario showed Kidman, pursued by paparazzi, desperately trying to escape her own celebrity through a brief love affair with a bohemian writer, the only person in the world who did not know who she was. Luhrmann wrote, produced and directed; Catherine Martin designed additional costumes and the sets, which recalled *Moulin Rouge!* and *La Bohème*; and Karl Lagerfeld, controversial head fashion designer at Chanel, was responsible for Kidman's dresses. The music was Debussy's melancholy 'Clair de lune', orchestrated by Craig Armstrong, who had worked on *Romeo + Juliet* and *Moulin Rouge!*.[53] *No. 5 The Film* was initially expected to take six weeks, but post-production took far longer than anticipated.[54] The film was released on television and in cinemas around the world in October and November 2004, accompanied by extensive media campaigns. It was given worldwide repeat screenings in the 2005, 2006, 2007 and 2008 Christmas period.[55] There were several versions of *No. 5 The Film*, which was cut for transmission as a commercial. The full-length film ran for three minutes, which included approximately one minute of end credits.[56]

It is difficult to measure the success of *No. 5 The Film*. The press response was generally positive,[57] and the fact that the advertisement has been screened at regular intervals since its release in 2004 suggests that it was effective in promoting the Chanel No. 5 brand. Perhaps more significant is the public visibility it bestowed on Luhrmann and the Red Curtain identity in the period between 2004 and 2008 when he was working on the first of his historical epics. Its life was extended in March 2006 when it appeared on the Internet via YouTube, where it has been viewed by more than 250,000 people to date, albeit in poor quality. In 2004, besides starting pre-production for *Australia*, Luhrmann participated in a two-hour British television programme titled *My Shakespeare*, in which he mentored, via video-link from the House of Iona, a group of young non-actors from Harlesden in north-west London who were producing their version of Shakespeare's *Romeo and Juliet*.[58] Luhrmann and Martin had their second child, William Alexander, in June 2005, and officially announced the new trilogy of period epics, which included an Australian-themed story. Luhrmann kept the choice of his next project closely under wraps;[59] after widespread media speculation, in February 2006 Luhrmann finally confirmed in the Australian press that the Australian epic would be the first of the new trilogy to be filmed. It was to be a sweeping romance (as yet untitled) on the scale of *Gone With the Wind* (1939), filmed on location in northwestern Australia and funded by Fox with a budget initially believed to be around $40 million. By August 2006, the budget estimate had risen to $100 million. The cast would be predominantly Australian and would include indigenous actors. Luhrmann was working on the script with Stuart Beattie, who had written *Collateral* (2004), and Ronald Harwood, who had adapted Wladyslaw Szpilman's book for Polanski's *The Pianist* (2002).[60] The title was announced as *Australia* in November 2006.

From the beginning, the production was surrounded by rumour and controversy. Kidman and Russell Crowe had apparently signed up as the leads, and allegedly both had agreed a substantial salary cut to work with Luhrmann. But in May 2006 Crowe dropped out due to salary disputes with Fox, stating that he did not do charity work for major studios. Hugh Jackman was recruited as his replacement to play the rough-and-ready Drover opposite Nicole

Kidman's English aristocrat Lady Sarah Ashley. The story focused on their romance, set against the backdrop of the cattle wars of the 1930s and the bombing of Darwin by the Japanese during World War II. Stories circulated that Luhrmann was having difficulty raising the necessary finance, but he denied this. After nearly two years of development and months of preparation and workshopping, shooting began in Sydney in late April 2007 and moved to Bowen, where 1930s Darwin was reconstructed, in May amid strict security. A sense of secrecy surrounded the project as details of the stellar Australian cast were revealed bit by bit. The Australian press went into overdrive with coverage of the Bowen shoot and its impact on the town and its local community. The production was due to move to the remote Kununurra region in western Australia in late July, but because of torrential rain the crew returned to Sydney to shoot at Fox Studios, and the Kununurra shoot resumed in mid-August, continuing into September. Filming then moved back to Sydney for the final stages, wrapping in December. The media hinted that Luhrmann was running behind schedule, but he and the studio dismissed these reports.

Amid all the media hype, which tended to focus on the lead players, especially Nicole Kidman, and the romance, there were a few items about the film's indigenous actors. The most famous of them, David Gulpilil, whose appearances in films such as *Walkabout* (1970), *The Tracker* (2002) and *Rabbit-Proof Fence* (2002) are highly regarded, received some attention, as did the twelve-year-old newcomer Brandon Walters, who was cast as Nullah, the film's narrator and arguably its most important character. But the political centre of the story, the Australian government's policy of removing mixed-race indigenous children from their families and raising them as white, did not feature prominently in coverage of the production process, though it became controversial once the film was released. Luhrmann is adept at managing the media and does not release information until the time is right. His disarming frankness and accessibility are matched by a shrewd sense of how to generate and maintain interest in his work by not giving away too much too soon. All his films have been risky projects, but *Australia* certainly qualified as the most risky to date on its title alone. Another potential risk was the casting of the twelve-year-old non-actor Walters in a primary role. From the beginning, the subject matter was predicted to appeal more to Australian markets than to North America. As with *Moulin Rouge!*, *Australia* was accompanied by intensive marketing in different media. However, in *Australia*'s case the studio's prerelease publicity went beyond saturation levels, which may have alienated reviewers.[61] Although the reviews were by no means all negative, many from US critics in particular were scathing, and this unfavourable response was echoed in the press around the world.[62] Nevertheless, the film was nominated for several awards, including an Oscar for Martin's costume design.[63] Again echoing the fortunes of *Moulin Rouge!*, the box office in the USA was disappointing, but in Australia, Europe, China and Japan *Australia* performed well and its audiences gradually built worldwide.

Luhrmann courts controversy, and the mixed response to *Australia* was unlikely to have disturbed him too much, especially as the film generated widespread debate. He is also aware that his work does not appeal to everyone. With its sweeping panoramic landscapes and action-packed exterior settings, *Australia* inaugurated a new phase for Luhrmann and Martin's aesthetic, presenting them with fresh challenges. Nevertheless, the basic elements of the Red Curtain style survived. Despite the emphasis on real locations, Australia was presented as a mythical realm, consistent with Luhrmann's enduring approach to place; the narrative conclusion, though relatively open-ended, hinged on the inevitability of destiny; and the provocation of the audience remained in the theatrical performances, the rapid shifts in tone and the dense network of quotations. *Australia* revisited home territory in more ways than one, re-presenting on a vast canvas to diverse international audiences the questions about Australian history and national identity that motivated *Strictly Ballroom*, whose story unfolds in the following chapter.

Two
Strictly Ballroom (1992)

Baz Luhrmann's ebullient debut feature *Strictly Ballroom* evolved out of his experiences at Sydney's National Institute of Dramatic Art (NIDA), where he enrolled on an acting course in 1982 when he was twenty.[1] He has often expressed ambivalence about his time at NIDA; on a personal level, he was not entirely happy there, yet it also provided him with knowledge, skills and contacts that shaped his future direction. He had been rejected by the institute two years previously, and spent the intervening period busily building an acting career in film and television. When he was accepted by NIDA, he already had an impressive list of credits. He played Pete the pimp opposite Judy Davis and Bryan Brown in *Winter of Our Dreams* (1981), a drama written and directed by John Duigan; from 1981 to 1982 he appeared as Jerry Percival in six episodes of the long-running television series *A Country Practice*;[2] he had a small part as a student in Paul Harmon's thriller *The Dark Room* (1982), which went straight to video; and he conceived a drama-documentary about Sydney's homeless youth, for which he apparently slept rough for three months. Unable to get finance for this project, he took it to a television company, who made it into a sensationalist programme that generated a backlash in the tabloid press. The experience taught Luhrmann always to insist on creative control of his work.[3] In 1982 he set up his first theatre company, The Bond, some of whose members worked with him at NIDA.

Luhrmann was evidently a complicated, driven and ambitious young man; this, combined with insecurities about his Herons Creek background, led him to project an over-confident persona that did not endear him to everyone at NIDA. He was uncomfortable with some of the teaching there, which he found restrictive in its focus on traditional approaches to theatre. On the other hand, he was stimulated by what he learned about innovators such as Shakespeare, Molière, Brecht, Artaud and Strindberg. For a part as

Molière in *L'Impromptu de Versailles*, he researched the seventeenth-century French playwright and actor in depth and attempted to live as he had lived. NIDA students were encouraged to stage their own productions, and in 1984 Luhrmann devised in collaboration with a group of fellow students a thirty-minute play titled *Strictly Ballroom*, set against the background of competitive ballroom dancing. Luhrmann had been a ballroom dancing champion in his youth and had considerable experience of the context.[4] As part of the devising process, each member of the group was required to sit in a chair called the 'hot seat' and answer truthfully personal questions from the others. Luhrmann had devised projects with The Bond before NIDA, including a play called *American Days* that ran for a season at the Bondi Pavilion Community Cultural Centre in Waverley, New South Wales. NIDA gave him the training to refine and develop the collaborative methods of devised theatre that he had always instinctively used, and continues to use today. From the 'hot seat' sessions, it emerged that the group felt a sense of alienation about the state of the world, and a lack of political engagement. This led to the notion of the disenfranchised outsider expressed in the myth of David and Goliath and in Hans Christian Andersen's fairy-tale 'The Ugly Duckling', both of which formed central narrative threads in the play.

The version of *Strictly Ballroom* devised at NIDA dramatised a conflict between change and tradition with which Luhrmann and the group strongly identified.[5] The competitive ballroom dancing community acted as a microcosm for society in the grip of the Cold War, while its governing body, the Federation, stood for the rigid power structures of those in authority. The simple story-line showed a cultural revolution occurring as a result of an individual act of rebellion that inspired others. The production used a number of 'Brechtian' devices, such as direct address to the audience and the use of a plain black backdrop for the action. Costume changes were carried out on stage as the costumes descended from above. Tapes of radio broadcasts and pop music were played, and the staging used a montage technique in which different scenes were performed simultaneously rather than consecutively, cross-fertilising between radio, music, film and theatre. Luhrmann took the role of Ross Pierce, the hero Scott's father, while his close friend Catherine McClements, now a well-known film and theatre actress, played

Scott's mother Barbara.[6] This first production was a thinly disguised metaphor for Luhrmann and the group's frustration with the programme at NIDA and their sense of artistic oppression. At the same time, NIDA provided the conditions and the techniques that enabled the students to channel their disenchantment. While some of Luhrmann's experiences there were demoralising, his formative years at the institute paved the way for his creative development.

After the NIDA performance, following his graduation in 1985, Luhrmann and the group developed the play for the 1986 World Youth Festival in Bratislava, where the audience response was overwhelmingly enthusiastic.[7] This version was more overtly political, and tapes of speeches by US president Ronald Reagan and British prime minister Margaret Thatcher were included. As in the earlier production, Cyndi Lauper's 1984 hit record 'Time After Time' provided the soundtrack for a choreographed montage of dance, action and dialogue. The Czechoslovakian audience reacted with gusto to the message of creative freedom, which vindicated Luhrmann's ideas about the ability of myth to speak to people from different cultures. The performance won festival awards for Best Production and Best Direction, confirming Luhrmann's promise as an exciting new talent. In March 1986, he submitted a proposal to the Australian Film Commission for funding to develop a script for a thirty-minute film of *Strictly Ballroom*, to be co-written by himself and Nell Schofield, a founding member of The Bond who had worked on the NIDA productions, and directed by him.[8] The proposal identified certain key elements: a simple, fable-like story set against the background of world politics; a theatrical, non-naturalistic style; a hybrid music score combining opera, orchestrated dance music and original arrangements; the use of contrasting colour and black-and-white photography; design that veered towards absurdity; a collaborative workshop as part of the development process; and a young target audience. Although the proposal was not taken forward, the seeds of the fully fledged film were clearly in place.

The next incarnation of *Strictly Ballroom* emerged in 1988. In 1986 Luhrmann was asked by the Sydney Theatre Company to form an independent theatre troupe with himself as artistic director, and the Six Years Old company was born. The project was part of Australia's 1988 bicentennial celebrations; in that year Six Years Old staged *Haircut*, an irreverent take on the musical *Hair*, and devised a new production of *Strictly Ballroom* in which the Spanish theme appeared for the first time, with 'ugly ducking' Jenny Ferguson transformed into Fran. Members of the Six Years Old group included Glenn Keenan, a NIDA graduate who had worked on the earlier play, Craig Pearce, who was an actor at the time, and Tara Morice, who played Fran in this version and in the film.[9] The extended *Strictly Ballroom* had a successful run in 1988 at the Sydney Wharf Theatre, and at World Expo '88 in Brisbane, Queensland. Australian music producer Ted Albert saw the Wharf Theatre performance and with his business partner, documentary film-maker Tristram Miall, approached Luhrmann about buying the rights. They planned to turn the play into a full-length feature for M&A, their new film production unit. When Luhrmann told them he intended to make the film *Strictly Ballroom* himself, they suggested that he direct it for M&A Film Corporation, but stipulated that he should hire a professional screenwriter. Playwright Andrew Bovell came on board and wrote the first draft of the screenplay. Luhrmann felt that this draft was too naturalistic, and between 1989 and 1990 worked with Bovell on a revised screenplay that brought back the metaphorical dimension of the play and introduced stylistic flourishes in the theatrical mode of classic Hollywood musicals. At the time, Luhrmann was heavily involved in the Australian Opera production of *La Bohème* as well as completing the financing of the film. M&A preferred the idea of a naturalistic scenario, but Luhrmann was convinced that he needed to develop a theatrical cinematic language and recommended that Craig Pearce, who had experience of the play's evolution, should write the script with him. M&A agreed and, in the first of their writing collaborations, Luhrmann and Pearce co-wrote the final screenplay, in which psychological realism was jettisoned and the exhibitionist style of what would become Red Curtain cinema took centre stage.[10]

The writing process took many months and fourteen redrafts until Luhrmann, Pearce, Albert and Miall were satisfied. The film was ready to begin casting, when Ted Albert unexpectedly died of a heart attack in November 1990. His widow Antoinette took on the role of executive producer

so that pre-production could proceed.[11] Paul Mercurio, a member of the
Sydney Dance Company, was cast as Scott Hastings in his first appearance as
a screen actor. Dance rehearsals and workshops with choreographer John
O'Connell extended over a ten-week period, with some of the actors devising their own dances.[12] The budget of around A$3 million was very tight. A
fruitless visit to Cannes to raise funding for the film had been met by scepticism from overseas distributors that the ballroom dancing setting would
have any interest. The development and production were financed by M&A
and the Australian Film Finance Corporation (AFFC) with the assistance of
the New South Wales Film and Television Office. The AFFC apparently
wanted an American actress for the part of Fran, but with Tristram Miall and
Antoinette Albert's support, Luhrmann held out for Tara Morice.[13] The
seven-week shoot began in Melbourne with the complex final sequence, the
Pan-Pacific championship competition, which was shot with five cameras
while an actual ballroom dancing contest was in progress in front of a large
crowd of spectators.[14] The rest of the film was shot in Sydney. Budget and
time constraints imposed a gruelling schedule on the shoot, and some
severe financial cuts that particularly affected Catherine Martin and Bill
Marron's art department. In order to deal with these pressures, Luhrmann
planned each step in minute detail. Despite the budget cuts, the costume
and sets were visually splendid and meticulously constructed. The costumes
alone took 5,000 hours of labour, and for Paul Mercurio's matador-style
bolero jacket worn in the climactic sequence, two people worked for four
weeks to embroider and decorate it with imported braid, crystals and
sequins.[15]

Further pressures arose from the fact that, apart from Paul Mercurio, the
actors did not have professional dance training and had to acquire ballroom
dancing skills in a very short time. There was additional stress for those
members of the creative team for whom this was their first experience of
film-making. Everyone was stretched to the limit, including editor Jill
Bilcock. When post-production got under way, the editing process in
Melbourne took four-and-a-half months rather than the anticipated six
weeks. The Pan-Pacific championship finale consisted of shots from two
cities and four different locations spliced together. The matching of sound

and image in this sequence proved particularly difficult. Eventually, a year after production began and with everyone physically and emotionally drained, *Strictly Ballroom* the film was completed in January 1992 and shown to AFFC executives, who left the screening room in silence.[16] The initial response from some exhibitors was negative, leading Luhrmann to think that his film-making career was over as soon as it had begun. Then came the phone call from Pierre Rissient inviting *Strictly Ballroom* to join the Un Certain Regard section at the 45th Cannes Film Festival and programming a special midnight screening on 10 May 1992. The screening ran late, the cinema was not full, and one or two audience members walked out in the first five minutes. Luhrmann and his team were extremely nervous, but then at the end the film received a standing ovation from the notoriously difficult Cannes critics, and word-of-mouth reports spread like wildfire. Festival director Gilles Jacob immediately set up additional screenings, which received an equally rapturous response. As a result of this success, *Strictly Ballroom* was sold to eighty-six countries and later went on to gross an estimated $70 million worldwide.[17] The Cannes awards jury, which was led by Gérard Depardieu and included Jamie Lee Curtis, Pedro Almodóvar and John Boorman, gave the coveted Caméra d'or prize to John Turturro for his debut feature *Mac*. However, *Strictly Ballroom* was awarded a Special Mention and it won the Prix de Jeunesse for best foreign film. It went on to gather further accolades at film festivals and awards ceremonies around the world. Although it was not universally praised by critics, the reception was generally positive and the film received some high-profile endorsements. Writing in *The Times*, David Robinson described *Strictly Ballroom*'s triumph at Cannes as an unprecedented Cinderella story and included it in his list of all-time favourites.[18]

Strictly Ballroom's Cannes experience demonstrates the important role that international film festivals play in the success or failure of low-budget independent productions and in actors' and film-makers' careers. Gaining film festival awards for one project can make a difference to chances of acquiring finance for the next, and the reaction of festival critics can have a positive or negative impact on a film's future.[19] Major studios and production companies scouting for new talent are influenced by the buzz that film festivals generate around their tips for 'the next big thing', which also affects world press and media coverage. The significance of festivals creates a type or genre of festival film, with certain recognisable features. The typical festival film falls into the category of art cinema; it has 'European' qualities such as narrative ambiguity and an emphasis on the cinematic image, marking itself as different from what are perceived as conventional Hollywood movies; it celebrates its national provenance and use of national talent, while drawing on international elements that will appeal to wider audiences; it demonstrates stylistic originality, often using controversial subject-matter or unusual methods of storytelling; it displays technical ingenuity in overcoming its low-budget status. To distinguish itself from mainstream entertainment, a festival film will often be downbeat and focus on dark psychological themes in an elliptical manner. It addresses niche, sophisticated audiences, demanding their participation on the level of interpretation and appreciation. Above all, a festival film draws attention to itself as innovative while at the same time promising rewards, financial and cultural, for future backers.

Strictly Ballroom had many of the characteristics of a festival film. It showcased young Australian talent in performances and cinematic technique, but it also had hybrid qualities, combining a local Australian setting with a classical story structure and a theatrical style that drew on Hollywood musicals. Its garishly colourful visuals were matched by an eclectic soundtrack that mixed classical, pop and dance music. It featured no major international stars and used established character actors together with unknown performers, enabling as much as possible of its small budget to go into elements such as costume and sets. Its simple message of love crossing boundaries and overcoming oppression struck a chord with many different viewers, transforming familiar material with style and verve. However, in some ways the film differed from typical festival fare. It was assertively upbeat. Its sometimes strident tone and tendency to travesty did not conform to the tasteful principles of European art cinema, and its gleeful populism was unashamedly crowd-pleasing. Yet this was part of its appeal. *Strictly Ballroom* broke new ground by crossing over between traditional art cinema and commercial genre movies, re-energising both in the process. It injected new vigour into Australian cinema, and found a place in popular cultural vernacular.[20] It was the basis for the Red Curtain style, whose evolution preoccupied Luhrmann and the team for the next ten years.

*   *   *

Despite many transformations, the basic story structure for *Strictly Ballroom* remained constant. Twenty-one-year-old ballroom dancing champion Scott Hastings (Paul Mercurio) commits the cardinal sin of dancing his own steps rather than the correct ones laid down by the all-powerful Dance Federation. His partner Liz Holt (Gia Carides), desperate to win the Pan-Pacific Latin Freestyle Grand Prix, rejects him, and he incurs the wrath of his mother Shirley (Pat Thomson) and Federation president Barry Fife (Bill Hunter), who is determined to uphold the Federation's authority. A series of try-outs to find him a suitable partner is unsuccessful. Scott's hopes of participating in the Pan-Pacific contest fade, until 'ugly duckling' Fran (Tara Morice), a beginner at Kendall's dance studio where Shirley and Scott's ineffectual father Doug (Barry Otto) work, puts herself forward as his new partner. Scott refuses at first, but through sheer persistence Fran eventually wins him over and an unlikely partnership is born. But when champion dancer Tina Sparkle (Sonia Kruger) becomes available, Scott is persuaded to partner her in the Pan-Pacifics. Fran stands down for Scott's sake, but Scott has a change of heart and follows Fran to the home of her Spanish family at the Toledo Milk Bar, where her father Rico (Antonio Vargas) and grandmother Ya Ya (Armonia Benedito) introduce him to the passionate rhythm of the genuine paso doble. Scott is inspired by the experience to declare his love for Fran. The night before the Pan-Pacifics, Barry Fife tells Scott that his father Doug once tried to dance his own steps at the competition, and was disqualified, his dance career finished. Confused, to save his broken father's sanity, Scott once more turns his back on Fran and agrees to partner Liz Holt at the championships. Minutes before the contest begins, Doug reveals that Barry Fife has lied and that Shirley was persuaded to dance in the Pan-Pacifcs with Les Kendall, with the result that they lost. Released from the past, Scott finds Fran and they take to the floor with a virtuoso display of the paso doble that the crowd loves. Barry Fife stops the music, but the crowd, led by Doug, shows its support for Scott and Fran by starting a slow handclap. The couple dance to the rhythm of the clapping, the music is turned on again, Fife is humiliated and soon the floor is flooded with celebratory dancers.[21]

Earlier versions of the script had included devices to indicate the political context for the story, such as the 1989 Tiananmen Square protests in Beijing, and had a background in a working-class steel mill town. In the final script, the naturalistic backdrop was abandoned and the principal settings were tied to the fantastical world of ballroom dancing: the Town Hall, Kendall's Dance Studio, the Toledo Milk Bar and the championship stadium. The documentary-style sequences that took place in Scott's family home, the Federation offices, the hair salon, garage and Spa-orama were brief and cartoon-like. Remnants of social realism could be glimpsed in the set for Fran's home, the Toledo Milk Bar, with its nearby railway line, cramped interiors and run-down exteriors, the arena for Scott and Fran's budding relationship. The set was clearly a construction, but its dilapidated charm had the necessary romanticism and authenticity. This authenticity was linked to Scott and Fran, who had an ingenuous air that identified them as heroes of the story, in contrast to the exaggerated performances of the Anglo-Celtic Australian characters. In 1989, art director Bill Marron had drawn a *Strictly Ballroom* comic that encapsulated the dynamic visual style of the production.[22] The final version retained this comic-book energy, cutting rapidly between scenes that alternated between big close-ups and medium and long-shots to maintain a punchy rhythm. The overall tone was satirical, sending up the pretensions of the ballroom dancing community, but the love affair between outsiders Scott and Fran and their unconventional dance partnership was presented as genuinely sympathetic and a focus for audience identification. This enabled the film-makers to celebrate the potentially liberating ambience of ballroom dancing as a space for self-expression and creative reinvention.

The film's central relationship had wider cultural implications arising from the earlier Six Years Old stage version, in which the Spanish dimension had appeared for the first time. The play was devised for the 1988 Australian bicentennial celebrations, which were embroiled in controversy

Fairy-tale romance: Scott (Paul Mercurio) and Fran (Tara Morice) in *Strictly Ballroom*

because they marked the beginnings of white settlement. This may have provided the impetus for the inclusion of ethnic characters whose contribution to Australian society was recognised and celebrated. Although Scott and Fran's cross-cultural romance was not presented in overtly political terms by the film, it pivoted on a sub-text about the marginalisation of ethnic minorities. Scott and Fran's bravura performance in the rousing finale was not simply an act of individual defiance, it was also an affirmation of cultural diversity, epitomised by the mêlée that thronged the dance floor in the closing moments. The satire was reserved for the Anglo-Celtic Australian characters whose fear of change and deference to authority were seen to be at the root of cultural oppression. But while they were ridiculed, there was also sympathy for those, like Scott's father Doug, who were unable to throw off their chains and realise their creative potential. The approach to creativity was not elitist or sectarian, rather it was utopian and inclusive, reflecting the film-makers' commitment to communal artistic endeavour. In national terms, the film depicted Australia as a place where rigid social hierarchies were under pressure from multiculturalism. It affirmed the country's foundations in multi-ethnic immigration and the promise that every citizen could achieve success and fulfilment. Its visual flamboyance had a touch of carnival, dramatising cultural renewal through the overturning of the ruling order. This aura of cultural regeneration contributed to its status as instigator of the 1990s Australian cinema revival.

Strictly Ballroom's fairy-tale romance, comic-book vitality and utopianism are all part of its broad appeal. However, the film's apparent simplicity is deceptive. The theatrical cinematic style has different levels, nowhere more evident than in its approach to time and place. It has often been remarked that the film is not set in a particular era; rather, a mix of period styles in sets, costume and music creates a sense of collapsed time in which different decades merge together. The costumes, hair and make-up, usually reliable indicators of a film's period setting, span several eras. The collage technique enables references to be threaded through the fabric of the text like the sequins embroidered on the dancers' garments. The music soundtrack is carefully compiled from a melange of classical tracks (Bizet's 'Carmen'; Chopin's 'Etude'), dance music ('La cumparsita' tango; Strauss's 'Blue Danube Waltz'; 'Happy Feet'; 'Os quindins de yaya'; 'España cañí' paso doble; 'Rumba de burros') and popular songs (John Paul Young's 1970s hits 'Yesterday's Hero', 'Standing in the Rain' and 'Love Is in the Air'; Doris Day's 1965 version of 'Perhaps, Perhaps, Perhaps'; Cyndi Lauper's 1984 hit 'Time After Time'; Chuck Rio's 1958 'Tequila'; and the traditional Irish anthem 'Londonderry Air'). The music helps to tell the story and convey mood, but it also underlines the film's anachronistic character. 'Time After Time', played over Scott and Fran's rooftop dance, which is cut against Doug's secret cavorting, sets the tone for the central idea of memory, repetition and the persistence of the past, the destructive cycle that Scott has to break, and the restorative power of love. The music plays a large part in supporting the Latin theme, with several of the songs, including 'Love Is in the Air', 'Perhaps, Perhaps, Perhaps' and 'Tequila', of Hispanic origin.

The dance numbers also operate at more than one level. They trace the development of the love story, while at the same time contributing to the layers of allusion. Scott and Fran's behind-the-scenes rehearsals recall backstage musicals while their couple-dance to the strains of 'Perhaps, Perhaps, Perhaps' evokes classic Hollywood partnerships such as Gene Kelly and Cyd Charisse. Scott's narcissistic solo in the dance studio echoes John Travolta's performance in *Saturday Night Fever* (1977) and conjures up the heyday of disco. *Saturday Night Fever*'s rites-of-passage story-line, in which the young protagonist acquires a sense of morality through love, is paralleled by Scott's maturation process. The accumulation of references in *Strictly Ballroom* could be seen as nostalgic. There are certainly elements of nostalgia in Luhrmann's homage to his beloved Hollywood musicals. However, the film's underlying principle is one of appropriation rather than reverence; the source material is plundered, reworked and added to the heterogeneous mix to create a new, hybrid concoction. The result is a kaleidoscopic effect in which images and sounds collide with one another. Rather than look back to a golden age, the film uses references to the past to illuminate its message of the need to move forward, and to carve out its own aesthetic.

The manipulation of cinematic time is evident in the opening sequence, which begins with a monochrome, slow motion, medium-long shot of Scott and Liz with Scott's friend Wayne (Pip Mushin) and his partner Vanessa (Leonie Page) excitedly preparing to enter the ballroom. They are in costume, and the Blue Danube waltz plays as they move in slow motion through the glass doors at the entrance towards the camera. This is the audience's first glimpse of ballroom's enchanted world, which appears dreamlike. There is an explosion of sound and colour as the dancers burst onto the dance floor to begin their exhibition. It is not clear initially whether this is set in the present; the sudden switch to a pseudo-documentary scene in Scott's home, in which a distressed Shirley tells the story of Scott's rebellion at the state championships, indicates that the ballroom episode belongs to the past. However, the strategy of cutting the two scenes against one another, combined with the histrionic, non-naturalistic performance by Pat Thomson as Shirley, produces an impression that both are taking place simultaneously. The confusion about time scale is exacerbated when the next sequence at Kendall's dance studio carries the title 'Three days later', which could refer either to the documentary or to the ballroom scene, but is in any case redundant. The theatricalised performances in this sequence erase any generic differences between the documentary and the dance studio, and the inclusion of a fantasy scenario, in which Liz Holt's wish that Pam Short would break both her legs and Ken Railings would ask her to be his partner comes true, sets the seal on the film's non-realistic, atemporal character. Editing is also used to extend time, as with Scott's backwards knee-slide in the Pan-Pacific championship, where different shots are spliced together to make it appear to last longer than it actually did.

Another example of play with time is the retro sequence that accompanies Barry Fife's story about Doug's disastrous rebellion at the ballroom championships. The monochrome photograph of Doug and Shirley comes to life as they quickstep on to a proscenium stage framed by red velvet curtains. The time and place are obscure; on one hand the black-and-white image evokes 1930s and 1940s Hollywood, on the other Shirley's high beehive hairstyle and the intensified colour recall the 1950s and 1960s. The set mixes 1950s-style red curtains with 1970s disco mirror balls, while the costumes span the 1940s, 1950s and 1970s. A banner displays the title 'Championship 1967' as Shirley and Doug dance 1950s jive to the strains of John Paul Young's 1975 song 'Yesterday's Hero'. Doug's make-up and performance echo Joel Grey's as the Master of Ceremonies in Bob Fosse's groundbreaking musical *Cabaret* (1972). Although this glance into the past is more stylised and dreamlike than the main body of the film, because the red curtains and the monochrome image exploding into dramatic colour resonate with the opening scene, no absolute distinction is made between 'then' and 'now'. The retro sequence is a bold statement about what would become the Red Curtain aesthetic. Its heightened theatrical staging depicts a self-contained artificial world in which stereotyped characters are deliberately devoid of psychological depth. It uses pastiche, travesty and burlesque to satirise theatre and cinema conventions and establish a defiantly non-naturalistic style. The use of travesty gives a parodic edge to the film's homage to classic Hollywood, which becomes grist to the mill of Luhrmann and the team's reinterpretation of classic modes of representation. Cross-dressing, as a central feature of travesty, intimates a carnivalesque fluidity of class, gender and ethnic identities that chimes with the film's socially inclusive politics.

Strictly Ballroom's approach to place is as slippery as its treatment of time. The setting is recognisably Australian, but Australia is conceived by the film-makers as an imaginary location. It has identifiable national features, but the representation of the ballroom dancing world as a microcosm and its depiction through the filter of Hollywood mean that it could also be situated elsewhere. There are indicators of place; the opening competition occurs at the Waratah State Championships, which identifies the setting as New South Wales,[23] but the designation is intentionally vague. One of the exteriors, the rooftop above Kendall's dance studio, is the stage for Scott and Fran's dance to Cyndi Lauper's 'Time After Time', which plays out against a giant Coca-Cola sign on a glittering red-spangled background, offset by an Australian icon, the Hill's Hoist rotary clothes dryer. Behind the rooftop the city skyline, streets and traffic suggest a real location. The star-studded sign is reminiscent of the towering Coca-Cola masthead that dominates Sydney's King Cross. It might also refer to the film-makers' love of American culture,[24] and to the aspirations of the characters to celebrity status. It could appear ironic, as a statement of US cultural imperialism. The irony is doubly marked by the mundanity of the Hill's Hoist, a metaphor for 1950s and 1960s Australian suburbia. Like the rest of the film's settings, the rooftop is an amalgamation of specific signs of location and creative reconstruction.

The depiction of place in *Strictly Ballroom* was both local and global; it belonged to and spoke from a particular national context while at the same time reaching beyond national borders to wider international communities. Even at this early stage, then, Luhrmann's work could be classified as transnational, in the sense that it sought to make cultural connections across national boundaries. As already noted, *Strictly Ballroom* was a multi-layered melange of ideas and styles from diverse origins. Yet the film's overriding sensibility could be defined as Australian, not least in its investment in travesty and burlesque. It had strong affinities with the wickedly surreal comic lampoons of Barry Humphries,[25] and with the carnivalesque spirit of Sydney's annual gay and lesbian Mardi Gras. While travesty is not confined to Australian culture, it has found a home there, perhaps because Australia is a nation rooted in postcolonial rebellion, many of whose people

can identify with popular culture's unseemly impulse to challenge the
established order.

*   *   *

Strictly Ballroom's success at Cannes had dramatic consequences. Suddenly
the film became the focus of international media attention, and Luhrmann
was pursued by major Hollywood studios and agents eager to sign up the
talented newcomers. Marketing moved into gear to capitalise on the situation. The Australian distributors, Ronin Films, were a small independent
outfit based in Canberra who had guaranteed the film to the AFFC in order
to secure funding. International markets, including the UK, were handled
by Beyond Films, with Miramax in charge of US distribution. The mini-
major company Miramax, who had a maverick reputation for backing idio-
syncratic productions such as *sex, lies, and videotape* (1989) and *The Crying
Game* (1992), were attracted to *Strictly Ballroom* because of its reception at
Cannes. However, there was no guarantee that a low-budget, foreign production lacking international stars would achieve success at the US box
office. Miramax's strategy was to promote the film as a 'hot ticket' discovery movie,[26] and the support of influential critics such as Janet Maslin of
the *New York Times*,[27] *Variety*'s Todd McCarthy and *Rolling Stone*'s film col-
umn[28] helped *Strictly Ballroom* to become a winner in the USA, where it
went on general release in February 1993.[29] It was also a runaway critical
and box-office hit in the UK following its October 1992 release there, and
in Japan, where it achieved the best sales for an Australian movie since
Crocodile Dundee (1986).[30] In Australia, where it was released in August
1992, *Strictly Ballroom* was hailed by the press as a small masterpiece that
reflected a new multicultural spirit abroad in the nation, and was rated by
some as a worthy successor to the legendary *The Man from Snowy River*
(1982) and *Crocodile Dundee* in artistic terms as well as in its encapsulation
of what it meant to be Australian.[31] Both had been domestic and international money-spinners, and occupied a place high in Australian movie
pantheons. One or two press reviews were less enthusiastic,[32] but the general response was positive,[33] with the result that the domestic box office
quickly took off. Within six months of its initial release, *Strictly Ballroom*

had taken almost $18 million in Australia alone, an astonishing result for such a risk-laden project.[34]

Strictly Ballroom had been made at a difficult time for the Australian film industry. The AFFC, which was responsible for two-thirds of the film's budget, had been set up in 1988 after the controversial and costly 10BA government tax concessions available to Australian productions since 1981 had been drastically reduced.[35] The AFFC had a commercially driven agenda, with the expectation that it would recoup its investment in the films it financed. In 1992, the government announced a four-year diminishing financial allocation aimed at generating a self-funding film industry.[36] Those films with AFFC funding would be expected to return that money over the four-year period. *Strictly Ballroom*'s unprecedented financial success would not only enable it to repay the AFFC's investment, but would go towards making up the shortfall from those productions that failed to recoup their costs, since any profits above and beyond the investment money would be shared between the private investors,[37] the AFFC and key members of the production team.[38] This was an extraordinary achievement for a project that broke the usual AFFC criteria by having no stars and a lead creative team with no track record in film-making. Part of that achievement could be put down to proactive marketing. Early preview screenings in Australia for school children aged between twelve and eighteen years had been held in April, May and July 1992 to gauge the response of young viewers to the film, with the aim of using this information in media campaigns.[39] Public relations companies put together plans for the theatrical release, acknowledging that competition from bigger-budget Hollywood movies would be fierce in the home marketplace.

The marketing plans proposed that the target audience should be carefully and accurately defined, and creative promotional strategies should be devised to generate interest in *Strictly Ballroom*. Both leading actors were important in the campaign, but most attention focused on Paul Mercurio. The target audience was identified as people between sixteen and thirty-nine years, strongly angled towards female viewers. A high-impact television campaign across all channels at key viewing times, with 'top and tail' advertisements appearing before and after commercial breaks, was concentrated in higher viewing periods from Sunday to Wednesday. Coverage on the SBS channel[40] addressed the higher socio-economic sections of the target market. A 'making of' documentary and a teaser campaign for television broadcast were suggested. Radio was considered an important medium for reaching younger members of the target audience, especially the Austereo network, which was geared towards female listeners. Radio stations were also possible sites for promotional offers such as free tickets to preview screenings. Full-page advertisements in the press publicised the launch; Paul Mercurio featured prominently in these and advertisements in other media. Possible outdoor promotional activities were twenty-four-foot-high posters in prime positions with live ballroom dancers performing next to them as a means of generating a 'buzz'. Magazines such as *Cleo*, aimed at younger women, featured the sex appeal of Paul Mercurio.[41] A tie-in to television broadcasts of the 1992 summer Olympic Games, held in Barcelona, was mooted.

Ronin Films' marketing materials comprised trailers, street posters and press kit focusing on Paul Mercurio, as well as leaflets and a sixteen-page main press kit. A 'Love Is in the Air' music video, directed by Luhrmann and featuring John Paul Young performing a kitsch, updated version of his hit song, was produced by Albert Studios and released by Sony in 1992, to be used on cinema video walls and on television. A twelve-minute featurette consisting of interviews with Luhrmann, Paul Mercurio and other members of the cast and creative team was also made available.[42] Promotional materials included *Strictly Ballroom* t-shirts, some featuring Paul Mercurio, which had been hot property at Cannes.[43] In June 1992, Ronin issued a press statement announcing that it had entered into an agreement with the international company Columbia TriStar Hoyts Home Video, who would contribute to the Australian theatrical release marketing campaign, before launching *Strictly Ballroom* on home video.[44] Ronin indicated that the film's theatrical release in Australia on 20 August 1992 would be extensive, encompassing all state capitals and selected regional centres and using the major cinema chains, such as Hoyts, Greater Union and Village, as well as a range of independent cinemas. Initial release would be in forty-five screens, with more to follow.[45] The press announcement mentioned the widespread enthusiasm for the film among exhibitors, the marketing team and AFFC financial backers, a very different response from that initially experienced by the film-makers.

A few days prior to its general Australian release, on 17 August 1992 *Strictly Ballroom* had its gala premiere at the Greater Union cinema in Melbourne, in association with the AIDS Trust of Australia, for which tickets cost A$40.[46] Following its success at Cannes and screening at the 1992 Melbourne International Film Festival, where it won the audience vote for Most Popular Feature, the film achieved a high profile on Melbourne's art-cinema circuit. A special marketing plan was conceived to promote *Strictly Ballroom* to mainstream audiences in the city and suburbs through advertising, interviews and cover stories in the popular press, including street newspapers and specialist dance magazines. Television spots on programmes with wide appeal, including the light entertainment shows *Hey Hey It's Saturday* and *Tonight Live With Steve Vizard*, and the daytime television magazine programmes *Melbourne Today* and *Good Morning Australia*, were planned, along with features on news items such as *Melbourne Extra*, *Channel 10 News* and ABC's *7.30 Report*.[47] These marketing strategies were aimed at capitalising on the vast amount of interest that had built up around *Strictly Ballroom* in just a few months, which had also reached the higher echelons of the New South Wales government. Minister of the Arts Peter Collins QC wrote a letter of congratulations to Luhrmann on the film's outstanding success.[48] Marketing campaigns in countries outside Australia were equally intensive,[49] and the film rapidly became a global phenomenon.

Although the worldwide media attention generated by *Strictly Ballroom* was not on the scale of Luhrmann's subsequent films, it was greater than a low-budget Australian independent production would normally receive, and significant enough to make it an event movie in its own right. By October 1992, it had become the fourth-highest grossing Australian film ever. In the same period, the soundtrack album went gold and sold 50,000 copies.[50] The screenplay was published in 1992,[51] and in the same year the first VHS version was launched. In May 1993, Ronin took the unorthodox step of rereleasing the film in Australia less than a year after its debut, in more screens this time. Its impressive roster of awards, including eight at the 1992 Australian Film Institute (AFI) awards, reached record-breaking proportions.[52] It also performed exceptionally well on Australian television; screened on Channel 7 at 8.30 pm on 23 October 1994, it gained 41.3 per cent of an audience of 700,000 viewers against Hollywood fare such as *Lethal Weapon* (1987) at 26.5 per cent, *Darkman* (1990) at 10.75 per cent and *True Stories* (1986) at 4.25 per cent.[53] Before long, *Strictly Ballroom*'s renown was picked up in academic circles. Karl Quinn, writing in 1994 following the release of Stephan Elliott's *The Adventures of Priscilla, Queen of the Desert* (which, like *Strictly Ballroom*, had been lauded at Cannes) and P. J. Hogan's *Muriel's Wedding*, linked Luhrmann's film with a brash new wave of Australian cinema that broke with the tasteful costume dramas, landscape-centred rural epics and European-art-cinema imitators that had become the norm, to address young, urban, street-wise audiences. Quinn saw a connection between the three films' trashy aesthetics, nostalgia for the 1970s in music and design and use of surrealist fantasy, taking them to task for exploiting 'dagdom' in their camp parodies of suburban Australia.[54] For Quinn, the films' reliance on irony was a sign of a society that had lost the means to respond directly with emotion and desire, and took refuge in distanciation and insincerity. *Strictly Ballroom* was accused of treating all its characters and key moments of reconciliation with the same degree of self-mockery. The new wave was founded in ambivalence, in that its celebration of Australian talent was based on a sense of self-loathing that historically permeated the home culture. The most that could be said of these films was that they energetically rejected social norms in favour of their own, individualistic world-view. Rather than asserting a unified national identity, they recognised Australia as a more pluralistic, open society.[55]

Quinn saw the 'glitter cycle', as it came to be known, as foregrounding sexual dysfunction and deviance. This aspect was explored more sympathetically by John Champagne, who identified a tension in the cycle's solicitation of gay male viewers and its treatment of women. Writing in 1997, in the context of queer theory and postfeminism, he suggested that, much as he liked them, the films' sexual politics were flawed. Champagne claimed that there were a number of reasons why these Australian productions had queer appeal, including the reputation of Australia as an island haven for male

Self-parody: Pat Thomson
and Barry Otto as Scott's
parents in *Strictly Ballroom*

homosexuals; the popularity of Aussie outback fantasy porn featuring men
from 'down under'; Sydney's pan-sexual Mardi Gras; Dame Edna Everage;
the films' eroticisation of the male body; their camp aesthetics and use of
drag; and their deployment of the utopian conventions of the Hollywood
musical to enable the characters to find fulfilment and a sense of community.
In the case of *Strictly Ballroom*, Champagne pointed to the gay attraction of
Paul Mercurio and speculated that Luhrmann, on the basis that he had been
a ballroom dancer, had directed opera and theatre and lived with a man and
a woman, could be seen as queer-friendly, if not actually queer. The multilayered quality of *Strictly Ballroom* led Champagne to conjecture that it

'encoded' a gay discourse. He quoted Richard Dyer's influential definition of gay sensibility as holding together contradictory qualities such as theatricality and authenticity; intensity and irony; and fierce emotion with a sense of its absurdity. For Champagne, *Strictly Ballroom*'s use of a romantic couple that featured a de-glamorised heroine and a homoeroticised hero was further evidence of its gay appeal. He saw that appeal as founded on gynophobia, and therefore problematic for an alliance of queer politics with feminism.[56]

Champagne's critique made passing reference to *Strictly Ballroom*'s multiculturalist theme, subsuming it within the film's perceived queer discourse. This aspect had been flagged by Australian press reviews at the time of its 1992 release, when it was seen to reflect the nation's coming-of-age, and subsequently it had been discussed by academics too.[57] In a 2003 article primarily focused on Michael Powell's Australian production *They're a Weird Mob* (1966), Jeanette Hoorn engaged with the academic debates, arguing that in the context of the problematic shift from assimilationism to multiculturalism in official policies, the opposition in *Strictly Ballroom* between the Anglo-Celtic Australians and the Spanish immigrants placed authenticity, and thus cultural superiority, with the latter. Moreover, it was the young Anglo-Celtic hero Scott who must adapt to the immigrant culture, not the other way round. Hoorn paid more attention to the heroine Fran than earlier commentators, maintaining that her display of the paso doble at the climax was a triumphant appropriation of conservative Anglo-Celtic Australian mores that reinvigorated the community. For Hoorn, this gave *Strictly Ballroom* revolutionary potential.[58] Brian McFarlane, on the other hand, placed the film firmly within the traditional narrative structures of classic Hollywood cinema and the formal conventions of the musical. While he acknowledged its sympathetic approach to the young protagonists and its endorsement of the positive contribution of ethnic communities to Australian culture, he was critical of its treatment of Fran as a mere foil for Scott.[59] These widely varied approaches to *Strictly Ballroom* were an indication of its textual complexity, its openness to diverse interpretations and its lasting relevance.

Strictly Ballroom's cultural reach was extended in 2000 when it became one of the topics in a British television schools' education strand, Film

Focus for Channel 4's *The English Programme*. The series of three twenty-five-minute programmes directed at secondary-level students of Media and English included two devoted to *Strictly Ballroom* and *William Shakespeare's Romeo + Juliet* (1996), in which their production processes were examined in depth through interviews and film clips, supported by online teaching resources.[60] Because of their accessibility and perceived appeal to younger viewers, *Strictly Ballroom* and *William Shakespeare's Romeo + Juliet* were ensconced in the British media studies curriculum. The global success of *Strictly Ballroom* propelled Luhrmann into a different orbit. His reputation as an innovator, already strong in Australian theatre and opera circles, was consolidated on an international scale. After the difficulties in getting his debut feature off the ground, suddenly, at age thirty, he was the focus of intense media scrutiny and pursued by multinational media companies prepared to back him. His determination to preserve artistic control had strengthened during the development and production of *Strictly Ballroom*, as had his ideas about his personal world-view and theatrical cinematic language. The stage versions had employed elements from cinema and other media, and his first feature had translated the hybrid style he evolved in theatre into film form. With the movie, Luhrmann had successfully avoided producing filmed theatre; rather, he had used theatrical devices to create a non-naturalistic cinema that was identifiable as his signature style. His next film project, *William Shakespeare's Romeo + Juliet*, took his style, working methods and artistic credentials to another level, and to a place far removed from Australia. The team faced technological, aesthetic and logistical challenges that were exhausting, but helped to determine future directions. This transition marked a significant point in Luhrmann's progress towards attaining the cultural leverage that would enable him to establish an Australian working base and a degree of creative autonomy.

Three
William Shakespeare's Romeo + Juliet (1996)

The four years between the release of *Strictly Ballroom* and that of *William Shakespeare's Romeo + Juliet* were eventful for Luhrmann and Martin.[1] They were used to working on different projects simultaneously; amid the media circus surrounding *Strictly Ballroom* they were busy developing their Hindu version of Benjamin Britten's *A Midsummer Night's Dream* for the Australian Opera, which was staged in 1993. During research for this production they visited Rajasthan in India, an encounter that had long-lasting repercussions. The experience of going to see a Bollywood movie in which high tragedy clashed with low comedy, provoking a vociferous response from the audience, fed into both *Romeo + Juliet* and *Moulin Rouge!*. Their production of *A Midsummer Night's Dream* was set in colonial India and featured ambitious set design, including a raised bandstand constructed over a lake on stage. Luhrmann was struck by the fact that Britten had written his opera to celebrate the opening of a local church hall in Aldeburgh, taking it to a more popular audience than the London establishment. He discovered that links could be traced between Britten's interpretation of Shakespeare's play and Hindu mythology.[2] The process of working on an operatic rendition of a Shakespeare play may have influenced Luhrmann's choice of his next venture. Out of many potential topics, he decided to go with a film adaptation of Shakespeare's *Romeo and Juliet* that he would produce, co-write and direct. The idea was to make a film of the play that would translate the rambunctious context of popular theatre in Shakespeare's day into contemporary cinematic form, to make the film that Shakespeare himself might make. This would also take the theatrical cinematic style to the next level, updating the play for a modern audience while retaining Shakespeare's poetic language.

After *Strictly Ballroom* Luhrmann had considered offers from a number of major studios, and had decided to sign up with 20th Century-Fox on the grounds that the terms they offered would allow him and his team creative autonomy and the ability to develop their own work. The initial first-look deal was negotiated in 1993, and towards the end of that year Luhrmann pitched the *Romeo and Juliet* idea to Fox studio executives in Los Angeles. This was as risky a proposition as Luhrmann's debut feature had been; the bemused Fox executives found it difficult to grasp the concept and saw the use of Elizabethan rhyming couplets in the dialogue as a big stumbling block. However, they gave Luhrmann development money and he went away to refine the proposal. Meanwhile, Fox apparently had a second, more traditional version of *Romeo and Juliet*, with Broadway theatre director Desmond McAnuff scheduled to direct and Ethan Hawke to star as Romeo, in the pipeline.[3] To win over Fox, Luhrmann persuaded Leonardo DiCaprio, his first choice to play Romeo, to travel to Sydney, where Luhrmann had set up an office at the Fox Studios Australia site, and participate in workshops, which were filmed on Super-8 and video and then edited with music added. In 1994, armed with this footage and full-colour concept books displaying the costumes and style of the production, and with DiCaprio now officially on board, Luhrmann pitched the revised proposal to Fox executives, this time with success. The studio shelved the McAnuff version and pledged an estimated $14.5 million to Luhrmann's youth-oriented reinterpretation of Shakespeare's tragedy.[4] The concept books were based on collages of images from different locations and periods with the actors pasted in, geared towards building a coded, fictional environment to which modern audiences could relate.[5] This was intended to emulate Shakespeare's fanciful approach to the play's setting in an imaginary Verona.

Luhrmann went to great lengths to find a suitable Juliet, auditioning over sixty actresses in Australia, the USA and UK.[6] Natalie Portman was a serious contender, but when rehearsals revealed that she appeared too young to play against DiCaprio's Romeo, the search began again. Eventually, after studio resistance to using an unknown name was overcome, Claire Danes, an emerging star who had an award-winning performance in the US television series *My So-Called Life* (1994–5) to her credit, was cast in her first leading film role as Juliet. Danes had the necessary screen presence and air of maturity to hold her own with Leonardo DiCaprio, and the two immediately launched into an extensive period of rehearsals. Experienced British character actress Miriam Margolyes, one of several veteran players who gave the production gravitas, was recruited to play Juliet's nurse.[7] The combination of young up-and-coming stars with older character actors was one way of keeping costs as low as possible.[8] Fox and the film-makers were all too aware that this was a risk-laden project, and in order to keep the budget in check Luhrmann and co-producer Martin Brown teamed up with Canadian producer Gabriella Martinelli to find ways of economising.[9] The main cost-cutting strategy was to shoot outside the major US cities. They investigated several locations, including Cuba, Barbados, Toronto, Vancouver, Mexico and Sydney, with the intention of shooting two weeks of exteriors in Miami before moving elsewhere. When this plan proved uneconomic, Mexico was chosen as a cheap and viable alternative that also had the right ambience for the production, in that its society was divided between a wealthy few and a large poor population, its culture reflected the power of religion, and it was possible to believe that arcane potions might be acquired there.[10] Main shooting took place in Mexico City with its old European city centre surrounded by run-down suburbs.[11] Against this familiar yet exotic background, the production design drew on cultural sources from South America to Hawaii and Asia to conjure up a mythical faraway land that would nevertheless have recognisable iconographic reference points.

The core creative team was Australian; besides Luhrmann and Martin Brown, it included regular production designer Catherine Martin and co-screenwriter Craig Pearce; editor Jill Bilcock, costume designer Kym Barrett, choreographer John O'Connell and sound supervisor Roger Savage, who had all worked on *Strictly Ballroom*; and cinematographer Donald McAlpine. The mixed crew was gathered from Spain, Italy, England, the USA, Canada, Mexico and Australia for the seventy-day shoot that was filmed mainly in Mexico City and the port of Vera Cruz. Mexico City offered stark contrasts between ancient and modern, with ornate sculptures and religious shrines standing side by side with high-rise buildings, designer boutiques in contemporary shopping arcades, souvenir street vendors and snarled traffic. One location that featured prominently was a baroque church whose façade was topped by a giant statue of Mary. Its interior had a gold altar above which towered a huge figure of the Madonna and Child in pastel hues, framed by angels. On either side were brightly coloured panels depicting the story of Christ and painted on the wall above Mary's head was a pink Sacred Heart encircled by thorns that became part of the film's design. This building stood in for St Peter's church, the setting for Romeo and Juliet's secret wedding and the scene of their deaths. Mexico City, Vera Cruz's coastal site, the Churubusco studios and Texcoco on Mexico City's outskirts collectively became the film's 'Verona Beach'.[12] This ramshackle community was erected on the shores of the Gulf of Mexico, capturing the spirit of the place and of Shakespeare's context through the bars, restaurants, souvenir and sex shops with names such as 'Rosencrantzky's' and 'The Merchant of Verona Beach'. Shakespeare's Globe Theatre made an appearance as a pool hall. Other Shakespearian references included the Shylock Bank, advertisements for Prospero's whiskey and Out Damn Spot dry cleaners. The sycamore grove, not actually visited in the play, where the poet Romeo broods and the gangs hang out, was transformed into the shabby, decaying proscenium arch of an old theatre, scarred by time and climate, that opened on to the sea on one side and the amusement park set on the other.[13]

Theatricalised cinema: *Romeo + Juliet*'s sycamore grove

The playful approach to time and place was firmly anchored in the
Shakespearian background, and extended to the treatment of costume,
which was a key feature of Renaissance theatre. Kym Barrett designed the
characters' clothes to illuminate the Shakespearian language, sometimes
using literal interpretations. Romeo, dressed in knight's armour, echoed
his description in the play, while Juliet's angel wings referred directly to
her 'bright angel' designation. The feline imagery used to describe
Romeo's enemy Tybalt was visualised in his shiny black boots with their
silver heels embossed with a cat symbol. Barrett had fun with the custom-
designed guns carried by the warring gangs, which replaced the swords
used in the play, giving them the brand names of edged weapons such as
rapiers and daggers.[14] The guns were embellished with special stylistic
touches, including transparent handles, mother-of-pearl grips, religious
icons and family crests, so that they became extensions of the characters.
The gang members were distinguished from their parents, who were
dressed in 1960s/1970s high fashion, while the young turks sported flashy
street styles. The Capulet kids were decked out in expensive black tailored
garb inspired by Dolce & Gabbana, with bullet-proof vests as fashion
accessories, in contrast to the Montagues' more utilitarian Hawaiian shirts
and flak pants. The vibrant, acidic colour palette transmitted a dramatic

Kym Barrett's custom-designed gun for *Romeo + Juliet*

visual excitement that communicated the gangs' youthful energy as well as the film's anti-naturalistic character. The violence and hatred of the gangs' world, emanating from their parents' entrenched feuding, was opposed to the dreamy, lyrical tenor of the scenes between Romeo and Juliet. When it came to the star-crossed lovers, the look of their garments was toned down. Barrett felt that their costumes should be simple, and consulted the Italian fashion house Prada, whose streamlined style she perceived as appropriate. Prada supplied the suit that Romeo wore to his wedding. In other scenes, Romeo was dressed predominantly in blue or silver-grey, while Juliet's costume was mainly white. The simplicity of colour and line projected the innocence of the young couple and intimated their tenuous hold on life.[15]

The stylised visual design was only one way in which the film-makers differentiated their production from other movie adaptations of Shakespeare. In order to move as far away as possible from highbrow, stagy interpretations, they employed edgy camera movements, frequent changes of perspective and fast cutting. The traditional Hollywood patterns of shot-reverse-shot and two-shots were reduced to a minimum.[16] The use of anamorphic lenses allowed the actors to play out their scenes in wide shots without sacrificing the backgrounds. Swooping camera movements gave the illusion of transporting viewers into the onscreen space; hand-held shots in some scenes projected a sense of immediacy; and spectator involvement with the lead characters was intensified through underwater photography. The lighting and camerawork were in the metaphorical mode of the overall production, which worked to clarify the story, characters and the Elizabethan language through a cinematic form that deployed images and sound as a means of translation. From the initial stages, Luhrmann had declared his intention to devise a way of reviving Romeo and Juliet for twentieth-century audiences while remaining true to the Shakespearian text. For him, the truth of the earlier text lay in its sensational rendition of the violence, lust and murderous passions that characterised the imagined world in which it was set. This world resonated with modern society and its expression in popular forms, including cinema. As with *Strictly Ballroom*, Luhrmann created a complex texture of images, sounds and cultural references that produced an effect of a timeless zone where now and then, here

and there were merged. Shakespeare's play had gone through many transformations during its long history; indeed, it was itself a reinterpretation of
a prior text.[17] Luhrmann set out to capture the layers of adaptation that lay
beneath his own version, making them visible through a rhetorical language
that mobilised hyperbole at every level.

Technically, hyperbole is a literary device that uses exaggeration to evoke
strong feelings or for dramatic effect. Its converse is understatement, a
word that might be used to describe the cinematic naturalism that
Luhrmann wished to avoid. Hyperbole was commonly used in English
Renaissance literature, and by Shakespeare in his poetry and plays.[18] It is a
bombastic, vehement form of expression that assaults listeners, aggressively claiming their attention, and it has been associated by theorists with
the young and with comedy.[19] One of hyperbole's aims is to elicit amaze-
ment in the reader or listener in order to win them over, or to make an argument clearer. However, because it overtly distorts the truth, it carries with it
a risk that it will be revealed as deception, and thereby downgraded. The
danger and excess associated with hyperbole adds to the audience's excitement. Although as a rhetorical device hyperbole has often been considered
primarily in terms of formal expression, its use in Renaissance literature as
a strategy to expose the gap between appearance and reality lends it wider
implications. Used as an expression of love or infatuation, for example, it
can intimate a character's extreme depths of feeling while conveying the
added meaning that those emotions are unlikely to be fulfilled; in such cases
hyperbole's falsity points to a truth.[20] Part of that truth can be the speaker's
desire for attention or their tendency to self-aggrandisement masking a
personal insecurity. Hyperbole's ornateness can be perceived as deceptive,
and its forcefulness as intimidating, offensive or risible. In extreme forms,
it can overreach itself, alienating listeners by committing the 'error of too
much'.[21] On the other hand, its emphatic quality can be used to clarify or
illuminate, or to suggest doubt or social critique.[22] In some cases, hyperbole
is employed to indicate the existence of a prior source that has been transformed by reinvention, so that layers of meaning are created. In *William
Shakespeare's Romeo + Juliet*, for example, the hyperbolic visual style signals
the translation of Renaissance literary modes into modern cinematic form.

Hyperbole can become parody; in this respect, and in its tendency to over-statement and the grotesque, it has affinities with travesty.[23] In English Renaissance theatre, and in Shakespeare in particular, hyperbole was used in varied and complex ways: as a shock tactic; as irony; as social commentary; to elicit sympathy, horror and laughter; to exploit pleasure in language and, in the context of Elizabethan theatre, to capture the attention of mixed audiences who were boisterous, often inebriated but also sophisticated and aware of theatrical conventions. Shakespeare's use of hyperbole in the language of *Romeo and Juliet* linked comedy and tragedy, love and death with an analysis of the destructive effects of power and religion, and a challenge to the utopian notion that 'love conquers all'. In Luhrmann's film version, a heightened cinematic language was devised that encompassed performance, gesture, costume, sets, colour, dialogue, music, camerawork and editing, emulating Shakespeare but taking his language further by exaggerating it. This aesthetic strategy could be called 'hyperbolic hyperbole';[24] it translated Shakespeare's already grandiloquent style into an overwrought audiovisual experience that assaulted the audience's senses and many of their preconceptions. Luhrmann's use of hyperbolic hyperbole acknowledged Shakespeare's influence while grandstanding a modern reinterpretation of

Hyperbolic hyperbole: Leonardo DiCaprio as an anguished Romeo

Heightened cinematic language in *Romeo + Juliet*

his play. This was no reverential homage; the act of appropriation was
clearly marked, and Shakespeare's own piracy of the Romeo and Juliet story
was frequently mentioned by Luhrmann in interviews.[25] Furthermore, in
the adaptation process a third of the play devoted to visual description was
jettisoned and some of Shakespeare's rhetorical flourishes replaced with
more familiar rhymed couplets.[26] Other adjustments to Shakespeare's text
included the exclusion of Paris (Paul Rudd) from the film's conclusion.
While such deviations might be seen as evidence of the film-makers' lack of
respect for the source text, by their own account their revamp was an
attempt to remain true to the irreverent spirit of Shakespeare and his context in popular theatre.[27] Rather than mimic Shakespeare, Luhrmann and
his team set out to capture the essence of his work by transforming it.
Paradoxically, this strategy both acknowledged the playwright's prior
authorship and displaced it by asserting the updated version's innovative
qualities.

Luhrmann had used hyperbole in *Strictly Ballroom*, depicting the Anglo-
Celtic Australians in exaggerated, comic-book style in order to differentiate

them from the more authentic Spanish characters and the ingenuous young protagonists. Perhaps because the adaptation of *Romeo and Juliet* necessitated the translation of Shakespearian language into cinematic form, in Luhrmann's second film the distinction between the heightened artificial world of the gangs, their parents and other older characters and that of the star-crossed lovers was less clearly marked. Although the romantic scenes between Romeo and Juliet were sometimes less frenetic than the rest of the movie, the production design was no less ornate. Shakespeare's published plays offered little in the way of stage directions, so production designer Catherine Martin had free rein in interpreting the background to the action. However, the task was on one hand to enable the design to clarify the Elizabethan dialogue and on the other to reveal the complexity of the created world envisioned by Shakespeare and its modern cinematic counterpart. In order to present Juliet's bedroom in terms accessible to contemporary audiences, Martin dressed the space with pastel colours appropriate to the character's age and privilege, adding luxury items such as a large canopied bed piled high with cushions and quilts, and filling the room with collections of fluffy animals, dolls and porcelain saints. Religious votives were mingled with everyday personal items such as books, wall stickers, photographs, a hot-pink boom box and a beginner's computer.[28] The religious iconography here and elsewhere in the film was integrated as a natural part of the environment. For the death scene set in St Peter's church, the lavish interior, presided over by the massive Madonna and Child figure and the vivid Immaculate Heart, provided appropriate surroundings for the deathbed swathed in cream silk on the gold altar, encircled by 2,000 flickering candles and an array of ornate candelabras. The church was filled with white freesias and gladioli and festooned with floral crosses. Amid the grandeur, Juliet's collection of porcelain saints and angels added a poignant reminder of the fragility of life and the inevitability of destiny. Dramatic lighting and camera movement enhanced the powerful role played by religion in the demise of the lovers.[29] The elaborate theatrical staging of Juliet's apparent death both presaged the inescapable conclusion and added irony by commenting on the fissure between appearance and reality that led to the tragic outcome.

The production design for *Romeo + Juliet* was vital in providing icono-
graphical signals to communicate Shakespeare's play to present-day audiences. However, its role was more than instrumental; it extended to adding
layers of signification that acted as a form of annotation. In one of the film's
set pieces, the Capulets' ballroom was the stage for the ostentatious masked
party where Romeo and Juliet meet and fall in love. The ballroom, which was
constructed at Mexico's Churubusco Studios, was designed as a monument
to avarice and power, with a vast marble staircase reminiscent of Tara in
Gone With the Wind and Xanadu in *Citizen Kane* (1941). The room was dominated by a huge painting of the Madonna in gold and crimson, while on the
dark red walls golden cherubim and grinning eyeless masks looked down on
the revellers. Gilding was evident everywhere, in the mermaid lamp fix-
tures, the ornate frames of the giant mirrors facing the staircase and the
mammoth candelabra that acted as a focal point. The Capulet family crest, a
stylised cat bearing the motto 'Dios' and 'fuerza' ('God' and 'strength', or
'force'), was inlaid in the marble floor. Many of the props appearing in this
scene were rented in Mexico, which proved to be a rich source of antique
furniture and objects.[30] In this pretentious, excessive environment, Romeo
and Juliet appeared like babes-in-the-wood, their innocence in sharp contrast to the surrounding depravation. Both Martin and Kym Barrett took the
style of *Fellini-Satyricon* (1969) as a primary inspiration for the masked ball,
drawing on its dreamlike evocation of decadent ancient Rome in the lavish
set, costumes, hair and make-up, which were at once lurid, sinister and
captivating. The fancy dress mixed different eras and cultural sources, from
Dave Paris's astronaut garb to the Capulet parents' Anthony and Cleopatra
outfits. The reference to Fellini's film was more than homage. There were
parallels between his adaptation of Petronius's bawdy fiction and
Luhrmann's revival of Shakespeare's play, not least in the ironic titles
ascribing authorship. Fellini set out to reimagine the past as mysterious and
exotic, revising the surviving fragments of the source text, adding mythical
elements and evoking the incomplete nature of history.[31] This work of reinvention was related to Shakespeare's retelling of the Romeo and Juliet story
and Luhrmann's reconstruction of the play. The allusions in *Romeo + Juliet*'s
production design and costumes in the masked ball extended beyond the

Babes-in-the-wood: Romeo (Leonardo DiCaprio) and Juliet (Claire Danes) at the Capulet ball

quotation characteristic of postmodern cinema; it resembled a footnote pointing to precedents for Luhrmann's project.

The fantastical tenor of *William Shakespeare's Romeo + Juliet* was intensified when a series of bizarre incidents occurred during the Mexican shoot. Chief hair stylist Aldo Signoretti[32] was kidnapped and released for a $300 ransom; the Fox auditor who visited the set to look at the accounts was mugged at gunpoint; the aquarium through which Romeo and Juliet spy one another at the masked ball was broken; filming was suspended when some of the team, including Luhrmann, Claire Danes and Don McAlpine were laid low with a virus; the hurricane-force wind El Norte destroyed the Vera Cruz set, so that some scenes had to be shot later in San Francisco; and a plague of killer bees infested one location before being blown away by the wind.[33] Some of these disasters had a mythical, biblical quality suited to the aura of the production, and they became part of the folklore of the film. During the Mexican shoot initial editing began, with Jill Bilcock working with Luhrmann on the first cut, which was done under difficult technical conditions.[34] Unusually, sound editor Roger Savage became involved at an

early stage, so that work on sound and image overlapped. After shooting finished, editing moved back to Melbourne. The picture editing was a long,
complcated process, and the editing team was under increasing pressure
from Fox to deliver.[35] Eventually, post-production moved to Skywalker
Ranch, George Lucas's facility in northern San Francisco, to finish the picture edit and mix the sound and music. Some additional scenes were also
shot in San Francisco. The difficulties of communicating between
Melbourne, San Francisco and Fox's Los Angeles offices added to the time
constraints, with the result that the film's images and sound had a rough-
hewn flavour suited to its pop-culture style.[36] Luhrmann spent two weeks in
London working with composers Nellee Hooper, Marius De Vries and Craig
Armstrong (who also acted as music director and orchestrator) on recording the score before returning to San Francisco to finish the edit.[37]

The sound design for *Romeo + Juliet* echoed the stylised nature of the
images, using special effects to heighten sound beyond the demands of
realism while keeping within the bounds of the story.[38] The music was predominantly contemporary, featuring alternative rock and pop songs by
artists who were current and in some cases controversial ('#1 Crush' by
Garbage; 'Lovefool' by The Cardigans; 'Talk Show Host' by Radiohead;
'Whatever (I Had a Dream)' by Butthole Surfers; 'Local God' by Everclear).
Much of the music dramatised themes of nihilism, obsessive desire and
death and featured references to drug culture, which augmented
Luhrmann's vision of Romeo as a disaffected James Dean/Kurt Cobain figure. Some of it (for example, '#1 Crush') used hyperbolic language that res-
onated with the Elizabethan rhyming couplets and the film's style. Other
songs were more soulful ('Kissing You' by Des'ree, the love theme performed at the masked ball when Romeo and Juliet fall in love; 'When Doves
Cry' by Prince, performed by Quindon Tarver; 'Little Star' by Stina
Nordenstam) in keeping with romantic young love, and there were upbeat,
club and disco-style numbers ('Young Hearts Run Free' by Kym Mazelle;
'Everybody's Free (To Feel Good)' by Rozalla, performed by Quindon
Tarver; 'You and Me Song' by The Wannadies) that injected youthful energy
to match the overall frantic pace. Radiohead wrote and performed a dark,
despairing song, 'Exit Music (For a Film)', that played over the end credits.

Hooper, De Vries and Armstrong produced a dramatic symphonic score, with Armstrong performing his melancholy piano composition 'Slow Movement', while classical extracts (Richard Wagner's opera *Tristan und Isolde*, which accompanied the death scene; and Mozart's Sturm und Drang work 'Symphony No. 25 in G minor', which appeared at the opening) added further hyperbolic touches. The music, which mixed the surreal and grotesque with achingly beautiful romanticism, was an essential element of the theatrical cinematic aesthetic. It augmented the visual flourishes, and it had an expressive function, to symbolise the characters' emotions, suggest changes of mood and provoke audience response. In some instances it had an ironic edge, as in Quindon Tarver's choral renditions of 'When Doves Cry' and 'Everybody's Free (To Feel Good)'. Above all, it communicated the passion and power of Shakespeare's imagery. As Luhrmann pointed out, his use of music was inspired less by MTV than by Shakespeare's custom of inserting popular songs into his plays.[39]

With *Romeo + Juliet*, visual special effects became an overt element of the style. Rather than use US facilities, Luhrmann insisted, against studio opposition, on the Melbourne-based company Complete Post to carry out the majority of the digital effects. Chris Schwarze and Peter Webb of

Romeo + Juliet's imaginary cityscape created by special effects

Complete Post had advised Luhrmann's team in the early stages and were excited about the project. They provided Fox with sample work and budget breakdowns but were disappointed when some of the work initially went to Hammerhead Productions in Los Angeles. Fox's reason for keeping post-production in the USA was that it would be easier and quicker to obtain material for test screenings, and they needed Luhrmann there for marketing purposes. However, with some of the image and sound editing taking place in Melbourne, as the need for further digital effects became clear, Complete Post came on board. After Luhrmann and Bilcock returned to the USA, technical and logistical difficulties were overcome by using a video-fax machine to transmit and work on material in real time between Melbourne and Los Angeles.[40] Hammerhead had worked on the opening sequence, using scaled-down 3-D models to set up an imaginary cityscape dominated by the Montague and Capulet skyscrapers and the fifty-foot statue of Jesus seen from a helicopter-shot perspective.[41] Complete Post's first assignment was to add threatening storm clouds to the scene of Mercutio's (Harold Perrineau) death. In a sequence of twenty shots, using digital matte painting techniques they replaced the existing sky, added moving shadows on the ocean, ground and buildings and removed any inappropriate shadows. All shots were digitally colour graded for continuity. The digital effects contributed to the production's innovative take on Shakespeare; in the scene in which Father Laurence (Pete Postlethwaite) explains his plans to Juliet, his words were pictured behind him in a moving montage. The background footage was compiled from different sequences, treated, colour-graded and edited together by Complete Post and then combined with bluescreen shots of Father Laurence. The lighting was also digitally adjusted to enhance the separation between foreground and background. Digital effects such as crash zooms were added to other scenes to increase dramatic tension and add to the hyperbolic tone.[42] In the end, visual special effects took on a more active and extensive role in *Romeo + Juliet* than was initially anticipated.[43] Although post-production had been divided between Australia and the USA, it was predominantly the result of creative input from Australian technicians and craftspeople. Despite, or perhaps because of its apparently non-Australian identity, once the film was released, this fact was enthusiastically celebrated in the Australian media.[44] As well as box-office success, this element of local craftsmanship was instrumental in helping Luhrmann to set up his production base in Australia.

*   *   *

William Shakespeare's Romeo + Juliet's uncertain national provenance was not the only area of contention; as the irony in the title indicated, its authorship was also in question. In contemporary cinema, the director is usually nominated as the author by using the possessive form (for example, '20th Century-Fox presents a Baz Luhrmann film'), even if they do not actually own the work.[45] In this case, the title had several levels: it used the possessive to point to Shakespeare's prior text; it announced the film-makers' intention of producing a film of that text in the style of Shakespeare; and it heralded the adaptation process by changing 'and' to the graphic '+', sometimes reproduced as a religious cross. The latter, though it appeared to be a minor change, was decisive in affirming the film's modernity, and the act of appropriation of the play. However, as Luhrmann often commented, Shakespeare and his contemporaries plundered other works for ideas themselves;[46] indeed, there are long-running disputes about Shakespeare's authorship and identity.[47] The 'William Shakespeare' in the title of Luhrmann's film set up a challenge ('catch him if you can') and transported the issues surrounding Shakespeare's authorship into the context of contemporary film-making. While the title may have been intended as a homage to Shakespeare, it had the effect of posing a question about authorship and artistic production itself, particularly in light of the collaborative context of theatre and film. Yet, by inserting the '+', almost as a code for viewers to interpret, it signalled the stylistic gestures that were specific to this creative adaptation.

The '+' might also be interpreted in other ways: as a sign that the film drew on cultural sources other than the Shakespeare play; or as indicating that Luhrmann's film was an addition to the many different versions of the Romeo and Juliet story. The layers of meaning in the title were, as several writers have commented, a symptom not only of a crisis of authorship, but of a problem with the process of adaptation: how to stamp a signature on, or

More than other adaptations: *Romeo + Juliet*'s title card

claim originality for a work whose origins by definition exist elsewhere.[48] This was a problem that Luhrmann had encountered before in his operatic adaptations, and which led him to the conclusion that originality lay in the retelling of the source material. At the same time, the retelling was grounded in extensive research and respect for the source's context. Luhrmann's approach to adaptation could be described as founded in a contradictory impulse: an identification with the putative author of the prior work that was in tension with his desire to create a distinctively new object from it. This would seem to be an impossible task, but Luhrmann's creed that 'anything is possible' drove him to produce a text that was in excess of what had gone before, more than Shakespeare, more than the other antecedents on which his film drew – a 'more than' intimated by the '+' of the title and its extensive use in the film's design and promotional material.

Romeo + Juliet pivoted on a dilemma that Luhrmann had encountered as a student at NIDA: how to carve out a place in the history of theatre that was different from that of its great innovators. One of his solutions had been to 'act out' an identity, utilising performance to distinguish himself from his peers; another had been to use the collage technique in his stage productions to bring together different media and styles and create something new in the process. The first involved generating a myth of individuality; the second involved the deconstruction of that myth by breaking down elements from various sources and recombining them. Luhrmann was interested in myth, which in its oral manifestation has been characterised as a collective form without named authors. Theories of myth tend to play down the contribution of individual storytellers on the grounds that, whatever variations they introduce, they do not affect the story's basic structures. However, most myths exist in different forms; the David and Goliath story used in *Strictly Ballroom*, for example, is thought to have originated in oral traditions before emerging in written biblical manuscripts that changed certain elements without altering the heroic nature of the battle and its outcome; subsequently it surfaced in popular culture too.[49] Once a myth is written down, it becomes a legend, a story to be read. Legends were regarded as founded in historical events, until disputes about their historical accuracy caused them to be recast as unreliable.[50] There is a tension in both myths and legends between their origins, which can rarely be determined, and their multiple retelling across time and cultures. Their enduring popularity makes them rich material for writers and artists, but would-be authors of mythic or legendary material are faced with the fact that they cannot refer to an authentic, original version, nor can they originate a new rendition, because their work is only one in a series of adaptations.[51] The Romeo and Juliet story belongs to a tradition of tragic romances that reaches back to ancient times and existed in many different forms before Shakespeare wrote his play. In aligning the film with William Shakespeare's *Romeo and Juliet*, then, Luhrmann acknowledged Shakespeare's prior authorship and the predicament they shared in producing adaptations. Despite the differences in era and culture, both were practitioners of pastiche, creating hybrid works that could do no more than produce a surface aesthetic based on sampling and remixing previous versions. The title of Luhrmann's film was in some ways a hostage to fortune; many critics perceived it as recognition of the lack of authenticity of his own work in comparison to the Shakespearian masterpiece, despite Luhrmann's assertions that Shakespeare's play pirated other writers.[52] The film itself was often derided as an example of postmodern silliness.[53]

Pastiche: Tybalt (John Leguizamo) in *Romeo + Juliet*'s gas station sequence

Pastiche stands accused of lacking depth, emotional affect and a sense of history.[54] However, it can be used in ways that challenge this dismissive characterisation. A knowing 'wink' to the audience engages them in playful interaction with the text, while quotation and allusion build layers of references that present history as a process of accumulation of images rather than a linear narrative. Pastiche displaces traditional notions of artistic production and the writing of history, which can be seen as a strength rather than a weakness. A prime example of pastiche is *Romeo + Juliet*'s gas station sequence, which quotes from spaghetti Westerns, themselves appropriations of Hollywood movies, to make the Capulet and Montague gangs' showdown legible to modern viewers. The scene also refers to the Shakespearian text, not just in the dialogue but also in the signage, costumes, guns and cars, and in the choreography of the gun fight. A further level of representation is added by the film-makers' exaggerated treatment of Shakespeare and Italian Westerns, which are already hyperbolic forms. Luhrmann took his interpretation of these sources to extremes, producing an aesthetic excess that echoed the '+' of the title.[55] At the same time, this strategy placed the film as part of a continuum, making connections between apparently divergent artistic enterprises, crossing boundaries between high and low culture and suggesting a different way of looking at cultural history. It also suggested that artistic production, and indeed authorship, might be viewed less in terms of originality and more as an activity of producing variations on pre-existing works. The gas station sequence used pastiche and hyperbolic hyperbole to emphasise performance – of the actors, but also, in its stylistic excess, of the film itself, which could be said to 'perform', and thereby transform, the prior works on which it drew. It was a performance mode that identified itself as distinct from the widely accepted understanding of Shakespeare, claiming for itself innovation rather than originality.[56]

Pastiche operates in less overt ways too; there may be allusions and citations that are not necessarily consciously acknowledged, but which readers and viewers can decode on their own behalf. In her discussion of the relationship between Luhrmann's *Romeo + Juliet* and Shakespeare's play, Courtney Lehmann made a convincing argument that, like Shakespeare, Luhrmann took as his primary source Arthur Brooke's 1562 narrative poem *The Tragicall Historye of Romeus and Juliet*, evident in the water imagery prevalent in the film. Lehmann suggested that Shakespeare's use of overblown rhetoric in *Romeo and Juliet* was a symptom of his retelling, and desire to surpass, Brooke's prior work, arguing that Luhrmann's stylistic hyperbole reproduced Shakespeare's anxiety about stamping his signature on the legend. Although in interviews Luhrmann referred to Brooke's poem only in passing, Lehmann claimed that the water imagery in the film was actually closer to the poem than to the play. The fish tank sequence in which Romeo and Juliet first catch one another's eye at the Capulet ball, the love scene in the swimming pool and the storm over the sea, hailed by critics as Luhrmann's innovations, according to Lehmann were better seen as references to Brooke's poem, which haunted Shakespeare's text and Luhrmann's film.[57] Lehmann's deciphering of the allusions to Brooke's water imagery could be nuanced by factoring in the ubiquitous presence of water and beach imagery in the films of Federico Fellini, acknowledged by Luhrmann as one of the inspirations for *Romeo + Juliet*. The allusions to multiple sources in the play and the film deny the existence of a single, final origin or authorial signature, despite the authority bestowed on Shakespeare's work.

Lehmann mobilised psychoanalytic theory to illuminate the struggle for originality that beset Shakespeare and Luhrmann in the adaptation process. With respect to the film, that struggle takes on additional significance in the context of Australia's postcolonial history. In its genesis, production, promotion and reception, *Romeo + Juliet*'s defining problem was one of language, from the scepticism of Fox executives about the use of rhyming couplets, to the film-makers' drive to make the Elizabethan verse accessible to modern audiences, to the critics' response to the treatment of Shakespeare's text. The challenge of constructing an appropriate yet distinctively different cinematic language for a canonical work resonates with postcolonial struggles for cultural independence; it is no coincidence that modern Anglo-Australian vernacular does considerable violence to standard English.[58] The will to break free from a constricting colonial heritage is there in the film's mesmerising montages of Shakespearian references, on one hand recognising the weight of the past in the present, on the other resisting its overwhelming power by conjuring up a 'Shakespeare' who was a pirate rather than an establishment figure. In contesting myths of authorial origin, *Romeo + Juliet* proposes a model for creativity that is rooted in survival and revival and intimately connected to postcolonial experience.[59] Through the film's compulsive appropriations, the notion of adaptation comes to connote more than the activity of translating Shakespeare into modern cinematic form; it suggests the dynamic process whereby postcolonial societies both adapt to and adapt the ruling culture. The sense of urgency and ambivalence in *Romeo + Juliet*, its aura of what some perceived as hysteria or desperation,[60] could all be linked to a struggle for a new myth of origin and originality that is doomed to failure. In this light, the film's investment in transgression, reinvention and innovation is as much a statement about postcolonial artistic production as an example of postmodernist practice.[61] From this perspective, the water imagery and the placing of Verona Beach on the seashore could be seen as symbolic representations of fluid boundary areas, evoking liminal dream-spaces where geographic, ethnic and cultural obstacles cease to hold sway.

*   *   *

As the post-production work on *Romeo + Juliet* drew to a close, four test screenings were carried out in Los Angeles and San Francisco,[62] after which Fox requested some changes, including adding flashbacks to the final scene and adapting the gas station sequence to reduce the violence.[63] The film received a positive response from young female and male viewers, but the reaction of teenage girls was by far the most enthusiastic.[64] The studio's marketing in the USA reflected this by aiming at a young, urban, niche market; the soundtrack music was given extensive coverage on youth-oriented radio stations, carefully linked to the film's upcoming release. KROQ, Los Angeles' alternative rock station was one of several that gave away preview tickets. Posters featuring DiCaprio in a Hawaiian shirt and Danes as a 1990s-style Juliet surrounded by cars and guns targeted female viewers under twenty-four. Unlike *Strictly Ballroom*, for which Jill Bilcock had produced the material for the trailers and advertising spots,[65] the theatrical trailers and television commercials were handled by a US advertising agency who imitated the style of the film, making minimal use of the usual American voice-over.[66] The marketing campaign was a major expense, with a prints and advertising budget that rivalled the film's below-the-line costs. Fox exploited the teen-pic aspects of the production with promotion focusing on the young protagonists' problems with their parents. TV spots featuring post-grunge rock, flashy cars and guns were run during prime-time youth programmes such as *Beverly Hills, 90210*, *Melrose Place*, *Clueless* and *Sabrina, the Teenage Witch*, while MTV treated the movie as a major event by giving it saturation coverage. A dedicated interactive website with a youth-oriented tone was constructed by Fox, headlining the soundtrack, signage, fashions, cars, introductions to the story, the characters and family trees, but not the guns.[67] Promotional materials included t-shirts and postcards based on the film's design.[68] The music was central to the marketing campaigns; the soundtrack CD was released on the Capitol label at the end of 1996 and soon went platinum in the USA.[69] Two music videos were issued: one of Harold Perrineau's show-stopping performance in drag of 'Young Hearts Run Free' at the ball, and one of Des'ree performing 'Kissing You'.[70] The film's release was concentrated in urban markets rather than going for a platform opening.[71] It opened on 1 November 1996 in 1,200 screens and grossed around $14.5 million in the first week, with 450 more screens showing it in the second week.[72] On opening night, many cinemas were sold out and extra late-night screenings were scheduled.[73] The film topped the US box office for several weeks.[74] This strong performance could partly be put down to canny marketing, partly to the appeal of the young stars and partly to the MTV-style treatment of Shakespeare. The outstanding success of *Romeo + Juliet* astonished the studio and the film-makers. Whatever its box-office attractions, it was a Shakespeare film with dialogue in Elizabethan rhyming couplets, and such projects did not usually make money. Luhrmann had apparently achieved the impossible: his art-house picture had crossed over to become the sleeper hit of the season.[75]

The film's success was replicated in Australia, where it was released on 26 December 1996 and broke box-office records, beating Sylvester Stallone's disaster movie *Daylight* (1996) to take the top spot over the Christmas break.[76] A star-studded premiere was held in Sydney on 18 December[77] before preview screenings took place and Luhrmann began the exhausting round of promotional interviews. As in the USA, the biggest audiences were younger viewers.[78] *Romeo + Juliet* went on to triumph in Europe and the UK, garnering numerous award nominations, including the Golden Bear at the Berlin film festival, where it won the Alfred Bauer award. Luhrmann won the British Academy of Film and Television (BAFTA) David Lean award for direction and shared the BAFTA award for Best Adapted Screenplay with Craig Pearce. The Australian Film Institute (AFI) considered *Romeo + Juliet* a non-Australian production and nominated it as Best Foreign Film. Catherine Martin and Brigitte Broch received an Oscar nomination for art direction, and Don McAlpine won the Australian Cinematographers Society Award of Distinction.[79] While the Australian and European press write-ups were almost universally positive, some US critics issued vehement condemnations. This had been the case with *Strictly Ballroom* and became a pattern for Luhrmann's films. Although David Hunter in *Hollywood Reporter*, Peter Travers in *Rolling Stone* and Todd McCarthy in *Variety* admired *Romeo + Juliet*, Roger Ebert in the *Chicago Sun-Times*, Desson Howe in the *Washington Post*, Janet Maslin in the *New York Times*, Amy Taubin in *Village Voice* and Mick La Salle in the *San Francisco*

Chronicle were notable detractors, expressing in hyperbolic terms that matched the film's style their objections to Luhrmann's flashy, vulgar adaptation.[80] Some US critics who had liked *Strictly Ballroom* were alienated by *Romeo + Juliet*'s aggressively modern treatment of Shakespeare, but their negative reviews only added to the controversy surrounding the film and bolstered its status as an event movie. Apart from the stylised violence and drug references, which had been toned down in post-production, a further bone of contention was the effect that the depiction of teenage suicide might have on young audiences.[81] Other Australian writers expressed concern that the apparent glorification of violence might encourage social unrest, citing the recent Port Arthur massacre.[82]

The brouhaha extended to academic writing. Lucy Hamilton pointed out that the often extreme media response to the film was matched by a seeming reluctance on the part of scholarly publications to take it seriously, suggesting that the elevation of Shakespeare to the status of high art and *Romeo + Juliet*'s subversion of the established rules for the representation of his work were responsible. Hamilton argued that most adaptations of the play suppressed its carnivalesque energy, while Luhrmann's version brought this element back, showing disrespect not for Shakespeare but for the snobbery surrounding his corpus.[83] Hamilton defended *Romeo + Juliet* as renewal rather than travesty, using the term in its popular sense of caricature;[84] but the film's use of theatrical travesty in its revival of Shakespeare and in its own heightened cinematic language was not in conflict with the idea of renewal. As Hamilton noted, there was a paucity of analysis in film studies; most of the scholarly debate played out within Shakespeare studies and focused on issues of adaptation.[85] Whether the film was admired or denigrated, it raised burning issues in a variety of reception contexts, crossing borders between journalistic and academic writing. Shakespeare's play and his characters were already part of high and popular culture;[86] before long *Romeo + Juliet*'s cultural impact surfaced in television commercials, educational programmes and other media.[87] The film's unprecedented critical and box-office success had dramatic repercussions for Luhrmann's career. Not only was he now internationally recognised as an auteur; he was also regarded by Fox as having the Midas touch.[88] *Romeo +*

Juliet was a risky venture, but it was also a shrewd gambit through which Luhrmann and Martin had acquired the artistic credibility to give them bargaining power with Fox. Thanks to strategic thinking, they now entered a life-changing phase that would see the culmination of the theatrical cinematic style and the consolidation of their international prestige.

Four
Moulin Rouge! (2001)

In the weeks following the release of *William Shakespeare's Romeo + Juliet*, Luhrmann spoke in interviews about the personal and creative freedom he sought for himself and his team.[1] The film had not only played a part in his artistic and stylistic development, its unprecedented success put him in a position to make choices about his future direction. After the exhausting experience of working between opposite sides of the globe, he decided that he now wanted to be based in Australia, in his home town of Sydney. He believed that his relationship with Fox would enable him to do this, and would also help to boost the Australian film industry by returning money from successful productions to the independent sector.[2] In 1996 he signed a further two-year, first-look agreement with the studio stating that he would write, produce and direct exclusively for them.[3] For Luhrmann, a key factor in the deal was the understanding that he would continue to work with his Australian team. In 1997 he and Catherine Martin set up their independent company Bazmark Inq., with subsidiaries Bazmark Design, Bazmark Film, Bazmark Live and Bazmark Music, at the House of Iona in Darlinghurst, Sydney. The House of Iona was the production base for projects in various media they undertook over the next year.[4] During this period, Luhrmann was actively involved in the plans for Fox's extended studio complex in Sydney, for which Bazmark Live orchestrated the opening event on 2 May 1998, when Fox announced a revised first-look deal with Bazmark that allowed them to develop projects in any medium. In return for the rights to those projects, Fox paid Bazmark's overheads, staff salaries and development costs. The studio also handled the company's fiscal and administrative affairs, allowing the team to concentrate on creative matters.[5]

Luhrmann's next film venture emerged from discussions with his core team of collaborators. The project would represent the culmination of the theatrical cinematic style and would contain its basic elements: a story

based on primary myth in which the outcome was already known; a language, or form that would provide the key to a heightened created world; and
a demand that audiences should be actively engaged.[6] In 1998, work began
in earnest on a revival of the Hollywood musical set in Paris in 1899, to be
shot entirely on the sound stages at Fox's Sydney studios. Among the issues
that may have influenced the decision were Luhrmann and Martin's desire
to work on home territory, and their signing of a revised deal with Fox just
as the new Sydney studio facilities opened.[7] Another likely consideration
was the possibility of tax concessions for films that qualified as Australian
productions. Martin's personal connections with Paris may also have been
a factor. At the heart of the new project was a celebration of the classic musicals that Luhrmann loved as a child, combined with the reconstruction of
the decadent, bohemian ambience of fin-de-siècle Paris in a form that
would appeal to modern audiences. As with the previous titles, there was a
strong element of risk attached to the concept: the musical genre was
reputed to be moribund, or at least deeply unfashionable. Once again
Luhrmann took on a major challenge: to breathe life into the musical and to
give contemporary relevance to the period setting, while making a definitive
statement about cinematic style. The predominantly Australian creative
team was drawn from people who had worked on *Strictly Ballroom* and/or
Romeo + Juliet: Luhrmann himself was director, co-writer with Craig Pearce
and co-producer with Martin Brown and Fred Baron; Catherine Martin was
production designer and co-costume designer with Angus Strathie; Jill
Bilcock was editor; Donald McAlpine was director of photography; John
O'Connell was choreographer; and Marius DeVries and Craig Armstrong
were responsible for the soundtrack. The initial budget estimate was put at
$40 million, though this figure later rose to around $52 million.[8] The budget was far in excess of that for *Romeo + Juliet*, but it was relatively modest for
a major studio production. Nevertheless, the scale was ambitious, involving
a complex soundtrack, extensive visual effects, lavish production and costume design, sixty-five dancers, 400 extras and a crew of around 200.[9]

The new production incorporated many elements of Luhrmann's earlier
work. In addition to the theatrical cinematic style devised for *Strictly
Ballroom* and *Romeo + Juliet*, the story, ostensibly based on the Greek myth of

Orpheus, the poet who journeyed into the underworld to save his beloved Eurydice from death, closely resembled Puccini's *La Bohème*, staged by Luhrmann in 1990, 1993 and 1996. The central conceit of the play-within-the-film, familiar from backstage musicals, was also a trope in *A Midsummer Night's Dream*, which Luhrmann and Martin had produced for Australian Opera in 1993. The Bollywood influence, rooted in their experiences in India while researching their version of the *Dream*, surfaced explicitly in the latest enterprise at the level of design and in the conception and staging of the 'Spectacular Spectacular' show. Christine Anu, who had featured in the 1997 music video 'Now Until the Break of Day' and was cast as Arabia in the latest film, was a further connection to *A Midsummer Night's Dream*, while John Leguizamo, who portrayed Toulouse-Lautrec in *Moulin Rouge!*, had played Tybalt in *Romeo + Juliet*. The personal associations went deeper: Luhrmann likened the crazy bohemians of *Moulin Rouge!* to his creative circus at the House of Iona, marking the film with his particular ethos.[10] Although *Moulin Rouge!* was not an adaptation, it was a similar undertaking to the other films in that it set out to modernise classic material. Whereas *Romeo + Juliet* reproduced the creative ferment of Shakespeare's early-modern theatrical context, *Moulin Rouge!* recreated the social and cultural upheavals that gave rise to late-nineteenth-century modernism. In this case, the language bridging past and present was that of contemporary popular song, a device that both gave the idealistic hero Christian (Ewan McGregor) credibility as a poet and evoked the Moulin Rouge as a hedonistic nightclub akin to New York's Studio 54 in the 1970s and 1980s.[11] In 1998 Luhrmann, Martin and Craig Pearce began a period of intensive research, spending six weeks in Paris unearthing the history of the Moulin Rouge, the scandalous can-can, Toulouse-Lautrec and the cultural background of fin-de-siècle France. The design team collected period and present-day images that were collated with sketches and Photoshop material into regularly updated ideas folders.[12] Although contemporaneous film clips of the Moulin Rouge itself were unavailable, they gathered archive footage of similar entertainment venues that gave tantalising glimpses of the risqué ambience. The grainy texture of this material inspired the visual design of the movie.[13]

The Moulin Rouge conceived as a Studio 54-style nightclub

Writing the script was a lengthy and exacting process. Luhrmann and Pearce tried out numerous story-lines, most of which were discarded as they stripped away unnecessary information.[14] Every version was tested in meetings with other colleagues. Luhrmann and Pearce would read their own drafts to one another, and then each would read the other's draft back to them, often acting out the scenes. After eighteen months of collaborative back and forth, a first draft was ready to show to the lead actors, but script revisions continued during rehearsals and shooting and extended into post-production.[15] In 1998 Luhrmann began casting the film; among those apparently under consideration for the main role of the consumptive courtesan Satine were Catherine Zeta-Jones, Renée Zellweger, Courtney Love, Sophie Ellis-Bextor and Sharleen Spiteri, while Heath Ledger, Jake Gyllenhaal and Ronan Keating were mooted to be in line for the part of the penniless Christian.[16] Luhrmann was determined that the lead performers should be actors first and singers second, and finally settled on Nicole Kidman, whose performance in *The Blue Room* on Broadway he admired, as Satine, and Ewan McGregor as Christian.[17] British character actor Jim Broadbent, who had just finished work on Mike Leigh's musical *Topsy-Turvy* (1999), was selected to play Harold Zidler, the manager of the Moulin Rouge, whose obsession with turning it into a legitimate theatre has tragic consequences. John Leguizamo was initially approached to play the Unconscious Argentinian, but opted for the more pivotal part of Toulouse-Lautrec, for which he was subjected to difficult and sometimes painful measures to shorten his legs. Australian Richard Roxburgh, who had extensive theatre and film experience, was cast as the moustache-twirling, evil Duke. Once the principal roles had been finalised, the four-month workshop and rehearsal process began at the House of Iona,[18] with Luhrmann asking the performers to treat the production as a piece of theatre. The design team experimented with different looks in costume, hair and make-up for the central couple; early ideas had McGregor sporting a dashing pencil moustache, while Kidman's hair and dress were modelled on the late-nineteenth-century Gibson Girl.[19] These styles were anachronistic, and the playful approach to period styles was intensified by allusions in Kidman's hair and costumes to screen goddesses such as Marlene Dietrich, Rita Hayworth and Marilyn Monroe. Production design, costume and visual effects were deliberately eclectic, projecting the Moulin Rouge as an anarchic environment in which nothing was taboo. Documented history provided the basic material, which was then manipulated by the film-makers in the interests of telling the story and creating a heightened artificial world in which characters breaking into song would appear convincing.

The script went through innumerable drafts,[20] with endless rounds of readings in consultation with the core team, who were encouraged to contribute ideas to this and other areas such as production design and choreography. Improvisation was the order of the day, not only for the actors but also for the crew. In order to create the aura of heightened reality, everyone was required to experiment; director of photography Don McAlpine adapted the accepted rules of Hollywood-style lighting and used the anamorphic format that had worked so well on *Romeo + Juliet* to produce a widescreen effect that was closer to the experience of watching a theatre performance. At the same time, for close shots the wide-angle lens was positioned about three feet away from the actors to give viewers a sense of being in the middle of the action. Apart from some of the musical numbers, most of the film was shot using a single camera to avoid dissipating the actors' energy. The stylised lighting plan involved follow spot-lights for the

'Roxanne' tango number similar to those used in theatre, while the spectacular musical finale was lit almost like a rock concert.[21] The dramatic lighting
emulated and enhanced the excitement generated by the advent of electric-
ity at the close of the nineteenth century. The colour palette was based on
strong contrasts between primary shades to emulate the intense saturated
tones of 1950s Technicolor. When the camera could not produce sufficient
intensity, some features, such as the L'amour fou sign outside Christian's
garret, were pumped up using digital effects.[22] The vivid colour and
chiaroscuro effects contributed to the anti-naturalistic style of the production, in which both interior and exterior action played out on a series of
constructed sets. As with all Luhrmann and Martin's work, *Moulin Rouge!*
was design led and, despite the experimental imperative, every aspect was
carefully stitched together to produce an eclectic whole in which each contribution would be visible. The heightened artificial world was projected as
an illusion in which every detail was driven by the need to appear complete
and plausible, but which audiences would perceive and enjoy as a fiction.
The production design, striving for the theatrical look of 1940s and 1950s
Hollywood studio musicals, was crucial to this effect. Amid all the camp
artificiality, the love story provided an emotional core to which audiences
could connect.[23]

  Working from historical material, Catherine Martin and set decorator
Brigitte Broch reconstructed and reinterpreted the Moulin Rouge, supervising a large team of graphic designers, sculptors, model-makers, set
dressers and scenic artists, most of whom were local, who manufactured the
sets in fine detail. This team worked from one-fifth-sized replicas of the
Moulin Rouge and the Montmartre streets, from which they built a mixture
of full-scale sets and small-scale models. One particularly impressive full-
scale effort was the giant three-storey polystyrene elephant situated in the
gardens of the Moulin Rouge, for which several different sets had to be
made, including a forehead and back at ground level where Satine and
Christian perform their love medley.[24] Another separate construction was
the elephant's belly, which housed the red room with its elaborate heart-
shaped motif where Satine seduces Christian, and incorporated risqué
design elements such as erotic illustrations inspired by the ancient Indian

sex manual the *Kama Sutra*. Because of the movie's PG-13 rating, these images could only be glimpsed very briefly in the background.[25] The production design incorporated many influences from Toulouse-Lautrec's paintings, including his symbolic use of colour and stylised composition.[26] The design team worked closely with Don McAlpine to achieve the strong hues essential to the theatrical cinematic style, and to make the sets look as good as possible. Many props were sourced and hired in Paris to add period detail,[27] which then became part of the eclectic style mix. As with other creative areas, every step was subject to the workshop treatment and went through many revisions before Luhrmann eventually signed off the designs.[28] The costumes were similarly inventive; the aim was not to adhere strictly to rules of period correctness, but to capture the sensational and shocking arena where sex was not only on display, but was also for sale. The film-makers were restricted by the PG-13 rating from showing the authentic can-can skirts and underwear (or lack of it) that revealed everything underneath, but Martin and co-costume designer Angus Strathie came up with a series of petticoats with rococo touches that allowed the dancers to show flashes of suspenders and thighs, underpants and buttocks beneath the multicoloured skirts. The skirts were made from layers of ruffles that were dyed, pleated, ribboned and braided before being sewn onto the interior fabric. This was a labour-intensive business; there were five or six ruffles to each skirt, which took a week to make, and there were thirty dancers.

Erotic display: Catherine Martin and Angus Strathie's can-can costume

The completed skirts and petticoats were dazzling, especially when displayed in dizzying fast-motion by the high-kicking can-can girls. They were also so heavy that some dancers had to wear braces to support them.[29]

The men's costume was equally labour intensive. Jim Broadbent as Zidler had several 'fat suits' made from a full body-cast onto which his bulky shape was sculpted in foam, which took weeks to make. The suits worn by Broadbent, Ewan McGregor, Richard Roxburgh and John Leguizamo were a mixture of period and modern designs and took over a month each to hand-tailor. The costumes were revised and customised in tandem with the script as it developed in the workshops, so that the actors influenced the style of their garments and were familiar with wearing them when shooting began.[30] The costume team made the clothes in a large workshop at Fox Studios, though some detail work was done in India.[31] The costumes played an important part in projecting the Moulin Rouge as a carnivalesque space where different classes and ethnic groups mingled, artists and intellectuals came together and all manner of sexual fetishes were practised and bizarre habits indulged. In addition to visualisations of eccentric characters

A carnivalesque space: Satine (Nicole Kidman) entertains at the Moulin Rouge

At the edges of bourgeois society: travesty at the Moulin Rouge

immortalised by Toulouse-Lautrec, such as La Goulue and the clown
Chocolat, provocative sartorial themes were created for individual can-can
dancers, including a dominatrix, French maid, schoolgirl and baby doll.[32]
Burlesque was much in evidence, with bearded elderly gentlemen outra-
geously kitted out in formal jackets, bow ties and top hats with tutus and
tights.[33] The Moulin Rouge was conjured up as a liminal area at the edges of
bourgeois society, simultaneously compelling and fraught with danger. This
conception had affinities with the Ballets Russes, one of the significant
influences on Luhrmann. Diaghilev, the impresario of the Ballets Russes in
the 1920s, was a Zidler-like figure driven by a desire to innovate who brought
together dancers, musicians, designers and fine artists. The surreal, circus-
like ambience of the Moulin Rouge resonated with the collaborative spirit,
embrace of everything modern and disregard for convention that characterised the Ballets Russes. The analogy surfaced in the Erik Satie character,
one of *Moulin Rouge!*'s bohemians, who composed for the Ballets Russes in
the 1920s, and in the impact of painter and graphic artist Léon Bakst, one of
their principal set and costume designers, on Moulin Rouge's design.[34] The
bohemian ethos of both the Moulin Rouge and the Ballets Russes was an
inspiration for Luhrmann's own working methods. Indeed, the resemblance
between Luhrmann and Harold Zidler has been noted more than once.[35]

Montmartre, the area of Paris in which the Moulin Rouge stood, was
recreated using digital special effects that were deliberately de-naturalised

and integrated with the overall design. Against the trend to use digital technology to produce ever more perfect images, Luhrmann, Martin and supervisor Chris Godfrey pursued imperfection, replicating shaky camera movement and film stock from early cinema to give an illusion that the film was hand-made. Some imperfections arose from the digital processes themselves. The visual effects were carried out in Sydney by Animal Logic, who worked from Photoshop collages and rough-cut sequences put together by Martin and the design team to build a digital Paris. The number of visual effects exceeded 300 and ranged from digital corrections to long sequences that married live action to one-fifth-scale models, to computer-generated settings such as the railway station where Christian first arrives. The sweeping shot that travelled over Paris to Montmartre, through the Moulin Rouge to Christian's garret room combined matte painting techniques with miniature and full-scale models and live action to move from a two-dimensional postcard-style vista of Paris into a three-dimensional city and through a one-fifth-scale model of the Moulin Rouge to the full-scale main hall.[36] The digital effects were also used to augment the film's fantastical elements. Kylie Minogue's 'green fairy', seen by the bohemians when they were under the influence of absinthe, was produced using the actress suspended on a trapeze rig against a blue screen. Her wings were added later.[37] The green fairy, at first cute and Disney-like, transmuted into a nightmarish hallucination that sucked Christian into the vortex of the underworld. She was visualised by imitating the out-of-register colour techniques of early photography, which generated an effect similar to stereoscopic imagery.[38] Another virtuoso effect, the flight of Christian and Satine across the Paris rooftops to the star-studded night sky, referred directly to the trick films of Georges Méliès in the cartoon-like image of the moon. The task was to match the conception and style of the project, and many computer-generated elements were 'choreo-graphed', that is, animated and timed to the music, before the actual shoot.[39] The 'archival film' effects were treated to create a painterly look for some of the sets that harked back to MGM musicals such as *An American in Paris* (1951), for which a self-contained, imaginary Paris was constructed entirely on the studio lot.

Quoting Georges Méliès' trick films in *Moulin Rouge!*

The visual effects were instrumental in producing an aesthetic for *Moulin Rouge!* that was both nostalgic and ironic, on one hand celebrating the naivety and experimental energy of periods of technological innovation, on the other deconstructing the postmodern desire for perfect simulacra and the addiction to surface beauty. This aesthetic does not trade in the fake reality that is said to be the essence of the hyper-real;[40] nor does it substitute its images for those to which it referred. Rather, it points up its own trickery, seducing the audience into an unruly experience that is the obverse of the regulated theme park. Luhrmann's investment in artifice creates a world that is distinct from reality, but is nevertheless truthful in that it enables the audience to respond emotionally to the ideals of beauty, truth, freedom and love adhered to by the characters, and emerge from that experience with a changed perspective. The emphasis is on interaction between audience and film. In the course of watching the movie, viewers are confronted with unexpected events at every level; though they are aware in advance of the story's outcome, they are less prepared for the assault on their senses and preconceptions presented by the manner of its telling.

Overcoming obstacles: *Moulin Rouge!*'s death sequence

They are also on a learning curve, as the creative potential of the medium is pushed to its limits and audience expectations of the musical genre are tested.

While the visual effects support story and character, they also have another function: to break up the linear trajectory of the narrative by visualising magical alternative directions. As the classical cause-and-effect structure of the Orphean myth moves relentlessly to its tragic conclusion, the digital effects simulate camera movements that are physically impossible, giving an illusion of swooping in and out of three-dimensional space, or, as with the death scene, passing through the Moulin Rouge interior and over exterior rooftops as though walls are no obstacle.[41] The visual effects break with naturalistic conventions of space and time, pulling against the forward drive of the narrative towards death and despair and projecting a utopian fantasy that tragedy might be avoided. Because they are revealed as sleight-of-hand, they contribute to the tension between illusion and reality at the heart of the film. The death sequence encapsulates this, as the camera pulls up from the Moulin Rouge stage where a heart-broken Christian cradles the dying Satine, and appears to move across the rooftops past a mournful Toulouse-Lautrec, towards the garret where an older and wiser Christian struggles to overcome his grief through art. The unresolved tension shadows the conclusion, which does not provide the reassurance normally ascribed to the classic musical.

Other liberties were taken with the Hollywood musical. As Luhrmann frequently pointed out, *Moulin Rouge!*'s strategy of including modern popular songs in the period setting was common in the genre's heyday.[42] However, the device of tying in the songs to character and story development is a feature of 'integrated musicals', in which the musical numbers do not stand alone. Integrated musicals are generally written by individual composers, and owe something to opera in having a libretto, or 'book' that contains the text of the story, dialogue and songs. *Moulin Rouge!*'s score was compiled from many different sources, and did not have a conventional libretto. The script was developed alongside the music, with Luhrmann and Pearce trying out thousands of songs that would help to tell the story, or add an emotional or comic register that dialogue and action could not provide. In some cases song lyrics were used in place of spoken words, as with Christian's poems. The innovative score was developed by a core group that included music director Marius DeVries, composer Craig Armstrong, arranger Chris Elliott and producer Josh G. Abrahams. The process of choosing the songs, which were recorded before shooting started, began early on and continued through workshops and rehearsals. Advances in digital recording technology meant that redrafting could carry on throughout the film-making process, and facilitated recording of vocals and instrumentals outside the conventional studio environment.[43] Permissions had to be cleared and consent obtained from the many artists who agreed to collaborate on the film; only two of those approached declined.[44] Like *Romeo + Juliet*'s soundtrack, the music was an eclectic mix of styles from rock and pop to opera, with an eye to soundtrack album sales. A balance had to be achieved between the function of the songs as an integral part of the story and their ability to have extended life in CD and music video form. New technologies also made it possible to work between three continents in Sydney, Los Angeles and Glasgow, where Craig Armstrong was based.[45] During the three years it took him to compose the soundtrack, Armstrong brought together the intricate melange of popular songs, music not specifically written for the film and original score, a task that extended beyond the usual methods of film scoring. He fused arrangements for each song with the orchestral score to create a coherent soundtrack, an activity of collage on a par with that motivating the visual design.[46] The music had to underscore the drama and draw viewers in, to avoid alienating them with its overtly anachronistic mix. It played an important role in weaving together the disparate elements of the film, as well as creating the emotional tone for different sequences. Several methods were tried for achieving the best performance of the songs. Rather than lip-synching to pre-recorded vocal tracks, the principal actors sang live on set to keyboard accompaniment or a backing track, with the pianist following the direction in which the singer took the song on a particular day, giving their rendition a sense of immediacy and adding to the hand-crafted feel.[47] Kidman and McGregor sang their numbers, while the more operatic vocals required for Jim Broadbent's Zidler were dubbed by Anthony Weigh.

The collision of different musical styles was matched by the choreography. John O'Connell researched diverse dance genres, from the Ritz Brothers to Busby Berkeley, Bollywood and the can-can.[48] Inspired by the wit and imagination of Hollywood musicals from the 1940s and 1950s, he playfully reinterpreted the source material without straying into caricature. The dance moves are a mixture of classical, as in the 'Roxanne' tango that accompanies Christian's jealous pacing as Satine keeps her assignation with the Duke, and modern update, in the wild excesses of the can-can, the Bollywood-style 'Spectacular Spectacular' finale and the comedic travesty of the 'Like a Virgin' number between Zidler and the Duke, which has decidedly deviant overtones. Like the music and visual design, dance was used to recreate the anarchic ambience of the Moulin Rouge and drive the story forward, but it also signalled the fact that *Moulin Rouge!*, indebted though it was to musicals of the past, was a modern take on the genre. Jill Bilcock's editing was crucial to the film's collage effect, and to establishing its ever-changing rhythm. She developed a multifaceted cutting style that was able to augment and energise the main story-line, allowing space for Satine and Christian's romance to develop and the smaller dramas and comedies to unfold.[49] As with *Strictly Ballroom* and *Romeo + Juliet*, the film is characterised by fast cutting, although some intimate moments between the lovers are slower paced. Like other aspects of the production, the editing is not invisible, even though it is at the service of story. If editing in

classic musicals was geared towards revealing the song-and-dance rou-
tines, in *Moulin Rouge!* it reveals itself as well. Indeed, every element of the
film is characterised by performance, putting on display the talent and
expertise of those involved and drawing attention to the creative processes
that were as much part of the drama as the events that drove the story.

*   *   *

Moulin Rouge!'s emphasis on performance at every level was essential to the
theatrical cinematic aesthetic, which strove to make a statement about style
through a mode of storytelling that depended on producing surplus meaning. Those who condemned the 'stylistic overkill'[50] in Luhrmann's films in
one sense hit the nail on the head; however, such judgments also missed the
point. It was through its excess of signification that the work 'spoke' its
hybrid identity and uncertain origins, and pinpointed the activity of appropriation as the impetus for innovation. The mannered performances, theatrical travesty, pastiche and hyperbolic hyperbole had affinities with
melodrama and camp. Camp's association with gay culture caused some to
speculate about queer influences on Luhrmann's style. Luhrmann did not
deny or confirm such conjecture, other than to affirm the prominence of
gay culture in Australia generally,[51] and to accept that Sydney's Mardi Gras
had a formative impact on him. Others suggested that Luhrmann's work
might lend itself to a queer reading, without specifically addressing gay
audiences.[52] The camp artificiality of Luhrmann's style, its self-conscious
appropriation and reinterpretation of other forms, and its transgression of
cultural boundaries could be aligned with 'queering', in its radical sense of
disturbing and overturning what is perceived as normal or natural.[53] It
could also be linked to the postcolonial impulse to generate new meanings
and forms, as I argued in relation to *Romeo + Juliet*.[54] Camp can be elitist in
addressing a minority group of aficionados; while Luhrmann defies divi-
sions between high and low culture and addresses audiences across such
boundaries, the response to his work is divided between those who get it
and those who do not. In its mockery of established values and good taste,
camp satisfies a plethora of subversive interests,[55] many of which converge
in Luhrmann's performative aesthetic. The aesthetic also seeks to display

High camp: the Duke (Richard Roxburgh) and Zidler (Jim Broadbent) perform 'Like a Virgin'

the virtuosity of a group of practitioners who might be considered marginal or isolated in the context of global film culture. This use of camp is not directly political, but it can be seen as counter-cultural in its bid to recast the power relations between large media conglomerates and independent film-makers.

A hybrid mix of formal devices make up the theatrical cinematic style of *Moulin Rouge!*. The high camp of the 'Like a Virgin' duet between the Duke and Zidler uses grotesquerie and masquerade to sabotage the song's message of innocence regained through love, throwing into relief the romance between Christian and Satine. The early scene in which Christian first meets the bohemians approaches theatre of the absurd in the ridiculous acting styles and embrace of nonsense. Like the gas station sequence in *Romeo + Juliet*, this is a challenge to the audience's willingness to suspend disbelief and enter into the ludic spirit of the film. When Christian seduces Satine in the red room, the elements of mistaken identity, stylised performance and physical comedy are typical of farce. These strategies are primarily comedic or satirical; but the dramatic clashes of tone, investment in spectacle and drive to provoke an emotional response are closer to the neo-baroque. In cinema, neo-baroque aesthetics have been identified with the rise of global media conglomerates and tie-ins across multiple entertainment sites, which have transformed what were perceived as classical modes of production and consumption, generating different forms of storytelling.[56] Baroque

usually describes the artistic movement that arose in the seventeenth century and produced an exuberant, busy and chaotic style that reached beyond
the orderliness of neo-classicism, romanticism and realism. Baroque was
not confined to the seventeenth century; it surfaced in the extreme flourishes of nineteenth-century romanticism and the off-kilter follies of early
twentieth-century surrealism.[57] The neo-baroque, which has been linked
with postmodernism, emerged in the context of 1950s postcolonial struggle
in Latin America, where it often took on revolutionary force. This and later
neo-baroque are characterised by an obsession with illusionism that questions the 'truth' of ruling ideologies, aiming to create an alternative, imaginative world in which the carnivalesque, intertextuality and multiple
narrative voices are privileged.[58] The features of postcolonial neo-baroque
resonate with the drive to produce new cinematic forms that motivates
Luhrmann's work.

Baroque emerges at times of social and cultural upheaval;[59] in this
respect, it has affinities with melodrama, which, it has been argued, acts as
a safety valve for the painful contradictions experienced by human beings
caught up in social change.[60] The extravagant formal rhetoric of baroque can
be seen in some manifestations of melodrama; for example, in the histrionic performance styles of nineteenth-century theatre, which were incorporated into early and pre-sound cinema.[61] Like baroque, melodrama
extends across different cultural forms, periods and geographical locations,
and it expresses intense emotion in heightened visual and aural design.
Baroque and melodrama share a concern with myth and with elaborate storytelling devices. Despite such correspondences, baroque diverges from
melodrama in some ways: in its exploration of the possibilities and perils of
the new; in its desire to provoke awe and wonder; in its preference for illusion over reality; and in its display of artistic and technological virtuosity.
The heightened melodramatic aesthetic is said to represent and derive from
psychic repression or censorship,[62] whereas baroque style celebrates the
absence of regulation and directly challenges convention. Although baroque
can act as a safety valve for the contradictions attendant on social change, it
is more than a symptomatic response to cultural transformation. In dramatising chaotic and tumultuous events, it projects potentially revolutionary

alternatives and the power of the imagination to overcome obstacles. Its investment in illusionism is founded in a desire to flout the 'reality principle'[63] in favour of flights of fancy that depend on suspending disbelief.

Rather than representing a decisive break with classical traditions, baroque incorporates classical modes and transforms them in the interests of envisioning new configurations.[64] In contemporary cinema, neo-baroque emerges in the context of fundamental economic and structural changes in the entertainment industries in which cross-media synergies and different kinds of consumer experience are made possible by technological advances. These experiences may encompass imaginative encounters with fantasy worlds summoned up by theme parks or special-effects extravaganzas; they may involve participation in interactive engagement with electronic media; or they may give rise to creative activities, such as making music or producing videos, previously unavailable to individual consumers on a mass scale. Each of these refers outwards to other media that may or may not be based in new technologies, but are rendered accessible by them. Despite being owned by horizontally integrated, economically powerful conglomerates, many aspects of new technologies are relatively unregulated, offering the promise of consumer empowerment that seems to flout the logic of advanced capitalism. In this unstable situation, baroque's celebration of utopian possibilities beyond the boundaries of human knowledge thrives, and neo-baroque cinema delights in the proliferation of narrative forms, the seemingly limitless stylistic innovations and the diverse spectatorial relationships that have become available. It has been argued that the dispersal of the classic cinema spectator's experience across media events and locations has de-centred the viewer and given rise to a more democratic, collective understanding of the individual subject. This can also be applied to production processes, so that spectators are perceived as producers in their interactions with media texts as well as in their creation of their own texts.[65]

The concept of neo-baroque usefully gathers together the aesthetic devices that constitute Luhrmann's theatrical cinematic style, and its awareness of the context of contemporary media industries. The concern with myth and classical storytelling is offset by spectacular set pieces and hyperbolic performances that break the bounds of linear narrative and question its inevitability. This dynamic is replicated in the online sites, DVD versions and video games that rely on interactive processes that lead in non-linear directions. Spectacular visual and sound design, adventurous cinematography, ingenious special effects and inventiveness at every level assert the boundless possibilities of digital technologies, which are reproduced in the design of DVDs and other supplementary materials. The international scope and transnational collaborations characteristic of Luhrmann's production methods are a response to global production patterns, and at the same time project an idealistic vision of creative and business alliances that have the potential to transform existing power relations between financial backers, producers and consumers. The expansive, utopian discourse extends to promotional materials, press reports and media coverage, in which Luhrmann and his collaborators extol the virtues of new technologies and their benefits to the Australian film industry. The proliferation of such material is neo-baroque in itself, providing a running commentary on the dramatic events and pioneering production processes contingent on Luhrmann's creative activity. A kind of maelstrom of excitement, risk and adventure revolves around each project, whipping up emotions before, during and after completion. At the nub of the ballyhoo is the claim to innovation in working methods and aesthetic, whose status as novel and different depends on the acknowledgment, characteristic of baroque forms, that new ideas are forged from the old. The neo-baroque is visible in *Strictly Ballroom* and *Romeo + Juliet*; but its high point is *Moulin Rouge!*.

Moulin Rouge! uses digital technology to meld archive images with iconic depictions and techniques from the Hollywood musical's heyday to produce a multilayered work that wears its aspirations to stylistic novelty on its highly decorated sleeve. Three distinct periods characterised by social, cultural and technological upheaval (fin-de-siècle Paris, 1950s Hollywood and the modern global era) are synchronised to create an imaginary world where temporal and spatial boundaries are dissolved and obstacles can be overcome. This utopian construction, founded in bohemian ideals of freedom, beauty, truth and love, is in tension with its opposite, a Gothic netherworld pervaded by greed, lust and murder, which threatens utopian beliefs. The tension pivots on a collision between art and commerce, and generates a dynamic in which the protagonists oscillate between the utopian realm, visualised spatially in terms of upward momentum, and the dark underworld. The Moulin Rouge, where sexual liberation is a commodity, is situated somewhere between the two. This is a chaotic, anarchic environment in which the characters struggle to retain their integrity and beliefs against overwhelming odds. Despite the tragic outcome, a fragile sense of hope remains in Christian's growth to maturity and his determination to write the lovers' story as a triumph of art over death. A key feature of baroque aesthetics is the exhibitionistic display of artistic skill and ambition; as neo-baroque, *Moulin Rouge!* propelled Luhrmann's performative style to the next level, flaunting the creativity involved in every aspect of the film and its production process, and claiming international recognition for the virtuoso team that made it.

*   *   *

The filming of *Moulin Rouge!* took 192 days, including model shoots, inserts and pick-ups in Spain, where Nicole Kidman was working on *The Others* (2001).[66] There had been media speculation that the film was behind schedule and over budget. Shortly before the projected October 1999 start date, Luhrmann's father died;[67] this, combined with an injury sustained by Kidman during rehearsals, delayed the production by three weeks. Once shooting began in November, the process of making constant revisions to the script and the experimental nature of the way the team worked slowed down the progress of the highly complex production.[68] The secrecy surrounding the film added to the rumours that it was in trouble;[69] but although the Christmas 2000 release date was put back, dashing hopes of making the 2001 Academy Awards, this was not a major setback.[70] Indeed, it helped to consolidate Luhrmann's status as auteur pitted against the studio moneymen. Unsubstantiated reports circulated that audiences at test screenings in Los Angeles were confused and Kylie Minogue had been drafted in at a late stage to act as a narrator figure. These reports were denied by the filmmakers, who pointed out that Minogue's presence was planned from the start, and that her busy schedule had made it impossible to film her earlier.[71]

The final touches to the editing were still under way in Los Angeles as the studio marketing campaign, whose budget estimate was reported to be anywhere between $2 million and $40 million,[72] moved into gear. After test screenings in middle-class areas in the USA,[73] Fox's promotional strategy for *Moulin Rouge!* was to present it as a cultural phenomenon, to generate widespread interest so that even people who did not go to the cinema regularly would want to see it. The advertising onslaught spanned 'hero sites', with outsize billboards displaying lights and moving parts; posters at bus stops; 'road-block' radio and television commercials that ran simultaneously across more than one channel; and lavish features and photo shoots in fashion and lifestyle magazines such as *Vogue* and *Harper's Bazaar*, which put the film on two covers.[74] Fox's official website for the film, sadly no longer available, played on the film's design and included interactive elements. As with *Strictly Ballroom* and *Romeo + Juliet*, the music played a crucial part in marketing campaigns. The first soundtrack CD was issued on 8 May 2001, one day prior to the movie's opening at the Cannes Film Festival;[75] it became an immediate hit in the USA, went to the top of the Australian ARIA albums chart and to No. 1 in the UK.[76] The raunchy remix of 'Lady Marmalade', produced by Missy Elliott and performed by Christina Aguilera, Lil' Kim, Mýa and Pink, which was also released as a music video, was a smash hit and was reputed to be one of the most requested songs on American radio.[77] Music videos of Kidman's version of 'One Day I'll Fly Away' and a remix of the Kidman–McGregor duet 'Come What May', directed by Luhrmann, were also issued.[78]

The film's visual design, particularly the colour and costumes, and the French connection, triggered a host of commercial tie-ins. Christian Dior produced a Moulin Rouge lipstick and cosmetics range linked to promotional offers; Ponds did magazine advertising featuring the film; the French Tourist Bureau offered trips to Paris as *Moulin Rouge!* competition prizes; and French winery Moët et Chandon provided champagne for some events. The elaborate diamond necklace worn by Kidman as Satine, designed by Sydney jeweller Stefano Canturi and valued at close to $1 million, was displayed on US television shows such as *Oprah Winfrey* and *Today*. Canturi also designed a jewellery range inspired by the film. New York department store

Bloomingdale's commissioned designers such as Anna Sui and Max Azria to reinterpret the *Moulin Rouge!* look for a special fashion line, while the film's costumes revived interest in wearing bustiers and corsets.[79] A glossy book, designed by Bazmark and lavishly illustrated with full-colour production stills, gave behind-the-scenes stories and information on the history of the production and included portfolios by photographers Ellen von Unwerth, Mary Ellen Mark and Douglas Kirkland.[80] The book emphasised the film's design and its status as art, and devoted considerable space to its basis in historical research. Some newspapers published features on the history of the Moulin Rouge and Toulouse-Lautrec tied in to *Moulin Rouge!*'s release.[81] The notoriety of the production was inflamed by reports that Fox had a great deal riding on its success after the poor showing of titles that included *Anna and the King* (1999), *The Beach*, *Bedazzled*, *Woman on Top* and *The Legend of Bagger Vance* (all 2000). *Moulin Rouge!* was perceived as a test of Australian talent and Kidman's acting and singing abilities, and as a huge risk for the film-makers and the studio, while Luhrmann was regarded as poised to become a major force in the industry if the film succeeded.[82]

Moulin Rouge!'s artistic credentials were boosted when it was chosen to open the 54th Cannes Film Festival on 9 May 2001. The opening, attended by Rupert Murdoch, was accompanied by a spectacular Moulin Rouge-themed display featuring can-can dancers, modern tap dancers and music. Kidman, McGregor and Luhrmann posed for the cameras and gave press conferences and countless interviews.[83] This was the first opportunity to gauge international critical response, and the reaction of French critics. The first screening received a standing ovation, and initial reviews were generally positive, though *Hollywood Reporter* and *Variety* considered that the film would be tough to sell to general audiences, and the French press was deeply divided.[84] *Moulin Rouge!* was nominated for the Palme d'or award, which went to Nanni Moretti's *La stanza del figlio* (*The Son's Room*, 2001). The Cannes opening was followed by an intensive promotional tour of the USA. It was enthusiastically endorsed by the influential *Oprah Winfrey* show, with Luhrmann and Kidman interviewed for this and many other television and radio programmes. The interviews served a double purpose, to publicise the film and also to allow Luhrmann to provide background information about

Strictly utopian: Fran (Tara Morice) and Scott (Paul Mercurio) triumph at the Pan-Pacific Championship

Strictly Ballroom poster featuring the star power of Paul Mercurio

Catherine Martin's
set design for
Juliet's bedroom
in *Romeo + Juliet*

Water imagery:
Romeo (Leonardo
DiCaprio) spies
Juliet (Claire
Danes)

Lavish set for
Romeo + Juliet's
death scene

Quoting spaghetti westerns: Tybalt (John Leguizamo) in *Romeo + Juliet*'s gas station sequence

After Shakespeare and Fellini: Mercutio (Harold Perrineau) in drag at the Capulet ball

Dazzling display: can-can dancers at the Moulin Rouge

Bollywood influence: Satine (Nicole Kidman) and Christian (Ewan McGregor) in 'Spectacular Spectacular'

The lure of Absinthe: the green fairy (Kylie Minogue) leads Christian (Ewan McGregor) astray

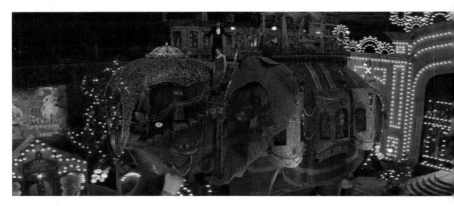

Polystyrene elephant constructed for the *Moulin Rouge!* set

Caged bird: Nicole
Kidman in *No. 5
The Film*

Buttoned up:
costume design
for Lady Sarah
Ashley in *Australia*

Under the boab tree: *Australia*'s sublime landscapes

Magical realism: Nullah's special powers

Sarah
Evening Dress

As THE DROVER and SARAH
slowly make their way
towards each other,
the crowd is reduced
to a murmur. When they
meet, SARAH looks up
into THE DROVER'S eyes,
a scab and some
bruising seem only
to amplify his
charm.

Costume Design by Catherine Martin
Illustrations by Ignacio Peña

Sc 147
Government House Ball

Transformed: costume design for Lady Sarah Ashley

its history, playing a vital educational role. The performative nature of the theatrical cinematic aesthetic was carried over into the promotional activities, which primarily depended on the performance of Luhrmann as director. The film was still being fine-tuned by the time of its Los Angeles premiere on 16 May; on 18 May it opened in two selected cinemas in Los Angeles and New York before being released nationwide in the USA on 1 June 2001.[85] The strategy of limited platform release was geared to building word-of-mouth that the movie was a special event. Luhrmann returned to Sydney on 20 May ahead of the 24 May Australian release to engage in another round of publicity work. It was at this point that the term 'red curtain style' was coined to link *Moulin Rouge!*, *Romeo + Juliet* and *Strictly Ballroom* together as a trilogy.[86] The fact that the Australian media did not universally praise *Moulin Rouge!* was used by Luhrmann in interviews to reinforce its innovative, rule-breaking status. The Sydney premiere took place on 21 May in eleven cinemas at the Fox studio complex, to an audience of 3,000 that included locals who had worked on the film.[87] Following its national release, it became the biggest local debut ever for an Australian film, surpassing the blockbuster *The Mummy Returns* (2001) at the box office in its first week.[88] On 27 May Luhrmann went to Taiwan for further promotional work before moving on to the USA for the national release. Here he did media interviews in the southern heartlands of Texas and Georgia, perceived as the most difficult territories to conquer, particularly

Red curtain cinema: *Moulin Rouge!*'s red velvet curtains

with an art-house musical. Trailers exploited the critical controversy surrounding the production, headlining it as 'the most talked-about movie of
the year'. The US nationwide promotional push seemed to have worked;
audience exit interviews were positive and the box-office figures for *Moulin
Rouge!*'s opening weekend exceeded expectations at $13.7 million.[89]

Luhrmann participated in a relentless, worldwide round of publicity
stunts, as marketing events continued throughout 2001 and into the run-up
to the US Academy Awards in March 2002. Luhrmann and Fox went all out
for the coveted best picture award, wooing potential voters through appearances at the writers, directors and actors guilds and advertisements in the
trade press featuring endorsements from Stanley Donen (*Singin' in the
Rain*, 1952) and Robert Wise (*The Sound of Music*, 1965).[90] The first double-
disc DVD, designed by Bazmark with an impressive array of extra materials,
including a 'Behind the Red Curtain' interactive feature, was issued in
December 2001, while the first *Baz Luhrmann's Red Curtain Trilogy* DVD
boxed set came out in September 2002, setting the seal on the Red Curtain
brand and Luhrmann's authorship.[91] *Moulin Rouge!* was rereleased theatri-
cally in 2002,[92] in advance of the Oscar ceremony, where the film was nominated in several categories, including Best Picture, Best Leading Actress,
Best Cinematography, Best Sound, Best Editing and Best Make-Up, and
won awards for Best Art Direction and Best Costume Design. It went on to
garner a host of award nominations, among them several from the
Australian Film Institute (AFI), who considered the Australian involvement
sufficient for it to qualify as an Australian production,[93] and from the
British Academy of Film and Television Arts (BAFTA), where Luhrmann
picked up a nomination for the David Lean prize for direction.[94] Thanks
largely to Luhrmann's efforts as communicator, the promotional drive was
successful in achieving maximum visibility for the film and its director,
reaping substantial rewards at the box office.[95] Members of the press, however, were more difficult to convince. As with *Romeo + Juliet*, US critics were
particularly hostile;[96] but many supporters of the earlier film disliked
Moulin Rouge!'s postmodern take on the musical, comparing it to pan-
tomime and finding its style too distancing and Kidman's performance
mannered and cold.[97] The words 'kitsch' and 'camp' were often used to

describe the film, usually as a way of dismissing it, though some saw its perceived lack of emotion as appropriate to its critique of commercialism.[98]

Australian critics were generally kinder. Some appreciated the film's departure from classical aesthetic norms, and others saw its artificial style as a logical outcome of Luhrmann's background in theatre.[99] *Moulin Rouge!*'s international scope and ambition were seen as evidence that the domestic film industry had come of age.[100] However, the status of the production's national identity came into question when the Australian Taxation Office rejected concessions for its overseas financial backers on the grounds that they qualified as tax evasion. This controversial decision was perceived as having serious consequences for international investment in the local industry, and on Australia's future success as a viable off-shore production alternative.[101] Through all the dissent, *Moulin Rouge!* gradually built a reputation for innovation, particularly among those who responded positively to its sophisticated engagement with digital technologies.[102] Its cultural influence was affirmed in September 2001, when the London National Film Theatre (now BFI Southbank) mounted a season of films under the umbrella of 'Red Curtain Cinema' that took *Moulin Rouge!*'s style of magical illusionism as a starting point. Besides Luhrmann's *Strictly Ballroom* and *Romeo + Juliet*, the eclectic programme included *Sunrise A Song of Two Humans* (1927), *Cabaret* (1972), *An American in Paris* (1951), *Lola Montès* (1955), *Gentlemen Prefer Blondes* (1953) and *The Red Shoes* (1948).[103] These had in common an exhibitionistic aesthetic that depended on delighting the cinema spectator with artful displays of technological ingenuity and spectacular visual design. The reference to *The Red Shoes* is intriguing. In addition to sharing Powell and Pressburger's disregard for boundaries between realism and artifice, Luhrmann's industrial set-up and his collaborative working methods resonated with their company The Archers' situation as part of J. Arthur Rank's Independent Producers Ltd (IPL) in 1940s Britain.[104] Despite *Moulin Rouge!*'s cultural impact, academic writing about it was surprisingly scarce.[105] However, the film generated online fan and information sites that grew in popularity and sustained public interest in Luhrmann's activities.[106]

The marketing strategy of building an audience base for *Moulin Rouge!* recognised its niche appeal, cross-over potential and extended life in ancillary media. It was a tactic that incorporated commercial advertising techniques such as saturation-level promotion, while using branding to create an immediately recognisable style that traded on its difference from the mainstream. The Red Curtain Trilogy name provided Luhrmann and Martin with a singular identity that reflected their position as independent film-makers operating on the borders of major studio production. *Moulin Rouge!*'s theme of art versus commerce commented on their situation, not least in the Duke's insistence on tying Satine to an exclusive contract, as Fox had with Bazmark. Yet the relationship between art and commerce in their dealings with Fox seemed to be successful, enabling them to produce ambitious works that achieved high visibility, with minimal studio interference. To an extent, Bazmark's alliance with Fox could be seen as mirroring the production patterns of contemporary US film-makers who occupy 'Indiewood' territory, the area between mainstream and independent Hollywood that grew up in the late 1990s with the establishment of the mini-major companies.[107] *Moulin Rouge!*, the pinnacle of the Red Curtain aesthetic, was testament to the benefits gleaned by both sides. For Fox, the rewards were not just financial; indeed, this was one of the riskier areas of the partnership. While they banked on some profit, they also stood to gain cultural credibility from investment in unconventional art movies that appealed to popular audiences. For Luhrmann and Martin, the Red Curtain Trilogy also resulted in economic gains, but more importantly its completion consolidated their reputation as major players on the world stage. Their next film project would be on an even grander scale; they planned to leave the studio-based aesthetic behind for a new trilogy of epic works that would face enormous challenges of historical reconstruction, and test their creative and organisational skills to the limit.

Five
No. 5 The Film (2004) and *Australia* (2008)

Moulin Rouge! may have taken the Red Curtain Trilogy to its flamboyant limits, but the style was not quite exhausted yet. In December 2002, Luhrmann staged his production of *La Bohème* on Broadway, following a six-week run in San Francisco, where it was greeted with enthusiasm despite the director's fears that a post-9/11 America might not be receptive to his exuberant, modern take on the classic opera. The production was praised by aficionados and novices alike, and Luhrmann's attempts to woo a younger audience to opera were apparently successful.[1] The cross-fertilisation between *Moulin Rouge!* and *La Bohème* was evident; in a sense, the opera represented the final encore to the three acts of the Red Curtain films. Luhrmann and Martin appeared to be riding the crest of a wave; however, the reality was more precarious, and the months following the release of *Moulin Rouge!* were professionally and personally tumultuous. Extracts from Luhrmann's diary published in American *Vogue* in 2004 revealed the disheartening events that brought about the delay and eventual abandonment of the *Alexander the Great* project and led them in a different direction from the envisaged large-scale epic.[2] The planned new cycle would move away from the studio-bound aesthetic of the Red Curtain movies to a more authentic, exterior mode focused on landscape as the background for the drama. The Red Curtain Trilogy pivoted on a tension between artifice and naturalism, both of which played a significant role in the storytelling. The privileging of illusionism in the Red Curtain style would give way to an emphasis on naturalism that would subtly reveal its underlying artifice, rather than confront the audience with it. Luhrmann was now interested in externalising the interior thoughts and emotions of characters through vast landscapes, in the mode of *Lawrence of Arabia* (1962).

Initial preparations for the *Alexander the Great* biopic began in 2002 while Luhrmann and Martin were heavily involved with *La Bohème*. Work on the script, design, locations and casting were well under way, the main backers and the estimated $150 million budget were in place, and considerable thought had been put into the question of how to represent the complex and sophisticated ancient world. Luhrmann and Martin travelled the globe in an exhausting round of investigative journeys. In December 2002 they received news from producer Dino De Laurentiis that Oliver Stone's production of a film about Alexander for Warner Bros. was going ahead, and they would have to move fast to begin shooting first. Under extreme pressure, they decided to have a short break and take stock.[3] In February 2003 Luhrmann was approached by Chanel, on the advice of Nicole Kidman, who had recently become the new face of the iconic No. 5 perfume, to conceive, produce and direct an advertising campaign starring Kidman. Luhrmann was attracted to the idea of collaborating again with the *Moulin Rouge!* actress, who had signed up to play Alexander's mother Olympias in the next project. He was also interested in making an advertising film that would use Chanel No. 5 as a backdrop to a fairy-tale romance in the Red Curtain style. However, with his *Alexander the Great* epic due to begin shooting in October 2003, it was difficult to see how he would be able to find time for the Chanel commercial. To add to the stress, Luhrmann and Martin then learned that they were expecting their first child in October 2003. During this period, Luhrmann drafted the *Alexander the Great* treatment, this time without his long-time collaborator Craig Pearce. The break with the Red Curtain aesthetic demanded a new team of creative partners, and British playwright and film-maker David Hare was recruited to work with Luhrmann on the script. With the support of De Laurentiis and backers Universal and DreamWorks,[4] the decision was made to allow more time for *Alexander the Great* to be developed; while David Hare tackled the next draft of the screenplay, Luhrmann and Martin would take on the ostensibly smaller task of producing the Chanel No. 5 commercial. This would enable them to work with Kidman again and to extend their visual-effects language in a painterly direction suited to the style of the new trilogy.[5]

Initial preparations for the Chanel No. 5 project began in July 2003 and involved discussions with Chanel executives in New York, who wanted the campaign to maintain the position of the fragrance as the world's best-selling perfume.[6] For his part, rather than produce a commercial centring on Chanel No. 5, Luhrmann conceived a short film that would use the perfume as a backdrop for a romantic encounter and would be a cinematic event in its own right.[7] Despite its more modest scale, the work went through the same process as any Luhrmann project, beginning with extensive research and total immersion in the history of the company, the perfume and its promotion, and Coco Chanel herself.[8] Images of the stars and personalities featured in previous campaigns were collected and Luhrmann sifted through commercials from earlier periods.[9] He was particularly taken with those from the 1970s featuring Catherine Deneuve.[10] A full-page magazine advertisement displayed a black-and-white photograph of Deneuve in black tailored jacket, white shirt and black bow-tie, wearing the Chanel trademark white camelia on her lapel and with blonde hair scraped back.[11] This androgynous image surfaces in Luhrmann's commercial when Kidman emerges onto her lover's garret roof wearing a black tuxedo, shorts and unbuttoned white shirt, with an untied bow-tie hanging loose around her neck. As well as recalling Deneuve's association with the perfume and playing on Chanel's trademark black-and-white look, this get-up suggests a

Androgyny in black and white: Nicole Kidman in *No. 5 The Film*

The most famous woman
in the world: a composite
of female icons

tomboy identity for the character that is very different from the haute couture dresses and jewellery that signify her celebrity status. Luhrmann envisaged 'the most famous woman in the world' as a composite of female icons
who had, or may have had some relationship with Chanel, such as Marilyn
Monroe, Jacqueline Kennedy, Maria Callas, Catherine Deneuve and
Princess Diana.[12] The story revolves around the character's attempt to elude
her fame and responsibilities through a passionate, short-lived love affair
with a bohemian writer, played by Brazilian actor Rodrigo Santoro, who does
not know who she is.[13] Her agent, a Zidler-like figure, reminds her of her
duty, whereupon she returns to her former existence, leaving behind the
memory of her kiss, smile and perfume. There is irony in the fact that the
character's escape, which is achieved through taking on yet another iconic
image, is a chimera, while the love enjoyed by the romantic couple is no
more than a daydream. The ubiquitous Chanel signage that entraps her in
the city streets is also there on the garret roof, as if there is no refuge from
the image-saturated commercial world she inhabits.

The fantasy nature of the story was underlined by the production design,
which created a mythical urban setting that was a hybrid of New York and

Paris. On a three-day fact-finding visit to Paris, Martin's team filmed Coco Chanel's apartment above her studio and the company's black-and-white offices in Neuilly-sur-Seine, and took photographs of Paris rooftops that might be suitable for the garret.[14] In New York, photographs were taken and video footage filmed of buildings around Manhattan.[15] Back in Sydney, the drafting of the script and the creative workshop process took place at Bazmark headquarters at the House of Iona. Working from the collated materials and stock images, the team built sets on Fox Studios Australia sound stages that were a mixture of full-size constructions and scale models, which were embellished by Sydney-based company Animal Logic's visual effects.[16] The costumes were in similar fairy-tale mode. Working from Catherine Martin's presentation boards, Karl Lagerfeld designed Kidman's extravagant dresses, which were hand made by seamstresses at the Chanel studio, while Martin contributed additional costumes. The pink-feathered gown worn by Kidman in the opening sequence suggests an exotic caged bird, while the black jacket and shorts outfit she sported on the garret roof intimate the anonymity and freedom she longs for. The long, figure-hugging, backless black dress and the neat hairstyle displayed in the final sequence on the red carpet show that she has regained control of her life, thanks to her brief escape. Her new-found independence is associated with the perfume by the diamond pendant carrying the Chanel No. 5 insignia that adorns her back, the only symbol of the product that appears in the film.[17] Kidman's jewellery was custom designed by Chanel's fine jewellery department, who produced small give-away promotional pieces as well as several different versions of the No. 5 pendant, which was reputed to contain 687 diamonds and became a feature of the media hype surrounding the production.[18] The shoot took place over four days on Fox Australia sound stages, finishing on 23 December 2003.[19] The music soundtrack was Claude Debussy's 'Clair de lune', performed by the Sydney Symphony Orchestra and arranged by Craig Armstrong, who also plays the piano for the melancholy rendition of the theme. The plangent score underlines the sense of loss and the elusive nature of love and emotional connection in the modern, commerce-driven global environment.

The Chanel No. 5 film took a year to complete. Post-production stretched out longer than expected, and different versions were made for television and cinema screenings.[20] Luhrmann and Martin were busy with other matters, not least their baby daughter Lillian Amanda, who was born on 10 October 2003.[21] *No. 5 The Film* was unveiled in October 2004, and as predicted was a spectacular media event.[22] Promotional materials included a lavishly produced book of photographs titled *No. 5*, bound in white with a cover image of Kidman in pink-feathered gown cradled by the rooftop Chanel sign, and packaged in a luxurious box-case bearing a photograph of the night-time cityscape; outsize replica No. 5 perfume bottles; and a card featuring one of Andy Warhol's silkscreens of the Chanel No. 5 bottle. A full-page colour advertisement in the French newspaper *Le Figaro* carried an image of Nicole Kidman in black backless gown and No. 5 diamond pendant, and invited the reader to an exceptional event, the screening of the film on French television channel TF1.[23] As with earlier promotional campaigns, Luhrmann himself played a key role in explaining the story, the ideas and the processes involved in completing the project through the twenty-five-minute 'making of' documentary.[24] The commercial was screened on television and in cinemas around the world in October and November 2004,[25] accompanied by extensive media campaigns, and annual worldwide repeat screenings followed. Despite its success in promoting the Chanel No. 5 brand, the mini-film's relationship to a commercial is tangential. The role of the perfume in the central character's bid for freedom and independence is obscure; indeed, it is possible to interpret the film, albeit against the grain of the director's intentions, as asserting the illusory nature of the ideals of beauty, truth, freedom and love celebrated by *Moulin Rouge!*. The idea that the writer's garret provides a peaceful haven is unconvincing, as is the notion that he is unaware of his lover's identity. The conflict between commerce and art at the centre of *Moulin Rouge!* is weakened in *No. 5 The Film*, which, partly because of the need to condense the story into a two-minute format, has an overwhelming claustrophobic quality. There is no implication that the bohemian artist will overcome his loss by writing the lovers' story, nor is there any suggestion that the couple might reunite in the future. All that remains of their ephemeral liaison is a memory, or more precisely, the memory of a dream.

It is tempting to see *No. 5 The Film* as Luhrmann's acknowledgment that the Red Curtain style was now completely played out. Its visual design is dominated by barriers and cage-like imagery, while the melancholy tenor of the music intimates an ending rather than a beginning. Indeed, it can be understood as a transitional piece between the studio-bound Red Curtain aesthetic and the expansive exterior mode of the projected series of epics. The central character's flight through imaginary city streets is conceived as a panic-stricken response to a hostile environment, similar to Sarah Ashley's desperate rush to save Nullah in war-torn Darwin in *Australia*. Her desire to find a place of refuge elsewhere anticipates *Australia*'s Faraway Downs and the 'Somewhere Over the Rainbow' motif. The character's trans-formation due to her experience of a place removed from the pressures of urban existence is also the motivating force of *Australia*'s story-line and its accompanying tourism advertising campaign. The use of slow motion in the mini-film's opening sequence is a technique extensively employed in *Australia*, and seems to imply a slowing-down of the frantic pace of the Red Curtain Trilogy. The slow motion also supports the notion that the charac-ters are dreaming, looking forward to *Australia*'s deployment of Aboriginal Dreamtime mythology and its connections between memory and dream. Although at this point Luhrmann was still committed to the *Alexander the Great* biopic, he was also preparing for what might happen if he had to aban-don it when Oliver Stone's film was released in late autumn 2004.[26] The links between the Chanel No. 5 film and Australia are speculative; however, it is likely that Luhrmann was already working on the Australian-themed epic so that he would have a replacement if necessary. Cross-fertilisation between the two projects was therefore possible. As it happened, the much-delayed *Alexander the Great* film was finally dropped at the end of 2004 when Oliver Stone's version was met by poor reviews, and though the subject of Luhrmann's next work was not confirmed for several months, the Australian-themed epic moved into first place. One of the factors undoubt-edly influencing the decision to produce a film on home territory was Luhrmann and Martin's discovery that they were expecting their second child in June 2005.

In May 2005, they officially confirmed that the new cycle of epic works would begin with the Australian-themed story, as yet untitled, starring Nicole Kidman and Russell Crowe. Luhrmann intimated that he would like to return to the *Alexander the Great* project at some stage, and he also revealed that a Russian story would be part of the epic trilogy. The first epic would be shot on location in Australia, backed by Fox and Dune Entertainment with a budget of around $130 million, and would be co-scripted by Luhrmann with fellow Australian Stuart Beattie, who had written the screenplay for Michael Mann's *Collateral* (2004).[27] The story centred on a romance between an English aristocrat, played by Kidman, and a tough Australian drover played by Crowe, and would be set against the backdrop of the 1930s cattle wars and the advent of World War II. The visual style would be less dominated by artifice than the Red Curtain films, but would nevertheless project a heightened romanticism reflecting the characters' emotions. By the time the official announcement was made, exploratory research was under way and the first concept book had been put together. Locations were investigated in and around the Northern Territory, a large, sparsely populated region stretching from the central mainland to the northern coast. The capital city was Darwin, a port situated at the northernmost tip of the Territory, which had been bombed during World War II by the same Japanese task force that had attacked Pearl Harbor. This little-known event was one of the central narrative threads; another was the Stolen Generations, the mixed-race Aboriginal children who were removed from their indigenous families to be brought up as white; and a third was the white European settlement and ownership of cattle stations in the area during the run-up to World War II. All these themes pivoted on relationships to the land, enabling an examination of Australian colonial history and national identity that took the concerns of *Strictly Ballroom* several stages further.

The Northern Territory's ethnically diverse population included white Europeans, Chinese and Japanese, and indigenous Australians who had lived in the region for an estimated 50,000 years.[28] A substantial part of the initial research was devoted to talking to people in various indigenous communities about their different histories and cultures. These discussions fed into the script and its ideas about storytelling and ownership of the land.[29] The remote area around Kununurra in far northern Western Australia close to the border with the Northern Territory, a region of spectacular natural beauty and grandeur with ravines, mountainous terrain, waterfalls and rivers, was chosen as the setting for the homestead and cattle-drive. The production was complicated by the fact that permission to film on the land in Western Australia had to be obtained from different government agencies and private individuals who held overlapping territorial rights, as well as the traditional indigenous owners who held equal rights with the pastoral leaseholders.[30] The complex negotiations with local inhabitants and communities affected many aspects of the creative process and gave the project and its participants an intimate emotional connection to the land and its history. In the early stages, the large Asian community and the pearling industry in northern Western Australia had a significant presence; as the script was honed via workshop discussions, this element was relegated and survived in the minor character of the Chinese cook Sing Song, played by Yuen Wah, the Pearl Picture Gardens cinema and the Chinese influence on the costume and production design. Other ethnic groups were represented in minor roles, such as the Russian hotel owner Ivan, played by Polish actor Jacek Koman, who had played the Unconscious Argentinian in *Moulin Rouge!*, and the Filipino band that featured in the ball sequence. Australia's multiethnic population was key to the film's portrayal of the country's national identity. However, Luhrmann's primary interest was in the relationships between the Anglo-Celtic Australians and the indigenous characters, which provided a focus for the representation of the nation's colonial and postcolonial history. This focus was dramatised through fictional storytelling devices, performance, visual design and music, woven together with references to classic cinema to produce a multilayered, hybrid work that reflected the cross-fertilisation between Australia's mix of cultures. To avoid didacticism, the story centred on the transformation of Kidman's English character through her encounter with the land, her romance with the Drover and her attachment to the mixed-race Aboriginal boy Nullah (Brandon Walters).

Nicole Kidman and Russell Crowe were the first cast members to be factored in to the production in 2005; Crowe in particular played a considerable role in early word-of-mouth publicity through press interviews. Since the *Alexander the Great* epic had fallen through, anticipation about

Luhrmann's new project was high, particularly among the Australian media. As usual, the secrecy surrounding the project contributed to speculation that sometimes reached fever pitch in the three-and-a-half years it took to complete. The controversy began when Russell Crowe left the film in June 2006, citing 'creative differences' with the studio as the reason, and Hugh Jackman was signed up as his replacement. It was rumoured that filming, due to start in July 2006, was delayed until 2007 because the studio would not approve the budget.[31] Further details of the characters, story, cast members and locations emerged bit by bit, feeding media conjecture. In November 2006 the title was officially announced as *Australia*. This was a bold move that risked alienating international audiences; in interviews, Luhrmann explained that the title was a metaphor for a faraway exotic land and the female protagonist's emotional journey.[32] He was interested in expressing his country's history through a fictional work that would have universal relevance. Despite these disclaimers, the production was overwhelmingly Australian. Luhrmann co-wrote, produced, directed and contributed additional music, with Catherine Martin as co-producer, production and costume designer and Ian Gracie as supervising art director. The music team included David Hirschfelder, who composed the score for *Strictly Ballroom*; folk music expert Felix Meagher, who worked with Luhrmann on the 1988 experimental opera *Lake Lost*; songwriter and singer Angela Little;[33] local folk/rock musician Stephen Pigram;[34] and Bazmark music producer Anton Monsted as music supervisor. Director of photography Mandy Walker had worked on *No. 5 The Film*, as had producer Catherine Knapman, who also co-produced *Moulin Rouge!*.

Risks were also taken with the casting. Luhrmann and Ronna Kress adopted the tried and tested approach of combining international stars with veteran character actors and less well-known performers. The line-up included established Australian players such as Bryan Brown in the role of cattle baron King Carney; David Wenham as corrupt station manager Neil Fletcher; Jack Thompson as alcoholic accountant Kipling Flynn; David Gulpilil as the Aboriginal elder King George; Ben Mendelsohn as the British Captain Dutton; David Ngoombujarra as the Drover's brother-in-law Magarri; and Lillian Crombie as Bandy Legs. Barry Otto, who played Scott's

David Gulpilil as tribal elder King George

father in *Strictly Ballroom*, appeared as Administrator Allsop. Ursula Yovich, who featured as Nullah's mother Daisy, was a relative newcomer, while the part of Nullah himself was given to total novice Brandon Walters, who was chosen after an extensive search.[35] Nullah is a major figure in the drama; Luhrmann's biggest gamble was to give centre stage to an indigenous character who was the film's narrator and crucial to the story development, and to cast an unknown name in the role. Nullah is a special boy with magical powers, harking back to the 'Nature Boy' theme of *Moulin Rouge!*. He is the focal point for the film's ideas about storytelling, dream, myth and music, and for the exploration of relationships to the land. His supernatural abilities, bestowed on him by the tribal elder King George, introduce an element of magical realism, associated with Aboriginal culture in the story. Luhrmann wanted to use a naturalistic mode that would nevertheless incorporate undercurrents of the fantastic. This aesthetic was no less self-conscious than the theatrical cinematic style, and retained many of its features, including histrionic performances, particularly from the Anglo-Celtic Australians, heightened romanticism and cinematic references. But it was less overtly concerned with revealing the artifice, and more inclined to present a subtle challenge to realism by weaving Gothic and fairy-tale tropes into the adventure story. As an outsider who belongs nowhere, Nullah moves between the naturalistic and the supernatural worlds. His name, which in Hindi signifies a ravine or gully that carries rainwater in drought-stricken territory, has additional resonance because of its association with the Aborigine nullah-nullah club, a weapon made from an uprooted young tree.[36] Through his name, Nullah is closely connected to the land and in a sense represents its resistance to colonisation and the redrawing of geographic and cultural boundaries.

The son of his Aboriginal mother, Daisy, and Anglo-Celtic Australian father Neil Fletcher, Nullah is an offspring of colonisation, a 'creamy' who has no place in white European Australian society nor in his indigenous community. Yet his undecided status gives him certain advantages. Nullah is related both to the mischievous land-sprite Puck and to the Indian boy-child at the centre of the quarrel between Oberon and Titania in *A Midsummer Night's Dream*. He also has affinities with the spirit-child of Australian Aboriginal myth. In his role as magical hero, and in the etymology of his name, he is connected to the youthful Hindu deity Krishna.[37] Thus he is simultaneously a character founded in documented history, and a mythical being whose significance reverberates across cultures. His cross-cultural identity is evident in the quasi-Australian Aboriginal English speech that characterises his narrator's voice-over.[38] It was another audacious step by Luhrmann to use a hybrid language to tell the story from the point of view of a mixed-race child. This was appropriate to the project of depicting the impact of Australia's colonial past on its indigenous population; indeed, the prominence given to language in *Australia*, as in other Luhrmann films, can be viewed as motivated by a postcolonial search for alternative modes of expression. The decision to make Nullah's the dominant perspective was critical in other ways. *Australia*'s story of its heroine's journey into unknown territory and her subsequent transformation through contact with a mysterious place and its people is a characteristic of the Gothic women's picture, in which events are usually filtered through the female protagonist's viewpoint. The Drover's story and the cattle wars scenario are the stuff of the classic Western, focusing primarily on a solitary white male hero and his need to find a feisty female counterpart. The action-adventure and war film motifs that feature in the second half also revolve around predominantly white male heroics. In weaving the genres together and placing the romantic couple at the centre, Luhrmann risked the accusation that he had reproduced the conventional forms and ideological hierarchies of classic Hollywood cinema. His innovation was to introduce the myths and rituals of Australia's indigenous communities to offset the white European heroic myths of the nation's colonial history. The romance between the Drover and Lady Sarah is inflected and displaced by that between each of them and the mixed-race child, while Nullah's framing narrative, his magical interventions and the supernatural role of King George throw into relief the traditional storytelling devices of classic movies.

The mixture of genres provides the means to trace Sarah's transformation from tight-laced English aristocrat to dishevelled tomboy and cattle queen, while bringing together different storytelling strategies enables connections to be made across cultures. When Sarah tells the recently bereaved Nullah the *Wizard of Oz* story and sings 'Somewhere Over the Rainbow', he responds by citing the Rainbow Serpent, a powerful figure in Aboriginal creation mythology who replenishes stores of water, forming deep gullies and ravines in the landscape.[39] Nullah's name links him to the Rainbow Serpent, while Sarah's narrative role, described by King George as healing the land, connects her to the mythical beast and to Nullah. The complex soundtrack, which incorporates ancient tribal chants, mission choirs, country and western, bush ballads, American classics and Filipino guitar music, enhances the rich cultural mix.[40] In addition to the recurring motif of 'Somewhere Over the Rainbow', which acts as an ironic counterpoint in scenes such as the one in which Nullah, his face blackened with dirt so that he is allowed to enter the Pearl Picture Gardens, watches Judy Garland's rendition of the song in *The Wizard of Oz*, 'The Drover's Ballad', composed by Elton John with lyrics by Luhrmann, plays over the end credits. The popular Australian folk music band The John Butler Trio contribute 'All Night Long', while two versions of 'Waltzing Matilda', one featuring Rolf Harris, whose famous wobble-board is also heard over the closing titles, and the other an update performed by Angela Little, are included. Little also performs the lilting number 'By the Boab Tree', for which Luhrmann wrote the lyrics, over the end credits; the words celebrate the iconic tree that features prominently in the film and underline the ability of music to speak to people across space and time.

Swing numbers from the 1930s, including period classics such as 'Begin the Beguine', 'Tuxedo Junction', 'Brazil' and The Ink Spots' 'Whoa Babe', are interpolated into David Hirschfelder's score, while 'Nimrod' from Edward Elgar's *Enigma Variations* suggests the mysterious, unfathomable nature of the land and its history. Aboriginal wind instrument the didgeridoo and chants and indigenous music composed and performed by David Gulpilil appear alongside folk themes, traditional ballads such as 'Wild Colonial Boy' and the 1890s music-hall number 'Soldiers of the Queen', which was played over the end credits of Bruce Beresford's landmark war movie *'Breaker' Morant* (1979).[41] Hirschfelder's original music, created on computers before being recorded by the orchestra, operates in sub-textual ways: to underscore the action; to add emotional resonance; and to give extra meaning to some scenes.[42] Each of the lead characters has their own motif: 'Nullah's Primordial Theme' and 'I Will Sing You to Me' for Nullah; Bach's cantata 'Sheep May Safely Graze' for Lady Sarah; and 'The Drover's Ballad', mixed with strains of 'Waltzing Matilda', for the Drover.[43]

The orchestral score also contributes to imparting the mystery of the landscapes, captured in Panavision by director of photography Mandy Walker. Walker became involved with Luhrmann and Martin in the early stages of pre-production, working with them to put together material for the collage books that transmitted the look of the film.[44] The wide shots of the vast landscapes were filmed on location and supplemented by bluescreen material filmed on the Fox Studios sound stages under controlled conditions. Many scenes, such as the escape of the children from the fictional Mission Island, are a combination of location footage, studio work and special visual effects.[45] Of the five months of filming, several weeks were spent shooting the atmospheric terrain in the remote desert region in the far north-west in extreme heat. Some of the most romantic vistas were taken at the 'magic hour' just as the sun was setting to achieve a diffused, Turneresque quality. The dusty conditions in the region aided this effect. Filming the cattle drive and stampede through the Kuraman desert was a major operation that employed up to six cameras, including one tracking on a 2,000-foot overhead cable that was able to get close to the action.[46] One of the biggest set pieces, the bombing of Darwin and Mission Island by the

Visual effects set piece: the bombing of Darwin in *Australia*

Japanese, used a combination of restored footage from *Tora! Tora! Tora!* (1970), courtesy of Fox, and computer-generated images. Around 1,200 CG shots were used in *Australia*, and the process of integrating them with filmed material was complex, taking five weeks in post-production.[47]

The visual effects, which received a Satellite award, were far in excess of those for *Moulin Rouge!* and involved ten companies, headed by Animal Logic, who had worked on *Moulin Rouge!* and *No. 5 The Film*. Animal Logic designed and created a computer-generated Darwin harbour, wharf and ships across three time scales: the prewar cattle town, the wartime militarised zone and the post-bombing devastation. Using high-resolution scans of period photographs of Darwin wharf and ships, a CG harbour and backgrounds were created that captured a romanticised 1930s Darwin through replicating the faded colour tones of vintage photographs and movie footage. Cattle were added to footage of the harbour shot in three locations: the cattle-town set that was reconstructed in Bowen; Darwin harbour itself; and a bluescreen wharf set built on Fox's Sydney sound stage. Other CG effects included enhancing the harbour water and creating smoke,

Animal Logic's
digital effects
for Darwin
under siege
and overrun
with cattle

fog, clouds and cattle dust.[48] The visual effects have a deliberately hand-crafted appearance that contributes to the pictorial aspect of the images. Luhrmann's view of the effects was that they should strive for romanticism rather than realism, and should be used in a painterly manner to heighten the location footage. No attempt was made to disguise the presence of CGI work in the film;[49] this strategy conferred a fairy-tale, picture-book quality on the depiction of historical events and fictional episodes alike.

Much of the period reconstruction was effected by the production and costume design. Martin's teams began with meticulous research into the social history of the north-western region in the 1930s through books and biographies chronicling the experiences of the people who lived and worked there. They interviewed veteran outback cattlemen and stockmen and held extensive consultations with the owners of Carlton Hill cattle station in Kimberley, where the imaginary homestead Faraway Downs was built. The research involved several field trips and visits to local archives and museums. Material compiled during this process was supplemented by the online resource Picture Australia, a collection of digitised images from libraries all over the country.[50] The information gleaned was the basis for the authentic detail that went into the sets, props, costumes and accessories, many of which were custom-made by specialists.[51] One of the team's biggest tests was the five-acre set reconstructing Darwin in the coastal town of Bowen, which entailed building a two-storey hotel, a Chinatown area and a wharf, plus period features and redressing existing buildings to blend in. This set, which was a condensed version of Darwin, took ten weeks to construct.[52] For the ramshackle outback homestead Faraway Downs, a character in its own right that undergoes a transformation in the course of the story, location photographs and footage of the area were scanned and a digital model of the house produced. The model was repositioned until the right spot, in terms of the light, composition and demands of the drama, was found. The cinematography reflected the house's metamorphosis by imbuing early scenes with dark, dusty red tones that were replaced by white, airy hues as Sarah and the environment blossom. In contrast to the Red Curtain Trilogy, the film's colour palette was de-saturated with a bleached-out appearance that recreated the period aura of 1930s and 1940s colour photography.[53]

The costumes were on a far grander scale than those for the previous films. Vintage clothing from the 1930s was too small for the actors, and many of the 2,000 garments were created from scratch. Some period clothes were hired, so that the mix of custom-made and off-the-peg outfits would add a sense of authenticity, especially in crowd scenes.[54] Costume for peripheral characters received as much attention to detail as those worn by the principals, to ensure that everything in the scene was appropriate to the overall design. Kidman's wardrobe entailed a 'costume plot' that followed her character's transition from tightly controlled English aristocrat to unkempt cowgirl and confident ranch owner, while reflecting her modernity and independent spirit.[55] Her black riding suit and hat in the early scene set in England are elegant and in fashionable 1930s sportswear mode; they also reflect the androgynous styles adopted by modern, fashion-conscious women of the time. The outfit is, however, firmly buttoned and constricting, as are the clothes she wears when she first arrives in Australia. Her stylish, pristine blue-and-white nautical ensemble and matching Prada luggage are as inappropriate to the rough-and-tumble of Darwin as her gauze-veiled pith helmet, goggles and safari suit are to the outback terrain. Both these costumes are over-the-top, expressing Sarah's status as an outsider; but

Inappropriate: Sarah (Nicole Kidman) arrives in Australia

they also refer to 1930s screwball-comedy actresses such as Katharine Hepburn and Carole Lombard, both fashion trendsetters.

The cattle stampede, during which Sarah loses her luggage and fashionable clothes, is a turning point. As she comes to realise the importance of survival and human values over appearances, the change is represented by her tousled appearance and workman-like gear.[56] This shift is also communicated through a modification of Kidman's performance from arch, brittle Englishness to a softer, more relaxed demeanour. Italian shoe designers Ferragamo, whose founder supplied shoes to the rich and famous in the 1920s and 1930s, collaborated on Sarah's footwear, while her pearl earrings were custom-made by the Darwin-based company Paspaley, who were at the forefront of Western Australia's pearling industry in the 1930s. Sydney's Stefano Canturi, who designed Satine's elaborate necklace for *Moulin*

Character driven: costume design for Sarah

Rouge!, created Sarah's diamond jewels.[57] After the cattle drive, as Sarah's transformation progresses, a local Chinese influence is perceptible in the cheongsam-style dress she wears at the ball, while the military garb she dons in the wartime sequences emanates functional elegance and anonymity. Reflecting her forward-thinking independence, Sarah's costumes through-out display the androgyny that was characteristic of fashionable women's wear at the time. Some of her clothes appear too tight, intimating an unspo-ken desire to break free from social and emotional constraints.

While Sarah's clothing is character-driven, the Drover's style of dress is modelled on traditional stockman gear and says more about his outback way of life than about his individual personality. The archives of the R. M. Williams company, renowned leatherworkers and makers of bushwear

Traditional stockman gear: costume design for the Drover

since the 1930s, provided a wealth of detail about period cattlemen's garb that fed into the designs for each of the stockmen. Martin's wardrobe department turned the designs into patterns that were then handed over to the R. M. Williams workrooms, where most of the cattlemen's outfits and boots were made. Jackman's costume consists primarily of moleskin trousers, check shirt or sweatshirt, R. M. Williams leather boots and the distinctive Akubra hat worn in rural Australia. Several different styles of moleskin suitable for various postures and activities, such as sitting, standing, stunt work and riding were manufactured for Jackman, some of which were geared towards emphasising his athletic physique.[58] The costume designs for the indigenous characters were derived from extensive research, expert advice, and discussions and collaboration with the actors and were closely based on documented evidence.[59] The body decoration was an art in itself, and permission had to be sought to use certain forms, while many were taboo.[60] Two different indigenous communities are represented in the film, a Kimberley group and an Arnhem Land group, each of which has distinctive cultural practices. After consultations with the Miriwoong tribe, who were the traditional owners of the cattle station where Faraway Downs was constructed, the film-makers decided to represent the groups as an amalgamation of Kimberley and Arnhem Land. The primary aim of the detailed work on indigenous costume, body decoration and culture was to challenge stereotypes and to produce interpretations that celebrated the complexity and artistry of the traditional dress of the area.[61] Luhrmann and Martin always base their work on extensive research and preparation; with *Australia*, however, the striving for authenticity grounded in documented evidence was more strongly emphasised, even though the film-makers took liberties with some historical events. Although creative play with history is a feature of the epic, the balance between authenticity and poetic licence had shifted from that operating in the Red Curtain Trilogy.

Shooting began on 30 April 2007 at the colonial mansion Strickland House, a heritage site on Sydney Harbour. After filming in Bowen, Darwin and the outback region of Kununurra finished, on 6 September the cast and crew reconvened at Fox Studios for bluescreen work and pick-ups, which took several months. The shoot was completed on 19 December 2007.[62] The

massive scale of the epic project and the logistics of working across four
states, sometimes in difficult environmental conditions, were trying for
everyone concerned. The ambition of the enterprise and the high expectations of one of the biggest productions ever made in Australia generated
prodigious amounts of media attention.[63] From the announcement of the
film in May 2005 to its release in November 2008, the Australian press, radio
and television delivered increasing volumes of coverage, in which several of
the film-makers participated, that contributed to the speculation, anticipation and myth-making surrounding Baz Luhrmann's latest offering.[64]

*   *   *

In *Australia*, Luhrmann uses the epic form to revisit his country's troubled
colonial and postcolonial history. The epic contains within it classic
Hollywood genres such as the Gothic women's picture, the Western, the war
film and action-adventure, all of which engage with the past in one way or
another. To complicate the generic mix further, elements of Australian

Australia's generic mix: the Western (Hugh Jackman as the Drover and Nicole Kidman as
Sarah Ashley)

... and the Gothic women's picture (Nicole Kidman with Lillian Crombie as Bandy Legs inside Faraway Downs)

cinema's inflections of classic Hollywood, including the period romance, the wallaby Western, the outback film, the landscape film and the rites-of-passage movie are woven into the iconographic texture. Traversing these motifs are multiple storytelling devices from voice-over commentary, dialogue and oral performance to song, music and gesture, not to mention visual forms of narration such as costume, body decoration, sets and scenery. This is a heady brew, designed to create an image of the nation's identity and culture as a network of diverse, interlocking myths and histories that extends beyond its borders and back to ancient times. *Australia* engages with white colonial legends of the country's foundation in beleaguered settler communities struggling to forge a living in an inhospitable, uninhabited land. The heroic stereotypes of these traditional representations are juxtaposed with other legends, such as those of Australia's indigenous people, to de-familiarise and overturn them.[65] The different traditions sometimes appear to be in conflict; the outback myth of self-sufficient masculinity embodied in the Drover clashes with the ultra-feminine Lady Sarah

Ashley's sense of moral and cultural superiority, for example. Yet they are connected by the value placed by each on independence and courage, and via the overarching melodrama through which the characters' romance is shadowed by loss: by the death of the Drover's Aboriginal wife and the murder of Lady Sarah's husband, and by Sarah's infertility. A shared sense of grief links them to Nullah's story, in the course of which his mother Daisy is killed helping him to escape the authorities.

The convergence of genres and story-lines has been identified as a feature of contemporary Australian cinema's transgeneric quality.[66] It has been argued that Australian cinema itself, in its preoccupation with national identity, is an international genre with its own iconography, array of stereotypes, visual style and audience address.[67] Discussing the ways in which Australian cinema responded to the cultural shock of the 1992 legal decision that granted native land rights to indigenous people and rejected the fabrication of *terra nullius*,[68] Felicity Collins and Therese Davis used the metaphor of backtracking to illuminate the compulsive return to the past of so many 1990s films. The High Court ruling, known as 'Mabo' after one of the plaintiffs, Torres Strait Islander Eddie Mabo, overturned the nation's founding colonial myth and set in motion a process of collective anxiety, often characterised by guilt and shame, about the colonisers' relationship to the land and the indigenous population. The repercussions of Mabo are still being felt by a divided country and are fiercely contested by commentators, politicians and historians engaged in the 'history wars'.[69] The case raised issues of the reliability and veracity of documented evidence, so clearly biased towards Anglo-centric perspectives. In light of Mabo and Australia's struggle for postcolonial identity, Luhrmann's films, with their emphasis on marginal communities and cultural hybridity and their inclusive philosophy, could be seen to participate in the drive to reconfigure the nation's idea of itself. This is most explicit in *Australia*, which sets out to re-present the vicissitudes of the country's colonial past in the global arena. One of the ways it does so is to invoke catastrophic events that resonate across national borders, such as the bombing of Darwin by the Japanese during World War II (Australia's Pearl Harbor). The controversial issue of the White Australia policy and the Stolen Generations, given international visibility by films such as *Rabbit-Proof Fence*, is played out against the background of imminent world war, 1930s economic crisis and a drought-stricken terrain.

Collins and Davis employ trauma theory to illuminate the formal and thematic characteristics of post-Mabo Australian cinema, putting down the unsettling shifts between emotional registers, generic incoherence and inconclusive narratives to a crisis of representation under the impact of the loss of traditional certainties.[70] They detect a tension between complexities of theme and form and the requirements of mainstream cinema. If post-Mabo movies can be identified by the way they exhibit the symptoms of trauma, Luhrmann's films certainly qualify. In the Red Curtain Trilogy, the use of rapid cutting, the juxtaposition of comedy and tragedy, the proliferation of images and genres creating an excess of signification, the tension between historical research and poetic licence, the unsuccessful search for 'truth' and the ambivalence towards classic cinema could all be viewed as symptomatic responses to postcolonial anxieties, writ large for international audiences. *Australia* stands out as an evolved example of international trauma cinema, not least in the number of disasters packed into the narrative. In the first hour, three personal tragedies occur: the deaths and funerals of Sarah's husband, Nullah's mother and Kipling Flynn. During the cattle drive, the Drover tells Sarah about the death of his Aboriginal wife, and even the villainous Neil Fletcher is motivated by a sense of dispossession, since he perceives Faraway Downs to have been appropriated by the Ashleys from his family, who lived on and worked the land for generations. In his lust for power, Fletcher murders cattle baron King Carney and takes over his empire, actions that lead to Nullah's abduction to Mission Island. Sarah and the Drover become lovers and transform the run-down homestead, but their happiness is built on shaky ground as war and the bombing of Darwin bring about cataclysmic destruction. When the Drover and Magarri rescue the mixed-race Aboriginal children from Mission Island, Magarri is killed by Japanese soldiers; the trauma of his death is linked to the threat of Japanese invasion. The Drover's mistaken belief that Sarah has died in the attack on Darwin has a devastating emotional effect on him, and the couple's idyllic reunion with Nullah at Faraway Downs is cut short when the boy goes off on walkabout with King George, ending the film with separation and loss.

Australia's trauma-centred narrative portrays the country as scarred by bitter conflict over the land. It is a place where settlement and community are impossible, until some form of reconciliation between warring factions is brought about and a process of healing takes place.

Lady Sarah Ashley is one of the principal agents of healing. On the face of it, this is a strange choice, since she belongs to the British aristocracy. In a twist that reverses the more usual apportioning of blame to the British colonists, Sarah acts as a positive catalyst for change. Her transformation through contact with the harsh and beautiful country, her love affair with the Drover and her seduction by Nullah create alliances across boundaries of class and race. This unconventional family of outsiders provides a basis for optimism, in so far as they live together despite their differences. However, a utopian resolution along the lines of *Strictly Ballroom* is not forthcoming; when Nullah chooses to leave Sarah and the Drover for his Aboriginal community, the contradictions resurface as he walks off with King George into the mysterious Never Never Land, traditionally a no-go area for white Australians. The parting is a reconciliation of sorts, since Sarah recognises the significance of indigenous culture, and a dialogue between her and Nullah is inferred by the boy's declaration that he will sing to Sarah, and her promise that she will hear him. The closing moments affirm the capacity of music to connect people from different backgrounds, and the need for

Reconciliation and separation: Nullah (Brandon Walters) leaves Sarah (Nicole Kidman) to go walkabout

white Australians to listen to and learn from the country's indigenous people. However, the finale provokes mixed feelings of sadness, resignation and hope, implying that white Australians face further trauma in the process of national reconciliation. In a sense, the sequence replays the earlier scenario in which the Drover, Sarah and Nullah are torn apart by catastrophe, rupturing what appears to be a happy resolution. The compulsion to return to shocking incidents is an effect of trauma, but the prevalence of narratives of shock and loss in the film also underlines the Drover's philosophy that possession of people, things and land is unattainable, and that all anyone can own is their story. This belief system is born from melancholy, as the Drover, locked in grief over his wife's death, defends himself against attachments of any kind. Through the different stories of traumatic experiences, the complexity of Australians' relationship to the land is exposed, but with no clear indication of the way forward.

Australia's multiple narratives of conflict, death and loss project the country as essentially embattled. From the early scene in which the Drover brawls with the racist Carney men (a challenge to national ideals of white male 'mateship'), accidentally destroying Sarah's luggage before welcoming her to Australia, to the feud between the indigenous characters and the white authorities, the 'cattle wars', World War II and the clashes of class, gender and manners between the Drover and Sarah, this is a nation of battlers.[71] The 'Aussie battler', persevering in the face of economic and environmental hardship, is a national icon. However, rather than the conservative notion that confers white working-class aspirations to upward social mobility on the battler, the film revises the stereotype to include a broad spectrum of people fighting for a range of moral, political, social and personal causes. The solitary Drover distances himself from 'other people's battles'; but his attachments to Sarah and Nullah draw him to fight for and with them, while King George, Nullah and Daisy are portrayed as warriors struggling for survival in both physical and cultural terms. The revision of the battler is central to the film's project of revisiting Australian history in order to recast its myths. As tumultuous events impact on the characters' lives, moments of reconciliation are brief and transitory. Amid the upheavals, it might be expected that the outback landscape would offer a

The weight of water: Nullah (Brandon Walters) rendered invisible by white colonial history

reassuring image of stability and timelessness. However, in recognition of the part played by the terrain in Australia's national mythology, Luhrmann reinvents the landscape. In the opening sequence, Nullah 'makes himself invisible' by hiding beneath the surface of a waterhole to avoid capture by the authorities. The fairy-tale beauty of his hideout is shattered as a dead body, later revealed to be Sarah's husband Maitland, plunges into the stream and ends up floating face down above the boy, obstructing his way to the surface. This episode is horrific enough; but the symbolic resonance of its topographical imagery also conjures up the weight of white colonial history that renders indigenous culture invisible. At this moment of disruption, the film declares its intention to reinstate that culture in national memory. The 'hidden from history' metaphor reappears in the scene of Maitland's funeral, where his burial in the parched, ungiving earth consigns his secrets to the grave. By contrast, as Kipling Flynn lies dying after the cattle stampede, he whispers the truth about Maitland's killer and King George's innocence of the crime to the Drover, shifting culpability to Fletcher. As the Drover admits to Sarah, Fletcher's part in her husband's murder cannot be proved; by implication, the validity of 'evidence' and the veracity of accepted versions of history cannot be taken for granted.

As a counterpoint to the white European legend of *terra nullius*, the film invokes indigenous myths of the Dreamtime,[72] the primordial period when the land was brought to life by supernatural beings whose journeys created

rivers, mountains, trees, plants, birds and animals that formed the landscape. One such being was the Rainbow Serpent; another was the Tree God,
who made the totemic boab tree native to the north-west that features
prominently in *Australia*. After their work was finished, the ancestral beings
returned to the earth, which carries the marks of their existence in its rocks,
deserts, valleys and caves. Responsibility for caring for the land and maintaining its integrity passed to human beings living in the parallel moment of
the Dreaming, who were direct descendants of the creative ancestors.
Through storytelling, music, song, painting and ceremonial dance, the
Australian Aboriginal communities record the origins of life and preserve
the legal and moral codes laid down by the spirit ancestors. Songlines,[73] an
intricate system of song cycles that celebrates the journeys of the ancestors,
trace pathways across the terrain that act as an aid to navigation. The
Dreamtime creation myths are founded in an understanding that indigenous people do not own the land; rather, the land owns them. The earth and
its spirit beings are eternal, while human occupation is transitory. The
ancestral myths depend on the idea of continuous time in which past, present and future are co-existent; they are intimately connected to indigenous
peoples' everyday lives, governing their behaviour and their spiritual relationship to the land. Australian Aboriginal cultures understand the landscape as a living entity, a different interpretation from that of white
European settlers battling an antagonistic environment. In *Australia*, the
indigenous cultures' belief in magic and the importance of dreaming are
mobilised to offset white European values and are given a central role via
King George and Nullah.

However, there are also scenes that emphasise cultural correspondences. When Sarah comforts Nullah with the *Wizard of Oz* story, parallels
emerge between that film's dream narrative and indigenous storytelling.
The Wizard of Oz's use of music and magic, and its foundation in a fear-of-
loss scenario, echo *Australia*'s themes, while the sequence in which Nullah,
in blackface amid the racially segregated cinema audience, watches Judy
Garland sing 'Somewhere Over the Rainbow' intimates the similarities
between Australian and American experience. Sarah's first night at Faraway
Downs, when she is suddenly woken up by Nullah's eerie, unexplained

Australia's final frontier

presence in her bedroom, is reminiscent of Gothic literature's deployment
of the uncanny to suggest other-worldly realms outside human knowledge.
In such episodes, the focus is on cultural exchange and the connections
underlying social differences. The ending is a partial endorsement of
exchange between opposing cultures. As Sarah and Nullah part, it is clear
that their bond will continue. Nullah's journey is not yet over, and his destination, like his origins, remains unsettled. By invoking Nullah's uncom-
pleted rite of passage at the end of the film, Luhrmann implies that his
country is itself on the cusp of maturity, its destiny and identity still
unknown as it faces a final frontier. Before Australia can move on to modernity, it first needs to come to terms with its traumatic past.

*   *   *

As post-production on *Australia* drew to a close, the media hype surrounding the production went into overdrive amid rumours that the director was
still editing the film up to forty-eight hours before its Sydney premiere on
18 November 2008.[74] It was reported that Luhrmann was under pressure
from Fox executives to change the ending after negative responses to the
death of Hugh Jackman's character from test screening audiences. These
stories suggested that Luhrmann did not have creative control and that he
rewrote the final scenes to accommodate studio demands for a more uplift-
ing conclusion.[75] Luhrmann denied the reports and revealed that he had

several possible endings at his disposal.[76] Despite the change, which retained the love interest between Sarah and the Drover, *Australia*'s conclusion remains overshadowed by melancholy, partly because of the intensity of Sarah and Nullah's relationship. Another rumour circulated that in order to benefit from tax concessions, Luhrmann had been under government pressure to include a Stolen Generations theme.[77] In 2007, under the Producer Offset scheme, tax concessions offered to Australian productions were increased from 12.5 per cent to an unprecedented 40 per cent, reputedly due to negotiations between Luhrmann and the Federal Government. The concessions were intended to boost all Australian productions, building on recent international successes; but apparently this deal meant that Fox benefited from a rebate on *Australia*'s final budget of up to a quarter of its overall cost, resulting in a substantial reduction of its original estimate.[78]

Further controversy ensued when it was revealed that Luhrmann and Fox had secured a tie-in arrangement with the government agency Tourism Australia by which an ambitious advertising project, titled 'See the movie, see the country', exploiting the global interest in *Australia* in key overseas markets, would be launched. The arrangement included the production of two commercials, one set in New York and one in Shanghai, conceived by Luhrmann, shot by Mandy Walker, directed by Bruce Hunt and produced by Bazmark in association with Revolver. The cost of the campaign was estimated at $40 million.[79] The commercials were inspired by Sarah Ashley's transformation through contact with the Australian landscape, and featured Brandon Walters as a sprite figure seducing overworked executives to 'come walkabout' and find themselves by getting lost in the beauty of the country.[80] Although the poor showing of the film at the US box office sparked accusations that the campaign was a failure,[81] the New York version went on to win a prestigious industry award.[82] The campaign capitalised on the mythic, fairy-tale quality of the production, which was intensified by stories that Nicole Kidman had become pregnant after bathing in the 'magical' waters of the Kimberley region during filming.[83]

Australian media attention also focused on *Australia*'s marketing campaign, rumoured to be one of the most expensive ever lavished on a movie, though the actual costs were not revealed. The promotional push was relentless, geared towards reaching the widest possible audience, and involved a deal with the television channel Nine in which the film received wall-to-wall coverage. In addition to Tourism Australia, a long list of sponsors included Qantas airline, whose name appeared in the movie, outfitters R. M. Williams, who had been involved in creating the costumes, communications company Telstra BigPond, Coopers brewery, soft drinks manufacturer Kirks, News Limited and Jacob's Creek.[84] There was speculation that the saturation marketing levels and the over-the-top claims of the campaign could alienate potential viewers. A sophisticated, stylish interactive website allowed viewers to explore eight of the movie's themes via animated camera apertures, through which they could access video clips and download photographs. The site also offered production information and details of media coverage.[85] In a tie-in agreement with Apple, Luhrmann and Fox devised a series of podcasts directed mainly at HE students that invited viewers to respond to a creative challenge by submitting a project to the site. Prizes included a range of Apple products, the chance to win a visit to Australia and a tour of the film's US promotional sites, hosted by Luhrmann, and the publication of the winning project on the DVD release. Ten *Set to Screen* podcasts covering aspects of the production process, produced by Bazmark and featuring an introduction by Luhrmann to each one, were published between April and November 2008.[86]

A 'Meet the Filmmaker' podcast was released on 5 January 2009; this was a fifty-four-minute interview with Luhrmann by critic Jason Solomons, conducted at the UK Apple store in Regent Street, London, in which the director discussed the making of *Australia*.[87] In the UK, the promotion drive included 'roadblock' ad breaks on Channel 4's digital channel Film4 consisting of short introductions by Luhrmann, Kidman and Jackman to the experience of working on the film, and other mini-introductions by Luhrmann to the classic Hollywood titles that influenced *Australia*, some of which, such as *Red River* (1947) and *The African Queen*, were screened by Film4 as part of a season to tie in with the film's Boxing Day release.[88] A short season of Nicole Kidman movies was also tied in. The *'Australia* Special' ad breaks, between two and six minutes long, were repeated regularly in the run-up to the theatrical release. BBC2's *The Culture Show* devoted a special thirty-minute programme to the making of *Australia* in which pre-senter Mark Kermode travelled to Sydney to interview Luhrmann, Kidman, Jackman and other collaborators, and to witness the final stages of post-production.[89] Two trailers, two television spots and a featurette were pro-duced; the trailers appeared on numerous websites in addition to their theatrical and television screenings.[90] Although the popular media covered the theatrical release and featured promotional offers, the marketing blitz was primarily directed at thirty-something, affluent cinemagoers.[91]

Australia's style — the look of its sets and costumes — was widely used in promotion. Much of the coverage drew attention to Australia as a hub of high-end, sophisticated fashion design. Prior to the Sydney premiere, Catherine Martin launched a limited edition one-off clothing collection in association with R. M. Williams, and Canturi and Ferragamo both put on related events.[92] The sets were central attractions in an exhibition at Melbourne's Australian Center for the Moving Image (ACMI).[93] US *Vogue* put Nicole Kidman wearing a dress designed by Martin on the cover of its July 2008 issue, which included a sixteen-page illustrated feature on the film photographed by Annie Leibovitz, who issued a video diary of her on-set photo shoot.[94] *Vogue* concentrated on Kidman, while articles in male-oriented style magazines focused on Hugh Jackman.[95] The *New York Times* published an article about the costume design, displaying a slide show of seven images, initialled by Luhrmann, photographed and with commentary by Catherine Martin; interviews with Martin got wide coverage in the press generally.[96] Although the male and indigenous costumes were discussed, it was the costumes designed by Martin for Lady Sarah Ashley that attracted most media attention. Since expensive designer clothing was beyond the reach of most cinemagoers, such reports emphasised the fantasy and escapist aspects of the film.

The expenses and risks associated with the production were defended by Luhrmann, who argued that in times of social and economic turmoil, view-ers needed escapist entertainment to lift their spirits.[97] *Australia*'s market-ing overkill may have been motivated by Fox's anxiety that it would not perform well at the international box office at a time of economic instabil-ity.[98] In spite of the film-makers' emphasis on its entertainment value, and on the homages to classic cinema, the film was riven by a tension between its celebration of Australia's sublimely beautiful landscapes and its critical portrayal of the country's postcolonial history. This tension was potentially confusing to viewers who were not familiar with the events in question, nor with the copious references to Australian cinema. The intention to present Australia as an exotic place of refuge and regeneration, which was also the main impulse behind the tourism campaign, was undermined by the trauma-filled scenario in which the characters lurched from disaster to disaster. Yet such contradictions only increased the controversy surrounding the film, adding to the aura of risk and confirming its status as a major event.

It is likely that the scale of the budget, the high level of commercial tie-in arrangements and the excessive marketing onslaught alienated some reviewers. The promotional claims were often immodest,[99] and it would have been difficult for any film to live up to such overblown rhetoric. Not for the first time, Luhrmann trod a fine line between art and commerce, and it may have seemed to many that in this case the balance veered towards the latter. In Australia, where the film held its world premiere, critical response was mixed. While press reports prior to the 26 November 2009 theatrical release were generally supportive,[100] early reviews were often muted.[101] *Australia*'s foray into national history was controversial and provoked some scathing responses.[102]

Despite Luhrmann's attempts to bypass the 'history wars' by juxtaposing documented events with fiction, the implicit challenge to accepted views was enough to incite the wrath of those who felt the film's approach to indigenous issues was misconceived. Marcia Langton, Professor of Australian Indigenous Studies at Melbourne University, wrote an enthusiastic endorsement in the *Age* praising Luhrmann's reinvention of Australia's past, his credible rendition of indigenous experience and his celebration of the country's multiracial cultures. In response, Australian expatriate Germaine Greer penned a vitriolic piece in the *Guardian* pointing out the film's deviation from fact and attacking its (and Langton's) reconciliation-oriented politics. Langton replied with a robust defence of her argument, denouncing Greer's attachment to the stereotype of Aboriginal victimhood.[103] This heated

Luhrmann at work reinventing Australia's past

exchange generated a flurry of online comments, many of which encapsulated the entrenched positions characteristic of those engaged in the 'history wars'. The race controversy surrounding *Australia* extended to the USA
and UK.[104] Luhrmann's cinematic intervention in this emotive debate was
contested on grounds of realism and accuracy by many, while his poetic,
lyrical approach was appreciated by others. This polarisation was typical of
the critical response to his work. Although *Australia* aroused more political
commentary than the Red Curtain cycle, the contentious issues of representation and realism were common to all the films.

Following its New York premiere on 24 November 2008 and nationwide
release on 26 November, US media reviews of *Australia* were divided.
Influential critics such as Roger Ebert of the *Chicago Sun-Times* and
Manohla Dargis of the *New York Times* were positive, and Oprah Winfrey
issued an enthusiastic pre-release recommendation on *Oprah*.[105] Todd
McCarthy in *Variety* and Kenneth Turan in the *Los Angeles Times* expressed
qualified support, while Mick LaSalle of the *San Francisco Chronicle* delivered a damning critique, as did Sebastian Smee in the *Boston Globe*.[106]

Coverage in the popular media was generally favourable,[107] but even so, the negative critical response gathered pace, and predictions of the film's failure proliferated as award nominations appeared thin on the ground and chances of Academy Awards success receded.[108] Though the tally was less than for *Moulin Rouge!*, the film was nominated for several awards, including an Oscar for Martin's costume design.[109] Initial Australian box-office figures were respectable, outgrossing *Moulin Rouge!*,[110] while the film's results at the US box office in the run-up to Christmas were scarcely disastrous.[111] In the UK, where the London premiere on 10 December was followed by national release on 26 December 2008, articles in the quality press followed the trend of bewailing *Australia*'s perceived poor box-office business,[112] while reviews, with notable exceptions,[113] ranged from lukewarm to savage.[114]

In interviews, Luhrmann defended the film and Nicole Kidman's acting, which was praised by some but was the subject of much adverse criticism.[115] Luhrmann countered misconceptions about *Australia*'s lacklustre box-office showing by pointing out that *Moulin Rouge!* had followed a similar pattern of mixed reviews and slow box office followed by a gradual build-up of audience loyalty. He also took issue with media reports that misrepresented Kidman's self-effacing comments about her performance.[116] As with *Moulin Rouge!*, Luhrmann was a central character in the media furore that surrounded *Australia*. He played a crucial educational and informative role as well as contributing to the impassioned tone that characterised arguments about the film. Before long, it became clear that far from being a failure, *Australia* was set to become one of the highest-grossing movies of all time in Australia, while European box-office results were also strong.[117] Although it would not be a major money-spinner for Fox, it was predicted to make a small profit for parent company News Corporation.[118]

There is no doubt that neutral and negative media response contributed to the aura of failure, however misconceived, that clouded *Australia*'s initial release. Tempting though it is to demonise parts of the media for their parochial attitudes, the hyperbolic tone of many reactions, positive and negative, can be viewed as working in synergy with the studio's promotional strategies by adding to the film's contentious nature and bolstering its status as a cultural event. Fox's marketing plan for Luhrmann's films took a long view; the ballyhoo that accompanied the production from its early stages to the theatrical release fed into the publicity for subsequent DVD releases, a lucrative market in its own right. The first DVD/Blu-ray release of *Australia*, with limited extra features, was rushed out by Fox Home Entertainment on 3 March 2009 in the USA, hot on the heels of the movie's international release. A dedicated interactive DVD website was set up on the official movie site with coordinated features across both.[119] The Australian DVD/Blu-ray release followed on 1 April, with the European release in late April. Sales in the USA and Australia apparently exceeded expectations.[120] A divide between the press and popular audiences was identified in coverage of the film's growing financial success; this perceived divergence further nurtured the studio's and the film-makers' presentation of the movie as a hot topic. A special edition DVD, produced by Bazmark, was mooted for release in late 2009.[121] On 24 June 2009, the movie soundtrack, with digital booklet designed and produced by Bazmark, was made available for download through Apple iTunes. Two music videos, 'Waltzing Matilda' and 'By the Boab Tree', were also issued by Bazmark.[122] Meanwhile, it was reported that, despite widespread criticism, the tourism marketing campaign centred on *Australia* had been successful in generating unprecedented levels of interest and slowing the decline in visitors.[123] However, even this campaign was rife with controversy.[124]

The promotional synergies put in place for *Australia* extended the impact and life of the movie across a wider range of media locations than for the Red Curtain cycle. Although the film itself appeared to represent the centre of a subsidiary network of tie-in partnerships, its existence in diverse forms across different media suggests that it was one feature of a dynamic, de-centred operation in which the elements acted independently as well as in cooperation with each other. This is not to suggest that economic power did not rest with Fox as primary funders, nor that there were not tensions between the partners' commercial aims and the film-makers' artistic aspirations. Indeed, those tensions were evident in the course of the production and its critical reception. Although Luhrmann's film provided an opportunity to rebrand the country, he had not produced a work of national propaganda. Nevertheless, his navigation of the fraught relationship between art and commerce may have led him closer to the mainstream than was comfortable. With the increased scale of *Australia*'s production on every level, the next stage of Luhrmann and Martin's journey, and the issue of preserving creative and operational independence, remained open questions. Rumours about their next project started almost immediately, as Luhrmann hinted in interviews that it might not be produced with Fox.[125] This implied that the long-standing first-look arrangement might be coming to an end, inaugurating a reassessment of Luhrmann's current position and future as a player in the global media industries.

Six
DVD, the Internet and Nostalgia

Over the past fifteen years or so, Luhrmann's production methods and aesthetic have displayed an increasingly sophisticated engagement with new technologies. He has embraced the technological developments and the revised institutional and commercial synergies of the current global era in order to reinforce his identity as an innovator and to brand his output as Australian. Equally, the burgeoning of more direct forms of access and home consumption through television, DVD and the Internet[1] have had an impact on the dissemination and marketing of his films. The proliferation of opportunities for viewer interaction with audiovisual media, from micro-scale to big-budget productions, official websites to fan sites and discussion forums, and trailers, blogs and podcasts to online production notes and information databases, has encouraged the growth of cinephile communities who are ideal recipients of Luhrmann's homages to classic cinema. These consumers are nurtured by the availability of home cinema equipment providing viewing and listening experiences that surpass those of public theatres, while pay-TV and the Internet deliver a far greater range of titles than the local multiplex.[2] The rise of home entertainment systems has produced a situation in which the majority of audiences for cinema now watch films and related media in a domestic context,[3] so that the public theatre screenings that were once the primary point of reception have progressively become only one element in complex networks of audiovisual experiences. As a result, it has become increasingly difficult to consider a single element in isolation from others.

The explosion in domestic audiovisual equipment has also supported the theatrical viewing – for example, through the supply of supplementary information, clips and trailers prior to and following cinematic release. Dedicated official websites with interactive features offer downloads of clips, photographs, desktop displays and production details. DVD extra materials perform a similar function by inviting contact with the film-makers through commentaries, interviews and making-of documentaries in encounters that are playful as well as informative and educational. These materials have the potential to position both film and film-makers within a culture, whether it be one of personal vision and authorship or local context. In the current era of globalised film production and distribution, the elaborated content and resources of DVD and other interactive formats represent 'added value', positioning the local as a privileged source of information and reinforcing national specificity.[4] Opportunities have opened up for independent practitioners to gain a degree of control over the dissemination of their work and to communicate with large numbers of people. Like Luhrmann, many film-makers participate in the promotion process, with the result that cinematic auteurs have acquired renewed commercial value as they increasingly engage with the whole field of cultural production. They perform a role similar to that of stars, trading on a persona that they contribute to constructing that is exchanged in interactions between producers and consumers across geographical boundaries.[5]

Within this context, Luhrmann represents a highly evolved example of a transnational auteur who mobilises discourses of local production that conjure up utopian spaces of creative opportunities in which audiences are invited to participate. The local/global dynamic is evident in the films, but is particularly marked in the DVD boxed set *Baz Luhrmann's Red Curtain Trilogy*, released in 2002 by Fox Home Entertainment soon after the release of *Moulin Rouge!* (2001). The DVD boxed set performed a triple branding function: to identify the Red Curtain Trilogy as a coherent body of work with a distinctive style; to associate the style with a collaborative creative group led by Luhrmann; and to locate the work within his personal biography and his Australian base. The DVD versions of the films include extras such as commentaries by the film-makers, behind-the-scenes photo galleries and documentaries, interviews, uncut material, music videos, trailers and screenplay excerpts. Although the copyright to the boxed set is owned by Fox, the supplementary features were designed and produced by Bazmark and the creative voice and signature are clearly those of Luhrmann and his team. The 'Behind the Red Curtain' bonus disc offers a wealth of special

'Behind the Red Curtain'
DVD menu and showbag

interactive materials, including an in-depth exploration of the origins of
the Red Curtain aesthetic, presented by Luhrmann and featuring home
movie, documentary and archive footage. Another segment, 'The House of
Iona', focuses on Bazmark's operational set-up in Sydney. In line with the
Red Curtain cycle's approach to place, the House of Iona is depicted as an
imagined milieu evoked through a collage of images and re-edited film
footage.

This construction of place as imaginary, as both somewhere and elsewhere, might be seen as colluding with the eradication of local specificity
perceived by some as an inevitable consequence of globalisation. However, it
can also be understood as a means of negotiating local and global relationships. On one hand, the setting is recognisable as an actual location, on the
other, it is a pretext for an adventure that engages viewers in imaginative
exploits. The significance of locale, whether it is the Sydney suburbs, 'Verona
Beach', fin-de-siècle Paris or 1930s Australia, is that it is a fabrication

shared between a transnational creative group and a broad international community that either accepts its terms or does not. The places in Luhrmann's work emerge from a creative process and reflect the dynamics of cultural exchange that characterise his modus operandi. He refers to the interactive relationship between the work and viewers as a contract, implying a common perspective between film-makers and audiences.[6] The representation of the House of Iona in the DVD featurette as a locus for experiment and invention presents Luhrmann's local cultural business enterprise as a hub of artistic activity.[7] The ambience is playful and ironic, offering glimpses of the different areas in the house and the people who worked there. The view of the house's interior is deliberately confusing, collapsing boundaries between reality and imagination.

In an interview, Ewan McGregor talks about his surprise that the music for *Moulin Rouge!* was rehearsed and recorded in the Luhrmanns' living room.[8] McGregor distinguishes the space and the process from a professional recording studio, implying a more artisanal, collaborative working environment. The jerky, hand-crafted style of the re-edited documentary footage and the nostalgic allusions to early cinema and home movies intimate a mode of production geographically and aesthetically at a distance from the mainstream. These differences in style and production methods are played up rather than disguised, and project the house as a place where miracles are performed. The situation of the actual house and gardens is transformed into a virtual arena where viewers can also work and play. The evocation of the House of Iona as a utopian creative ambience, achieved through digital technologies, allows Luhrmann to position himself at the heart of a nucleus of collaborative creative energy situated outside the major centres of production. This in turn enables Australia to be viewed as a location for a vibrant independent film culture and industry. The nostalgic use of digital technologies, also evident in *Moulin Rouge!* and *Australia*, encourages audience participation in the individual and collective opportunities for expression opened up by technological change.

The House of Iona represents 'home', in both national and personal terms (in interviews Luhrmann repeatedly emphasises that Australia is where he and his family belong). In the Red Curtain Cinema segment on the bonus disc, this idea is reinforced by the use of home movie footage of his childhood. However, home is not envisaged as a self-contained haven or retreat from modernity. It corresponds to what Svetlana Boym has called 'reflective nostalgia', a form of collective memory in which fragments of the past embodied in everyday objects and memorabilia produce multiple story-lines, in contrast to the unified, teleological ideal proposed by nationalist memory. This nostalgia depends on shared social frameworks, but is marked by discontinuity and incoherence; rather than calling up a static golden age, it mediates between past, present and future and between self and other in a process that is both intellectual and emotional. It is associated with modernity, in that it negotiates the swiftly mutating landscapes of modern life by forming dialogic connections between people; but it meditates on, rather than evades the passage of time.[9] Boym accuses the current period of globalisation and digital technologies of tunnel vision in their propulsion towards an ever-more-perfect future, and in their subscription to an eliminatory model of history in which each new advance supplants what has gone before, rather than co-exists with it. Reflective nostalgia challenges this fast-forward ethic by favouring digression, detour and reverie that slows down the drive to modernity. Founded in the activity of reworking narratives of the past, it depends on the idea of memory as creative process, and it utilises irony and humour.[10] Luhrmann's use of reflective nostalgia displays many of the features identified by Boym. The spatial and temporal displacements and transmutations characteristic of globalised production and distribution, transnational cultural exchange and digital technologies are given form through forward-driven narratives, fast-cutting techniques and visual effects that emphasise the construction of artificial virtual worlds. At the same time, jarring tonal registers and collisions of cultural references and story-lines solicit heightened affective response and dialogue among viewers. The past is reconstructed through digital effects that are presented as illusion rather than aspiring to perfectly reproduce the real.

Luhrmann's construction of virtual areas on the borders of the mainstream might be seen as infused with the 'romance of the margins', as some have called the idea that independent film-making is more authentic because of its minor status.[11] It has been pointed out that this notion tends to view minority cultures and activity as permanently disenfranchised, victims of a monolithic global machine. Luhrmann's hybrid spaces do not aspire to authenticity, nor to minority status. Drawing on Boym's 'reflective nostalgia', his world-view can be understood in terms of 'nostalgia for the periphery'. In the context of globalisation and transnational flow, this nostalgia yearns for creative arenas positioned at the edges of the mainstream that will destabilise the field of cultural production and displace the hegemony of the centre. The transnational utopianism at the heart of Luhrmann's films envisions the relationship between global centres of economic power and peripheral cultural operations as one of negotiation and exchange that is not inevitably unequal. Transnationalism's focus on mobility and flow allows for a view of cultural and other forms of identity as fluid and in process. This has often been realised in terms of the dissolution of spatial and temporal boundaries and the opening up of new imaginary topographies. Such topographies can be characterised as utopian, in that they transcend geographic and cultural barriers, projecting floating worlds of artistic possibilities. They may also be underpinned by conflicting ideologies: on one hand they envisage shared cultural interests across national boundaries; on the other they depend on a notion of creative elites. One example of transnational utopianism was the Advance Party initiative, a collaboration between Danish film-maker Lars von Trier's Zentropa and the Scottish company Sigma Films, which involved a pooling of resources and experience in an attempt to build a creative community and funding infrastructure for Scottish film production.[12] Another is the collaborative ethos of Luhrmann and Martin's operational set-up visualised in the House of Iona segment on the DVD bonus disc.

This interpretation of the House of Iona incorporates elements of magic, irony, performance and play, celebrating the imaginative potential of new technologies. In this respect, Luhrmann's nostalgic gaze resonates with Boym, who characterises global culture's virtual worlds as engendering different kinds of cross-national communication and stimulating moral, ethical and political debates.[13] Nevertheless, she is ambivalent about their role as part of the entertainment industries, which she views as trading on ready-made nostalgias rather than nourishing a creative nostalgia that projects the past as it might have been, giving birth to imagined futures.[14] As already noted, Luhrmann's utopian nostalgic aesthetic plays a vital part in the branding process, and could be seen as compromised by the film-makers' apparent willingness to comply with commercial demands. However, such contamination is one of the risks inherent in navigating the borders of independent and mainstream production, which often involves sailing close to the wind. This activity resembles piracy, in that it travels back and forth across cultural boundaries in order to embellish personal territory, or home, with plunder appropriated from diverse sources. Luhrmann's nostalgic depictions of home and homeland, in a reversal of colonial myths of exclusive, unified national identity, view them as locations for interactions between cultural entities that do not necessarily cohere. This use of nostalgia harks back to unruly, transgressive impulses associated with the carnivalesque, whose influence on Luhrmann's work is discussed in Chapters 2 and 4. It also imagines a future in which home could be configured differently, not as a stable, settled haven but as an environment in flux. Boym notes that the contemporary high-tech, globalised ethos has given rise to counter-cultural movements that resist the encroachment of the capitalist machine on personal space and time.[15] It has also been argued that global mechanisation has inspired a nostalgic return by some writers and artists to myths and fairy-tales that explore primordial aspects of nature, tapping in to childhood fears as a way of rekindling a naive sense of wonder.[16] This evocation of unsettling, uncanny themes relates to Gothic literature's projection of familiar worlds that are made strange as dreams and fantasies invade reality.[17] In these liminal areas located between childhood and adulthood, youthful innocence is shadowed by uncertainty, danger and death.

Such boundary areas, mobilising the power of magic and illusionism, exist in all Luhrmann's films. They appear in the fairy-tale ambience of the House of Iona segment on the Red Curtain Trilogy DVD boxed set, and in the interactive features of the *Moulin Rouge!* official website, in which white rabbits materialised at certain points for viewers to click on and explore different avenues, embarking on journeys into the unknown.[18] Nostalgia pervades every aspect of the work, from period aesthetic to remixed song

versions and DVD and CD reissues. The reissues often include commentaries and other material recorded some time after production that take the
form of recollections of the past. A special edition DVD of *Romeo + Juliet*
issued in 2002 included commentaries by Luhrmann, Martin and cinematographer Don McAlpine recorded after the release of *Moulin Rouge!*,
looking back on the production from the perspective of the present. The
2007 music edition DVD of *Romeo + Juliet* celebrating the film's tenth
anniversary had commentaries and insider interviews reflecting on production and decision-making processes from an even greater distance in
time. At the same time, this version flagged technological advances in its
DTS soundtrack, providing an enhanced, specialised experience. These
strategies intensify nostalgia, reinforcing the work's status as memorable by
engaging viewers in shared pleasures of reminiscence. They also perform
the function of rebranding at regular intervals. The official theatrical website for *Australia* offered highly developed nostalgic devices such as an animated camera aperture on the menu page that invited viewers to 'experience
Australia' by clicking on one of eight themes. Clicking on the centre of the
aperture loaded rotating slide shows of photographs and video clips from
the movie accompanied by sound effects and music from the soundtrack.
The photographs featured smaller animated apertures strategically positioned to lead to different aspects of the eight themes, such as the love story,
the lead stars, the costume and production design, the indigenous actors,
the landscape and set pieces such as the cattle drove. The process of exploring the themes returned again and again to familiar images and clips while
also opening onto new and different areas in a repetitive activity of arrival
and departure. The website design presented its materials as a kind of
memorabilia, enabling viewers to relive moments from the film and to pos-
sess them by downloading images and clips. The repetitive structure mim-
icked the operations of memory and nostalgia, with the images recurring in
apparently random order as though viewers were rummaging through a collection of old photographs.

The website's nostalgic experience was related to consumption, in so far
as it encouraged viewers to recapture moments as a prelude to buying the
DVD and the soundtrack. A link from the website to Facebook opened onto

a fan site that carried information about the DVD/Blu-ray and iTunes soundtrack releases, as well as clips, photo galleries and a discussion board. Prior to the DVD/Blu-ray release in the USA on 3 March 2009, a dedicated website advertising its arrival was attached to the theatrical website, which could then only be accessed via a portal on the DVD/Blu-ray site. The sophisticated theatrical website was targeted at viewers who would appreciate its complexity and advanced design features and who would also be potential buyers of the DVD and/or Blu-ray versions. In addition to performing a commercial function, it explored the aesthetic, affective and intellectual elements of its inventive use of technology. The *Australia* soundtrack and accompanying digital booklet released on iTunes on 24 June 2009 were equally state-of-the-art. The booklet, designed by Bazmark and available to download, displayed seductive images from the film embellished with snippets of character dialogue, accompanied by Luhrmann's thoughts on each track and its research, development and performance. These personal reminiscences informed readers and listeners about the many influences on and contributions to the soundtrack, directing them to websites promising further listening pleasures. The words to the key songs 'The Drover's Ballad', 'By the Boab Tree' and 'All Night Long' appeared superimposed on the map of Australia. The digital booklet could be perused as a PDF document or as a paper printout, and at fifty-one pages was on a bigger scale and had higher production values than normal CD extra materials or digital downloads. One of its functions was to generate ancillary revenue as a commercial spin-off, but, like the theatrical website, it also provided a unique aesthetic experience. Its release through iTunes offered a direct form of delivery that intensified the relationship between viewers, the film and its music, while the partnership with Apple consolidated the connection between style and technology appreciated by Luhrmann fans.

The soundtrack booklet provided inside information about the film's local context, positioning Luhrmann as creative leader of a collaborative Australian team. The series of ten *Set to Screen* podcasts covering different aspects of *Australia*'s production published on the Apple website and via iTunes had a similar function, although nostalgia was less in evidence.[19] In addition to a documentary about the background to the production fronted by Luhrmann, each podcast featured a short introduction by the director to mini-films exploring editing, sound, music, costume, production design, cinematography and location shooting. Luhrmann's performative role was paramount, as he guided viewers through the different process and was also highly visible in the mini-films as director on set. He figured in the podcasts in an educational and inspirational capacity, encouraging the students to whom they were primarily addressed to become involved in making films themselves. The podcasts were issued at regular intervals during production between April and November 2008, which added immediacy to the contact with viewers. Once again, the Internet supplied direct access and delivery methods that the film-makers were able to exploit. Subscription to the podcasts was free, and their educational remit was more in evidence than their role in the branding process. Nevertheless, they were effective in consolidating Luhrmann's auteur status and his Australian roots, as well as celebrating the adventure of making a large-scale epic in Australia. They were also historical documents that recorded film-making activity at a particular time and in a specific place, and they remained online for future research and study. Luhrmann and Martin have wholeheartedly embraced the potential of digital technologies to transform their work and working practices, and the effectiveness of new communication systems in facilitating, producing and disseminating the work across geographical boundaries and different media sites. While some of this uptake is motivated by financial interests, it would be overly pessimistic to view it as totally defined by commerce.

The convergence of art, industry, technology and business resulting from institutional and technological change in the media industries demands new ways of conceptualising cultural production and distribution. It also requires rethinking the relationships between mighty multinational conglomerates and the multitude of medium- and small-scale national cinemas and independent film-making operations, not to mention the burgeoning micro-scale activity at group and individual levels.[20] Resistance and alternatives to economically powerful global companies are now possible in many different forms and arenas, and critical cultural activity is no longer solely the province of those who are perceived as working outside the major centres, or those who heroically attempt to subvert it from within.

Rather, each case needs to be approached on its own terms as an example of a particular relationship with the centre. As the borders between margins and mainstream, centre and periphery have become blurred, micro-level research on specific film-making ventures in local contexts has become increasingly important in delineating different approaches, not all of which aspire to resistance. Equally, purist notions of critical practice have begun to give way to a more pluralistic approach that allows for the co-existence of diverse oppositional strategies. Luhrmann and Martin's working ethos and output represent a challenge to established perceptions of independent activity because oppositional elements are often enmeshed with their own financial interests and those of their commercial partners. The idea that counter-cultural activities might be facilitated by such partnerships is not easily accommodated by orthodox approaches that rely on more clear-cut adversarial relationships. As it becomes increasingly difficult to pin down the origins or destination of audiovisual products, or to predict their reception and use by audiences, more nuanced models of cultural activity that recognise that cooperation with the centres of power does not necessarily equate to collusion become necessary.

In Luhrmann and Martin's case, a viable model might be one in which their local identity co-exists and is in tension with the global operations of major studio Fox and parent company News Corporation. This partnership enables them to benefit from funding opportunities, superior facilities and worldwide organisational networks while retaining independence and control at a local level. While this situation clearly involves compromises, the cooperation with Fox can be viewed as an arena of cultural struggle in which power relationships fluctuate. As discussed in Chapter 1, Luhrmann and Martin adopted a strategic approach in accumulating creative capital that gave them leverage in negotiations with the studio. On the other hand, up to this point, Fox has retained ownership of their work. The arrangement depends on a distinction between the fiscal and administrative responsibilities of the studio, and Luhrmann and Martin's artistic activities, though because of the increasingly ambitious scale of those activities this distinction is not always clear-cut. A further, related tension exists between Luhrmann's status as auteur and the studio's financial concerns. Luhrmann exploits this tension, often pitting his artistic concerns against those of profit-motivated studio executives. Yet there is also convergence between his reputation as an innovator and the studio's investment in an art cinema that appeals to sophisticated niche audiences, who are potential consumers of home entertainment systems and associated products. Tensions are also evident between different aspects of the work itself: the use of reflective nostalgia outlined above, which can be identified as a critical strategy in so far as it challenges official versions of nationhood, exists in tandem with less reflective, ready-made nostalgias that induce consumers to purchase DVD and CD reissues in order to enjoy ever more elaborated and refined experiences, with each new version supplanting previous ones.

Detailed analysis of specific situations helps to provide a clearer understanding of the negotiations involved between the labyrinthine networks of economic and cultural partnerships that make up the contemporary audio-visual media industries. Luhrmann and Martin's experience as independent film-makers, and their progression from low-budget to mega-scale production, are illuminating in this respect, not least because of their strategic thinking and willingness to grasp commercial nettles that others would avoid. Their adventurous spirit, unquenchable ambition and entrepreneurial aptitude have played a part in their own artistic and business success, and in drawing attention to their local production set-up. Their means of achieving this have not pleased everyone, either at home or abroad, but by stirring up controversy they have succeeded in building a distinctive brand for their work and for Australian cinema. While their story is grounded in their personal circumstances and is not applicable to other independent film-makers, it makes an important contribution to debates about the survival and significance of national cinemas in the current global age.

NOTES

Introduction

1. Besides the extensive research undertaken for *Alexander the Great*, a specially constructed studio had been built in Morocco. (Unless indicated otherwise, information about Baz Luhrmann is taken from interviews with the author, House of Iona, Sydney, 14 and 15 June 2005.)

2. In 2009 Luhrmann announced that he had obtained the rights to Scott Fitzgerald's *The Great Gatsby*, which led to unconfirmed media reports that this would be his next film project.

3. *Australia*'s budget, estimated at $130 million (£86 million), made it the most expensive film ever produced in Australia (see <http://www.guardian.co.uk/film/2008/nov/18/australia-film-world-premiere> 18 November 2008. Accessed 29 January 2009). Like *Moulin Rouge!*, it took four years to complete.

4. See <http://news.bbc.co.uk/1/hi/entertainment/7723865.stm> 12 November 2008. Accessed 2 December 2008.

5. See <http://www.guardian.co.uk/film/2008/nov/10/australia-nicole-kidman-hugh-jackman-baz-luhrmann> 10 November 2008. Accessed 2 December 2008.

6. The Australian Film Institute (AFI) research library in Melbourne has a vast collection of press clippings relating to all Luhrmann's films. The British Film Institute (BFI) library in London also has a strong collection, though it does not include all the Australian coverage.

7. See Justin Wyatt, *High Concept: Movies and Marketing in Hollywood* (Austin: University of Texas Press, 1994); Richard Maltby, 'Nobody knows everything: post-classical historiographies and consolidated entertainment', in Steve Neale and Murray Smith (eds), *Contemporary Hollywood Cinema* (London and New York: Routledge, 1998).

8. See Justin Wyatt, 'The formation of the "major independent": Miramax, New Line and the new Hollywood', in Neale and Smith (eds), *Contemporary Hollywood Cinema*; Geoff King, *Indiewood USA: Where Hollywood Meets Independent Cinema* (London: I. B. Tauris, 2008).

9. Wyatt, 'The formation of the "major independent"', p. 87.

10. Tom Gunning, 'The cinema of attractions: early film, its spectator and the avant-garde', in Thomas Elsaesser and Adam Barker (eds), *Early Cinema: Space, Frame, Narrative* (London: BFI, 1990).

11. Tom Gunning, 'An aesthetic of astonishment: early film and the

[in]credulous spectator', in Linda Williams (ed.), *Viewing Positions: Ways of Seeing Film* (New Brunswick NJ: Rutgers University Press, 1995).

12. Rupert Murdoch, CEO of News Corporation, the parent company of 20th Century-Fox, was quoted in February 2009 as predicting a small profit for *Australia* (see <http://www.news.com.au/business/story/0,27753,25015824-31037,00.html> 6 February 2009. Accessed 6 February 2009).

13. The term 'persona' is familiar from star studies, where it refers to the image constructed for a star that is used to forge coherence across different film roles. The construction of a persona for a director who is positioned as an auteur has been less widely discussed. See, however, Timothy Corrigan, 'The commerce of auteurism: a voice without authority', *New German Critique* 49, winter 1990, pp. 43–57.

14. The sense of a creative group at the heart of the Luhrmann oeuvre is evident in the House of Iona feature on the bonus disc Behind the Red Curtain included in the boxed set *Baz Luhrmann's Red Curtain Trilogy* (2006), in which the viewer is introduced to Bazmark's production set-up and working methods.

15. The Australian media response to *Moulin Rouge!*, available in the AFI Research Collection, offers ample evidence of celebration of Luhrmann as a national figure.

16. The 'stolen generations' have been the subject of several Australian films (for example, Phillip Noyce's acclaimed *Rabbit-Proof Fence*, 2002).

17. See Deb Verhoeven's analysis of debates surrounding national and local cultures in 'Introduction: (pre) facing the nation', in Verhoeven (ed.), *Twin Peeks: Australian and New Zealand Feature Films* (Melbourne: Damned Publishing [Australian Catalogue Co.], 1999), pp. 6–7.

18. See Thomas H. Guback, 'Hollywood's international market', in Tino Balio (ed.), *The American Film Industry* (Madison: University of Wisconsin Press, 1985).

19. Verhoeven's outline of the features of the post-1990s Australian film industry and its output coincides in many respects with my description of the popular art film and its context (see Verhoeven, 'Film and video', in Stuart Cunningham and Graeme Turner (eds), *The Media and Communications in Australia* (Netley: Allen & Unwin, 2002), p. 162).

20. Verhoeven identifies Campion as a transnational film-maker who emerged from the globalised Australian industry in the 1990s, and whose work challenged traditional art-cinema boundaries (see Verhoeven, 'Film and video', p. 162).

21. Bazmark Inq. is located in Sydney, Australia, while Fox's headquarters are in Los Angeles. Fox has studio facilities in Sydney that are used for the production of Luhrmann's films.

22. See Verhoeven, 'Introduction: (pre) facing the nation', pp. 7–9.

23. Tom O'Regan, *Australian National Cinema* (London and New York: Routledge, 1996), p. 353.

1 – Once Upon a Time in Australia

1. Unless indicated otherwise, all information about Baz Luhrmann is taken from two interviews with the author, House of Iona, Sydney, 14 and 15 June 2005.

2. See the Bazmark logo at <http://www.bazmark.com/>. Accessed 20 February 2009.

3. The motto is a Spanish proverb quoted by Tara Morice as Fran in Luhrmann's debut feature *Strictly Ballroom* (1992).

4. Australia became a Commonwealth country with an independent constitution in 1901, though it is thought to have been inhabited by indigenous Aboriginal people for more than 50,000 years (see <http://australia.gov.au/ Our_Country>). European settlement, predominantly British, began in 1788 ('History of Australia (1788–1850)', *Wikipedia, The Free Encyclopedia* 19 February 2009. Available at: <http://en.wikipedia.org/w/index. php?title=History_of_Australia_ (1788%E2%80%931850)&oldid= 271765699>. Accessed 20 February 2009). This date was marked by the 1988 bicentennial celebrations.

5. Tom O'Regan describes the Australian film industry as a medium-sized English-language cinema, with 'a minor place in the international trade in national symbolic images' (see *Australian National Cinema* (London and New York: Routledge, 1996), p. 77).

6. In June 2008 Australia's estimated resident population was 21,374,000 (see Australian Demographic Statistics Jun 2008, Australian Bureau of Statistics, available at: <http://www.abs.gov.au/ ausstats/abs@.nsf/mf/3101.0/> 12 February 2009. Accessed 20 February 2009). The majority of the population is concentrated in the south-east in New South Wales, Victoria and Queensland.

7. Baz had an older brother and a younger brother. His younger sister (Amanda Luhrmann) was born some time later and worked for Bazmark for seven years until 2009.

8. The rehearsals for *Guys and Dolls* can be seen in the Red Curtain Cinema feature on the Behind the Red Curtain bonus disc in the *Baz Luhrmann's Red Curtain Trilogy* boxed set (2006).

9. Some sources credit Luhrmann with a role as an Able Seaman in Peter Maxwell's *Southern Cross* (1982), which is a shortened and re-edited version of the Japanese/Australian film *Minami Jujisei* (Seiji Maruyama, 1982) about the Japanese occupation of Singapore (see Film Index International, Baz Luhrmann entry at <http://fii. chadwyck.co.uk/>. Accessed 24 February 2009; and BFI Film and TV Database, Baz Luhrmann entry at http://ftvdb.bfi.org.uk/>. Accessed 24 February 2009).

10. Amateur footage of parts of the Bratislava performance of *Strictly Ballroom* can be glimpsed in the Red Curtain Cinema feature on the Behind the Red Curtain' bonus disc in the *Baz Luhrmann's Red Curtain Trilogy* boxed set.

11. Some of the workshop activity for *Moulin Rouge!* can be seen in the Red Curtain

Cinema feature on the Behind the Red
Curtain bonus disc in the *Baz
Luhrmann's Red Curtain Trilogy*
boxed set.

12. This award-winning production of *La
Bohème* had further successful runs at
the Sydney Opera House in 1993 and
1996 and has been performed around
the world to great acclaim. A DVD
version of the 1993 performance filmed
for television is available from Arthaus
Musik.

13. Unless indicated otherwise, all
information about Catherine Martin is
taken from an interview with the author,
House of Iona, Sydney, 16 June 2005.

14. Martin is bi-lingual in French and
English.

15. See Karl Quinn, 'Catherine the great',
Age 1 April 2002.

16. Folders viewed at the Luhrmann
personal archive in Sydney, May–June
2005.

17. Concept books viewed at the Luhrmann
personal archive, May–June 2005, and
during interviews with the author, 14
and 15 June 2005.

18. Pastiche has been extensively discussed
by critics and academics. Recent studies
include Richard Dyer, *Pastiche* (Oxford
and New York, Routledge, 2006); Pam
Cook, 'Rethinking nostalgia: *In the Mood
for Love* and *Far From Heaven*', in
*Screening the Past: Memory and Nostalgia
in Cinema* (Oxford and New York:
Routledge, 2005).

19. A full list of Catherine Martin's awards
for her cinema work can be found on the
IMDb: <http://www.imdb.com/>.
Accessed 2 March 2009.

20. A full list of Baz Luhrmann's awards for
his cinema work can also be found on
the IMDb: <http://www.imdb.com/>.
Accessed 2 March 2009.

21. This music video is included in the extra
features on the Behind the Red Curtain
bonus disc included in the *Baz
Luhrmann's Red Curtain Trilogy* boxed
set. The song, written in 1940, featured
in the soundtrack of *Australia*.

22. The budget for *Strictly Ballroom* was
around A\$3 million.

23. Treatment and script for the music
video viewed in the Luhrmann personal
archive in Sydney, May–June 2005.

24. The IMDb has estimated budget (in
Australian dollars) and gross business
figures for *Strictly Ballroom* (see
<http://www.imdb.com/>. Accessed 3
March 2009).

25. Luhrmann's response to his experiences
in India are included in the Red Curtain
Cinema feature on the Behind the Red
Curtain bonus disc in the *Baz
Luhrmann's Red Curtain Trilogy*
boxed set.

26. *Vogue* cover viewed in Luhrmann
personal archive, May–June 2005. Clips
from the issue can be seen in the Red
Curtain Cinema segment on the
Behind the Red Curtain bonus disc in
the *Baz Luhrmann's Red Curtain Trilogy*
boxed set.

27. The IMDb gives estimated budget in
American dollars and business figures
for the USA and Europe for *Romeo +
Juliet* (see <http://www.imdb.com/>.
Accessed 4 March 2009).

28. A full list of *Romeo + Juliet*'s awards
can be found on the IMDb:

<http://www.imdb.com/>. Accessed 4 March 2009.

29. See Gerard Whateley, 'Luhrmann on the love of his life', *Herald Sun* [Melbourne] 26 December 1996, p. 49; also 'Luhrmann signs with Fox studio', *Western Australian* 12 November 1996, p. 7.

30. For an accessible account of Bourdieu's idea of cultural capital see David Swartz, *Culture and Power: The Sociology of Pierre Bourdieu* (Chicago: University of Chicago Press, 1997).

31. The name of the house implies an Anglo-Celtic ancestry, since Iona is a small island in the Scottish Hebrides.

32. The house was viewed during a visit by the author in June 2005. A tour of the house is included in the House of Iona segment on the Behind the Red Curtain bonus disc in the *Baz Luhrmann's Red Curtain Trilogy* boxed set.

33. The music video 'Now Until the Break of Day' can be seen in the extra features included on the Behind the Red Curtain bonus disc in the boxed set *Baz Luhrmann's Red Curtain Trilogy*.

34. The history of the Sunscreen speech and its influence is documented by *Wikipedia* (see 'Wear Sunscreen', *Wikipedia, The Free Encyclopedia* 27 February 2009, available at <http://en.wikipedia.org/>. Accessed 9 March 2009).

35. New South Wales government press release about the proposed development, dated Friday, 13 December 1996, viewed in Luhrmann personal archive, Sydney, May–June 2005.

36. The details of the Fox deals remain confidential.

37. See Joshua Smith, 'Fox Sydney Studios celebrate grand opening', *Oz Cinema* 19 May 1998. Available at: <http://www.ozcinema.com/articles/1998/may/foxstudios.html>. Accessed 5 March 2009.

38. See 'About the Filmmakers' in the 20th Century-Fox production notes for *Australia*, available online at: <http://www.ffwdweekly.com/listings/film/66284/>. Accessed 5 March 2009. A subsequent Grand Opening of the new studios took place on 7 November 1999. This star-studded, televised event was hosted by Hugh Jackman and produced by Fox and Nine Network. It aired in Australia on Channel Nine on 7 November 1999 (see entry for 'Fox Studios Australia: The Grand Opening' on the IMDb: <http://www.imdb.com/>. Accessed 5 March 2009).

39. James Schamus describes the arrangement with Fox in 'To the rear of the back end: the economics of independent cinema', in Steve Neale and Murray Smith (eds), *Contemporary Hollywood Cinema* (New York and London: Routledge, 1998).

40. Mike Wayne takes this view of the UK company Working Title's deal with Universal, which began in 1999 and was extended in 2007 for a further seven years (see Michael Wayne, 'Working Title Mark II: a critique of the atlanticist paradigm for British cinema', *International Journal of Media and Cultural Politics* 2 (1), January 2006, pp. 59–74).

41. During this seven-year period, Luhrmann and Martin had two children.

Lilly Amanda was born on 10 October 2003 and William Alexander on 8 June 2005.

42. See IMDb box office/business for *Moulin Rouge!* at <http://www.imdb.com/>. Accessed 9 March 2009.

43. See interview 'Baz Luhrmann talks awards and *Moulin Rouge!*', *About.com: Hollywood Movies*, n.d. Available online at: <http://movies.about.com/library/weekly/aa030902a.htm>. Accessed 9 March 2009.

44. See IMDb box office/business for *Moulin Rouge!* at <http://www.imdb.com/>. Accessed 9 March 2009.

45. See *The Numbers*, available at: <http://www.the-numbers.com/movies/2001/MOULR.php>. Accessed 9 March 2009.

46. The IMDb has a full list of *Moulin Rouge!* awards: <http://www.imdb.com/>. Accessed 9 March 2009.

47. A lavishly illustrated book, produced by Bazmark Design and authored by Baz Luhrmann and Catherine Martin, was published in hardback in the USA by Newmarket Press and in paperback in the UK by Pan Macmillan (under their FilmFour Books imprint) to coincide with the film's 2001 release. Fox owns the book copyright.

48. A 2001 BBC television programme, produced and directed by Adrian Sibley, followed Baz Luhrmann's promotional world tour for *Moulin Rouge!*. *Baz Luhrmann: The Show Must Go On* was televised on BBC2 in September 2001.

49. See Internet Broadway Database (IBDB) entry for Luhrmann's production of *La Bohème*; <http://www.ibdb.com/production.php?id=13346> for list of awards. Accessed 9 March 2009.

50. The excellent Baz Luhrmann fan site *Baz the Great!* has an archive of selected news reports about Luhrmann's *Alexander the Great* project. See <http://www.bazthegreatsite.com/alexandernewsarticles.htm>. Accessed 10 March 2009.

51. Material viewed in the Luhrmann personal archive in Sydney, May–June 2005, indicates that development of the Alexander project was at quite an advanced stage when it was abandoned. Although the lead actors had not been signed, David Hare had written a first script.

52. The IMDb has a news item on the News for Baz Luhrmann 2004 page about Nicole Kidman's record-breaking fee for the Chanel No. 5 commercial. See <http://www.imdb.com/>. Accessed 10 March 2009. The film's budget has been put at $42 million by *Wikipedia* (see 'No. 5 The Film', *Wikipedia, The Free Encyclopedia* 21 January 2009, available at <http://en.wikipedia.org/>. Accessed 10 March 2009).

53. Craig Armstrong plays the piano (uncredited) at the end of *No. 5 The Film*.

54. US *Vogue* magazine's autumn issue 2004 carried an illustrated feature based on Baz Luhrmann's personal diary entries between 3 January 2003 and 14 July 2004 detailing work on *Alexander the Great* and *No. 5 The Film* (see 'Take five', *Vogue* Fall 2004, pp. 717–21, 825–6).

55. A twenty-five-minute documentary charting the making of *No. 5 The Film*, directed by Fabienne Isnard, aired on Australian television's Channel Nine on

15 November 2004, but it has not so far been made available on DVD. See Daniel Mudie Cunningham, 'Chanel No. 5 The Film: le film du film', *PopMatters* 22 November 2004. Available at <http://www.popmatters.com/tv/reviews/c/chanel-no5.shtml>. Accessed 10 March 2009.

56. The three-minute Chanel No. 5 film has not so far been made available on DVD. It can be viewed online at YouTube <http://www.youtube.com/>. Accessed 11 March 2009. The Chanel 'Making of' film, divided into five segments, can also be viewed online at YouTube. Accessed 11 March 2009.

57. The fan site *Baz the Great!* has an archive of selected news reports about *No. 5 The Film*. See <http://www.bazthegreatsite.com/chanel.htm>. Accessed 11 March 2009.

58. *My Shakespeare* was produced and directed by Michael Waldman for Shine Productions and Penguin Television. It was transmitted on Channel 4 on 27 December 2004 between 7 and 9 pm. A DVD version (region 1 only) by PBS Home Video came out in 2006.

59. Luhrmann and Martin confirmed the Australian-themed epic as their next project in interviews with the author at the House of Iona, Sydney, in June 2005.

60. See *Baz the Great!* fan site for media coverage of the development of *Australia*: <http://www.bazthegreatsite.com/australiadevelopment.htm>. Accessed 11 March 2009.

61. See Michael Bodey, 'Abuzz about Baz in the bush', *The Australian* 4 February

2009, for an analysis of the film's performance and reception. Available online at <http://www.theaustralian.news.com.au/story/0,25197,25004481-15803,00.html>. Accessed 13 March 2009.

62. A high proportion of negative reviews centred on Nicole Kidman's performance in the film.

63. A list of awards for *Australia* can be found on the IMDb at <http://www.imdb.com/title/tt0455824/awards>. Accessed 13 March 2009.

2 – Strictly Ballroom (1992)

1. Unless indicated otherwise, all information about Baz Luhrmann and *Strictly Ballroom* is taken from interviews with the author, House of Iona, Sydney, 14 and 15 June 2005.

2. See Baz Luhrmann page on the IMDb for details of the episodes of *A Country Practice* in which he appeared, and for information about *The Dark Room*: <http://www.imdb.com/>. Accessed 18 March 2009.

3. See John Lahr, 'Strictly Luhrmann', *Weekend Australian Magazine*, 1–2 March 2003. Luhrmann features on the cover of this issue. The article previously appeared as 'The ringmaster' in the *New Yorker*, 2 December 2002.

4. Home movie footage of Luhrmann's ballroom dancing exploits can be seen in the Red Curtain Cinema feature on the Behind the Red Curtain bonus disc in the *Baz Luhrmann's Red Curtain Trilogy* boxed set.

5. The script for the NIDA production of *Strictly Ballroom* is included in the Show

Bag section of the Behind the Red
Curtain bonus disc in the *Baz
Luhrmann's Red Curtain Trilogy*
boxed set.

6. Barbara is the name of Luhrmann's
mother, who became a ballroom dancing
teacher while he was at NIDA.

7. The rehearsals and performance in
Bratislava can be seen in the Red
Curtain Cinema feature on the Behind
the Red Curtain bonus disc in the *Baz
Luhrmann's Red Curtain Trilogy*
boxed set.

8. Original proposal viewed at the
Luhrmann personal archive in Sydney,
May–June 2005.

9. See the Australian and British press
campaign books for the film *Strictly
Ballroom*.

10. Different versions of the script can
be seen in the Show Bag section of
the Behind the Red Curtain bonus
disc in the *Baz Luhrmann's Red Curtain
Trilogy* boxed set. The final screenplay
was published as Baz Luhrmann and
Craig Pearce, *Strictly Ballroom*
(Strawberry Hills, NSW: Currency
Press, 1992).

11. See feature on *Strictly Ballroom* in
Australian *Vogue* January 1994, p. 83.

12. See Australian press campaign book for
Strictly Ballroom.

13. According to feature on *Strictly Ballroom*
in Australian *Vogue* January 1994, p. 83.

14. See Australian press campaign book for
Strictly Ballroom.

15. See Australian press campaign book for
Strictly Ballroom.

16. See feature on *Strictly Ballroom* in
Australian *Vogue* January 1994, p. 84.

17. According to the feature on *Strictly
Ballroom* in Australian *Vogue* January
1994, p. 85.

18. Feature on *Strictly Ballroom* in Australian
Vogue January 1994, p. 85. According to
Luhrmann, Bill and Hillary Clinton also
rate *Strictly Ballroom* as one of their
favourite films.

19. For example, stories of the negative
response from Cannes critics to Sofia
Coppola's *Marie Antoinette* (2006)
are said to have produced rumours
that adversely affected the film's
critical reception and its box-office
performance.

20. The popular British television ballroom
dancing programme *Strictly Come
Dancing* took its title from *Strictly
Ballroom*.

21. This is a revised and extended version of
the synopsis provided by the Australian
press campaign book.

22. Bill Marron's *Strictly Ballroom* comic
viewed in the Luhrmann personal
archive, Sydney, May–June 2005.

23. The Waratah plant is the emblem for
New South Wales.

24. The Coca-Cola-style lettering featured
in a banner that appeared above the set
of Luhrmann and Martin's 1990
production of *La Bohème*. The banner
displayed the words 'L'amour' in red
letters. This sign became emblematic of
their style, and appeared in *Romeo +
Juliet*, in *Moulin Rouge!* outside
Christian's rooftop garret and in *No. 5
The Film*.

25. Barry Humphries is an Australian actor
and satirist who is responsible for
creating the internationally renowned

Australian characters Dame Edna
Everage and Sir Les Patterson.

26. See Sandra Lee, 'US critics blitzed by the
corn of Ballroom', *Daily Telegraph Mirror*
23 February 1993, p. 34.

27. Janet Maslin, 'Cinderella wins dance
palace prince', *New York Times* 26
September 1992, p. 3.

28. See feature article by Ruth Hessey,
'Stepping out: behind the scenes of
"Strictly Ballroom", Australia's new
cinema classic', *Rolling Stone* 474,
September 1992, pp. 72–5, 92.

29. See *Strictly Ballroom* release information
on IMDb: <http://www.imdb.com/>.
Accessed 27 March 2009.

30. See Nic Haygarth, 'Japanese go wild over
"Ballroom" and its cast', *Canberra Times*
31 December 1992, p. 16.

31. See Peter Crayford, 'More than just song
and dance', and Deborah Jones,
'Waltzing out of the outback into the
ballroom', in Luhrmann and Pearce,
Strictly Ballroom, pp. ix–xiv.

32. For example, Lynden Barber, 'Strictly
bauble', *Sydney Morning Herald* 20
August 1992, p. 52, objected to *Strictly
Ballroom*'s 'relentless desire to be
adorable' and 'awkwardly written and
clichéd' romance. Dougal Macdonald,
'Easy-to-watch feel-good fare', *Canberra
Times* magazine 12 September 1992, p. 6,
acknowledged that the film was 'not
without shortcomings', the chief of
which was that when Antonio Vargas
danced viewers were able to see only his
feet rather than his whole body. Adrian
Martin, 'Let's hear it for urban whimsy',
Business Review Weekly 21 August 1992,
p. 49, qualified his generally positive

review by calling the film 'reasonably
invigorating entertainment', and
Georgia Brown, 'Truly, madly, deeply',
Voice [US] 16 February 1993, p. 54,
described the antipathetic response of
many of her colleagues and accused the
film of 'positively terrible taste'.

33. For examples of rave reviews see Neil
Jillett, 'Stories retold in dazzling dance
comedy', *Age* 20 August 1992, p. 51; Des
Partridge, 'Move over mambo', *Courier
Mail* [Brisbane] 15 August 1992, p. 55;
and David Stratton, 'Quick, slow, quick
quick, go', *Weekend Australian* 22–3
August 1992, p. 56.

34. See the analysis of *Strictly Ballroom*'s
financial fortunes by Vicky Roach,
'Dance movie risk pays big dividend',
Mercury [Hobart] 26 December 1992,
p. 18.

35. See 'The operation of 10BA', in Get the
Picture, Screen Australia website,
available at <http://www.afc.gov.au/
gtp/mptax10ba.html>. Accessed 27
March 2009.

36. According to Vicky Roach, 'Dance movie
risk pays big dividend', the
A$61.9 million budget for the 1992–3
financial year was to be reduced to
A$50 million at the end of four years.

37. The Albert family invested a substantial
amount in *Strictly Ballroom* (see Vicky
Roach, 'Dance movie risk pays big
dividend').

38. See Vicky Roach, 'Dance movie risk pays
big dividend'.

39. Ronin Films' report on school preview
screenings viewed at Luhrmann
personal archive, Sydney, May–June
2005. The report identifies the film's

appeal to female rather than male students.

40. SBS (Special Broadcasting Service) is a government-funded public broadcasting service in Australia. Its brief is to educate and inform all Australians, reflecting Australia's multicultural society.

41. Proposal for media ideas and opportunities for *Strictly Ballroom*'s Australian theatrical release complied by public relations consultants Bray, Lyall and Partners, viewed at Luhrmann personal archive, Sydney, May–June 2005.

42. The 'Love Is in the Air' music video and behind-the-scenes featurette can be seen in the extra features on the *Strictly Ballroom* disc in the *Baz Luhrmann's Red Curtain Trilogy* boxed set. Script for this music video viewed at the Luhrmann personal archive, Sydney, May–June 2005. A music video of 'Time After Time' was released in October 1992 (according to M&A's report of activities relating to *Strictly Ballroom*'s performance to October 1992 viewed at Luhrmann personal archive, May–June 2005).

43. *Strictly Ballroom* t-shirts viewed in Luhrmann personal archive, Sydney, May–June 2005. Undated letter from Tristram Miall and Antoinette Albert confirming the t-shirts' success at Cannes 1992 also viewed.

44. The film's British distributors Rank acquired British video rights to *Strictly Ballroom*, which were transferred to television company Carlton when it took over the Rank Group's film distribution business in 1997 (see 'Carlton of Britain

buys Rank's film library', *New York Times* 3 April 1997, p. 16).

45. Ronin's press release viewed at Luhrmann personal archive, Sydney, May–June 2005.

46. Promotional material for the gala premiere viewed at the AFI Research and Information collection, RMIT, Melbourne, May–June 2005.

47. John Nicoll Media *Strictly Ballroom* publicity strategy for Melbourne viewed at Luhrmann personal archive, Sydney, May–June 2005.

48. Letter on NSW parliament headed notepaper from Peter Collins to Baz Luhrmann, dated 3 June 1992, viewed at Luhrmann personal archive, Sydney, May–June 2005.

49. For example the French promotional campaign by UGC, which included preview screenings with audience questionnaires, around fifty premieres across the country and in Paris, with tie-in events, and an advertising campaign in print media and on radio. The UGC publicity budget was an estimated F2,165,500 (€330,128). UGC plan, budget and timetable for the film premieres and supporting radio items viewed at Luhrmann personal archive, Sydney, May–June 2005. Despite the extensive marketing campaign, the French box-office figures were disappointing. (M&A's report on *Strictly Ballroom*'s international box-office results to October 1992 viewed at Luhrmann personal archive, May–June 2005.)

50. M&A's report on the performance of *Strictly Ballroom* to October 1992 viewed

at Luhrmann personal archive, Sydney, May–June 2005.

51. Baz Luhrmann and Craig Pearce, *Strictly Ballroom*.

52. See Vicki Roach, 'No last waltz for Ballroom', *Daily Telegraph Mirror* 6 May 1993, p. 37.

53. According to Mark Lawrence, 'Ratings report', *Age* [Melbourne] 'Green Guide', 3 November 1994, p. 3.

54. Dag refers to clumps of dung stuck to the hide of livestock that must be removed to prevent illness. It is used in Australia as an affectionate term of abuse to refer to people perceived as uncool.

55. See Karl Quinn, 'Drag, dags and the suburban surreal', *Metro* 100, summer 1995/6, pp. 23–6.

56. See John Champagne, 'Dancing queen? Feminist and gay male spectatorship in three recent films from Australia', *Film Criticism* 21 (3), spring 1997, pp. 66–88.

57. For example, by Graeme Turner, *Making It National: Nationalism and Australian Popular Culture* (Sydney: Allen & Unwin, 1994); and Jon Stratton, *Race Daze: Australia in Identity Crisis* (Sydney: Pluto Press, 1998). Both writers are cited by Hoorn.

58. See Jeanette Hoorn, 'Michael Powell's *They're a Weird Mob*: dissolving the "undigested fragments" in the Australian body politic', *Continuum: Journal of Media and Cultural Studies* 17 (2), 2003, pp. 159–76.

59. See Brian McFarlane, '*Strictly Ballroom*: old stories, new images', *mETAphor: Journal of the Australian English Teachers' Association* 3, July 2000, n.p.

60. 'Film Focus: The Films of Baz Luhrmann' consisted of two programmes (on *Strictly Ballroom* and *William Shakespeare's Romeo + Juliet*) narrated by actress Kathy Burke, directed by Jonathan Rudd and produced by Double Exposure and Film Education for Channel 4. *Strictly Ballroom* programme details available online at: <http://www.channel4 learning.com/support/programme notes/netnotes/program/programid 1506.htm>. Accessed 31 March 2009.

3– *William Shakespeare's Romeo + Juliet* (1996)

1. For details see Chapter 1, p. 25. Unless indicated otherwise all information relating to Baz Luhrmann and *William Shakespeare's Romeo + Juliet* is taken from interviews with the author, House of Iona, 14 and 15 June 2005.

2. The research process for *A Midsummer Night's Dream* and excerpts from the 1994 Edinburgh Festival performance can be seen in the Red Curtain Cinema section of the Behind the Red Curtain bonus disc in the *Baz Luhrmann's Red Curtain Trilogy* boxed set.

3. See John Brodie, 'Fox doth use its wiles to sell Shakespeare', *Variety* 11–17 November 1996, p. 7.

4. The budget estimate is taken from the IMDb *Romeo + Juliet* entry at <http://www.imdb.com/>. Accessed 7 April 2009. Documents viewed in the Luhrmann personal archive, Sydney, June 2005 suggest that the final cost was nearer $20 million.

5. *Romeo + Juliet* concept books viewed at Luhrmann personal archive, Sydney, June 2005.

6. See Martin Brown, 'All the way with R & J', *Sydney Morning Herald Metro* 20 December 1996, p. 45. The casting process for *Romeo + Juliet* features in the 'Film Focus: The Films of Baz Luhrmann' television programme on *William Shakespeare's Romeo + Juliet* made for Channel 4 in 2000. Programme details available online at: <http://www.channel4learning.com/support/programmenotes/netnotes/section/printyes/sectionid100663793_printyes.htm>. Accessed 8 April 2009.

7. Documents viewed at Luhrmann personal archive, Sydney, June 2005 indicate that Al Pacino, Robert De Niro and Marlon Brando were among those considered for the part of Fulgencio Capulet, while Judy Davis, Meryl Streep, Susan Sarandon, Glenn Close and Anjelica Huston were among the possibilities for Lady Capulet.

8. Leonardo DiCaprio apparently agreed to a salary cut in exchange for the chance to work with Luhrmann (see Brodie, 'Fox doth use its wiles to sell Shakespeare', p. 15).

9. According to some sources, *Romeo + Juliet* was a US/Canada co-production, though 20th Century-Fox is credited as the production company. Film Index International and the BFI Film and Television Database state that during production a company called R & J Film Productions was credited as co-production company. See *William Shakespeare's Romeo + Juliet* entry on Film Index International: <http://fii.chadwyck.co.uk/>. Accessed 8 April 2009. Luhrmann described the film as 'an Australian-Canadian co-production, […] an Australian film', in Mark Mordue, 'Romeo & Juliet "Appear thou in the likeness of a sigh"', *Australian Style* January 1997, p. 35.

10. See Martin Brown, 'All the way with R & J', p. 45.

11. Some scenes were shot in San Francisco after a storm destroyed the set in Vera Cruz, making it impossible to finish filming. See the commentary on the DVD version of *William Shakespeare's Romeo + Juliet*.

12. See 20th Century-Fox production notes for *William Shakespeare's Romeo + Juliet*, p. 18. Some of the team's early research in Miami also found its way into the production design.

13. 20th Century-Fox production notes for *William Shakespeare's Romeo + Juliet*, p. 19.

14. Kym Barrett discusses her costume and gun designs in the 'Focus on Film: The Films of Baz Luhrmann' television programme on *William Shakespeare's Romeo + Juliet* made for Channel 4 in 2000.

15. 20th Century-Fox production notes for *William Shakespeare's Romeo + Juliet*, p. 15.

16. Don McAlpine in the 20th Century-Fox production notes for *William Shakespeare's Romeo + Juliet*, p. 17.

17. Shakespeare's play reworks the legend of Romeo and Giulietta that became popular in late Italian Renaissance times. See Courtney Lehmann, 'Strictly

Shakespeare? Dead letters, ghostly fathers, and the cultural pathology of authorship in Baz Luhrmann's "William Shakespeare's Romeo + Juliet"', *Shakespeare Quarterly* 52 (2), summer 2001, pp. 189–221. Available online at: <http://www.jstor.org/stable/3648667>. Accessed 9 April 2009.

18. See Goran V. Stanivukovic, '"Mounting above the truthe": on hyperbole in English renaissance literature', *Forum for Modern Language Studies* 43 (1), 2007, pp. 9–33. Available online at: <http://fmls.oxfordjournals.org/cgi/content/short/cql112v1>. Accessed 9 April 2009.

19. Stanivukovic, p. 3. Available online at: <http://fmls.oxfordjournals.org/cgi/content/short/cql112v1>. Accessed 10 April 2009.

20. Stanivukovic, p. 9. Available online at: <http://fmls.oxfordjournals.org/cgi/content/short/cql112v1>. Accessed 10 April 2009.

21. Heinrich Lausberg, quoted by Stanivukovic, p. 11. Available online at: <http://fmls.oxfordjournals.org/cgi/content/short/cql112v1>. Accessed 10 April 2009.

22. Stanivukovic, pp. 13, 17. Available online at: <http://fmls.oxfordjournals.org/cgi/content/short/cql112v1>. Accessed 10 April 2009.

23. Travesty is discussed in Chapter 1, p. 22, and in Chapter 2 in relation to *Strictly Ballroom*.

24. Hyperbole is often interpreted as 'hype', that is, as something to be mistrusted. A useful example of a more sympathetic understanding of hyperbole is Ross Gibson's analysis of *Mad Max Beyond Thunderdome* (1985) in 'Yondering: a reading of *Mad Max Beyond Thunderdome*', in *South of the West: Postcolonialism and the Narrative Construction of Australia* (Bloomington: Indiana University Press, 1992).

25. For example, in Erik Bauer, 'Re-revealing Shakespeare: an interview with Baz Luhrmann', *Creative Screenwriting* 5 (2), 1998, pp. 32–5; and in Pauline Adamek, 'Baz Luhrmann's *William Shakespeare's Romeo and Juliet*', *Cinema Papers* 14, February 1997, pp. 10–14.

26. See Adamek, 'Baz Luhrmann's William Shakespeare's Romeo and Juliet', pp. 13, 14.

27. Baz Luhrmann and Craig Pearce in the 20th Century-Fox production notes for *William Shakespeare's Romeo + Juliet*, p. 18.

28. Catherine Martin in the 20th Century-Fox production notes for *William Shakespeare's Romeo + Juliet*, p. 10.

29. 20th Century-Fox production notes for *William Shakespeare's Romeo + Juliet*, p. 19.

30. 20th Century-Fox production notes for *William Shakespeare's Romeo + Juliet*, p. 11.

31. See Peter Bondanella, *The Cinema of Federico Fellini* (Princeton, NJ: Princeton University Press, 1992), pp. 239–61

32. Aldo Signoretti worked as hair stylist on Fellini's *Ginger e Fred* (1986).

33. See Brown, 'All the way with R & J', p. 45. Some of the disasters affecting the shoot are discussed in the commentary on the *Romeo + Juliet* DVD.

34. See 'AFI conversations on film: Jill Bilcock and Roger Savage on the making of Baz Luhrmann's *Romeo + Juliet*', *Metro* 113/114, 1998, pp. 20–4, for an account of the editing process. Technical difficulties included the absence of up-to-scratch telecine equipment, which meant that footage was presented to the editors on a flat-bed, linear device and transferred onto non-linear editing equipment (p. 21).

35. Jill Bilcock in 'AFI conversations on film', p. 22.

36. Jill Bilcock in 'AFI conversations in film', p. 22.

37. Brown, 'All the way with R & J', p. 45.

38. Gareth Vanderhope, 'AFI conversations on film: Jill Bilcock and Roger Savage on the making of Baz Luhrmann's *Romeo + Juliet*', *Metro* 113/114, 1998, pp. 23–4.

39. See Adamek, 'Baz Luhrmann's *William Shakespeare's Romeo + Juliet*', p. 14; Peter Cochrane, 'Baz finds his place in the sun', *Sydney Morning Herald* 23 December 1996, p. 9; and Mark Mordue, 'Romeo & Juliet "Appear thou in the likeness of a sigh"', p. 34.

40. See Fred Harden, 'Characterizing Mr Storm ... and other stories', *Cinema Papers* 14, February 1997, pp. 50–3.

41. See Chris Schwarze in Harden, 'Characterizing Mr Storm ... and other stories', p. 52.

42. See Peter Webb in Harden, 'Characterizing Mr Storm ... and other stories', p. 52.

43. See Sue Hewitt, 'Storm troupers', *Sunday Age* [Melbourne] 16 March 1997, p 5; and Fred Harden, 'Virtual Verona',

Weekend Australian, 14 December 1996, p. 3.

44. For example, Mark Mordue, 'Romeo & Juliet "Appear thou in the likeness of a sigh"', p. 35; Julietta Jameson, 'The Bard big at box office', *Courier-Mail* [Brisbane] 5 November 1996, p. 3.

45. The copyright owner is usually the principal funder(s).

46. See note 23 above.

47. See 'Marlovian Theory' page on *Wikipedia, The Free Encyclopedia*: <http://en.wikipedia.org/w/index. php?title=Marlovian_theory&oldid= 279191355>. Accessed 20 April 2009.

48. See, for example, W. B. Worthen, 'Drama, performativity, and performance', *PMLA* 113, October 1998, pp. 1093–107, one of several writers cited by Courtney Lehmann in 'Strictly Shakespeare? Dead letters, ghostly fathers, and the cultural pathology of authorship in Baz Luhrmann's *William Shakespeare's Romeo + Juliet*'.

49. More recent manifestations of the David and Goliath story are found in films and paintings: see 'Goliath' page on *Wikipedia, The Free Encyclopedia*: <http://en.wikipedia.org/w/index. php?title=Goliath&oldid=283825727>. Accessed 21 April 2009.

50. See 'Legend' page on *Wikipedia, The Free Encyclopedia*: <http://en.wikipedia.org/ w/index.php?title=Legend&oldid= 285162669>. Accessed 21 April 2009.

51. Lehmann distinguishes the Romeo and Juliet story as legend rather than myth, and deploys Roland Barthes's concept of the 'déja-lu' (the 'already read') to illuminate legend's pre-scripted

nature ('Strictly Shakespeare?', p. 190, note 6).

52. See Evan Williams, 'Dazzle the eye, but not the ear', *Weekend Australian* 28 December 1996, p. 8; Roger Ebert, *Chicago Sun-Times*, 1 November 1996, n.p; Janet Maslin, 'Soft! What light? It's flash, Romeo', *New York Times* 1 November 1996, n.p. However, Tom Ryan, *Sunday Age* [Melbourne] 22 December 1996, p. 7, praised the film's success in remaining faithful to the spirit of its source.

53. See Jim Welsh, 'Postmodern Shakespeare: Strictly Romeo', *Literature/Film Quarterly* 25 (2), April 1997, pp. 152–3; cited by Lehmann, 'Strictly Shakespeare?', p. 189, note 3.

54. See Fredric Jameson's influential writing on postmodernism, particularly 'Postmodernism, or, the cultural logic of late capitalism', in Thomas Docherty (ed.), *Postmodernism: A Reader* (New York: Columbia University Press, 1993); cited by Lehmann, 'Strictly Shakespeare?', p. 190, note 7. A counter-view is offered by Richard Dyer, *Pastiche: Knowing Imitation* (Oxford and New York: Routledge, 2006). José Arroyo, in one of the best reviews written about *Romeo + Juliet*, also counters Jameson's negative approach to postmodernism: 'Kiss kiss bang bang', *Sight and Sound* 7 (3), March 1997, pp. 6–9.

55. See discussion of hyperbole and Luhrmann's use of 'hyperbolic hyperbole' above, pp. 64–7. Details of the making of the five-minute gas station sequence are given in the extra features on the *Romeo + Juliet* DVD included in the *Baz Luhrmann's Red Curtain Trilogy* boxed set.

56. Lehmann, 'Strictly Shakespeare?', pp. 196–7, puts forward an intriguing argument about the relationship between performance and authorship.

57. Lehmann, 'Strictly Shakespeare?', pp. 210–18.

58. Rob Sitch's *The Dish* (2000) is a witty celebration of the opacity of Anglo-Australian vernacular.

59. Gibson makes a compelling argument about Australian postcolonial struggle for creativity in 'Yondering: a reading of *Mad Max Beyond Thunderdome*', in *South of the West*. When *Romeo + Juliet* was released in Australia, Luhrmann forcefully expressed his views on Australian independence in Cochrane, 'Baz finds his place in the sun', p. 9.

60. Arroyo, 'Kiss kiss bang bang', p. 9; Ebert, *Chicago Sun-Times*, n.p.

61. Useful discussions of the film's postmodernist strategies are: Arroyo, 'Kiss kiss bang bang'; and Peter S. Donaldson, '"In fair Verona": media, spectacle and performance in *William Shakespeare's Romeo + Juliet*', in Richard Burt (ed.), *Shakespeare After Mass Media* (New York and London: Palgrave Macmillan, 2002).

62. Brown, 'All the way with R & J', p. 45.

63. Jill Bilcock, 'AFI conversations on film', pp. 22, 24

64. See Fox executive Tom Sherak in Inara Verzemnieks, 'Wherefore it's at, Romeo: teen girls relate to screen's star-struck lovers', *Washington Post* 8 November 1996, n.p.

65. Jill Bilcock, 'AFI conversations on film',
p. 22.

66. See Bernard Weinraub, 'Audiences are
in love with the doomed lovers', *New
York Times* 5 November 1996, p. B2. One
of the trailers can be viewed on the
IMDb: <http://www.imdb.com/video/
screenplay/vi5872053 7/>. Accessed 17
April 2009.

67. Official website viewed online at
<http://www.romeoandjuliet.com/
contents.html>. Accessed 16 April
2009.

68. T-shirt and postcards viewed at the
Luhrmann personal archive, Sydney,
June 2005.

69. According to Brown, 'All the way with
R & J'. p. 45. The CD featured the songs
that appeared in the film, with the
exception of Radiohead's 'Exit Music
(For a Film)'. A number of hit singles
emerged from the soundtrack, including
'Lovefool', 'Kissing You' and 'Young
Hearts Run Free' (see *Romeo + Juliet*
(soundtrack) page on *Wikipedia, The Free
Encyclopedia*, <http://en.wikipedia.org/
w/index.php?title=Romeo_%2B_Juliet_
(soundtrack)&oldid=283919739>.
Accessed 16 April 2009). Fox also
produced an interactive CD-ROM that
included the play's text and Luhrmann
and Pearce's screenplay (see Lee
Perkins, 'Apres-movie Romeo browser',
Age [Melbourne] 27 May 1997, p. D9).
The screenplay was published in the US
by Bantam Doubleday Dell in November
1996 as *William Shakespeare's Romeo &
Juliet: The Contemporary Film, The Classic
Play*. It included the original text of the
play, the screenplay, an introduction by

the director, notes on the play and stills
from the film.

70. Both music videos are included in the
special features on the *William
Shakespeare's Romeo + Juliet* DVD in the
Baz Luhrmann's Red Curtain Trilogy
boxed set.

71. See Brodie, 'Fox doth use its wiles to sell
Shakespeare', p. 15.

72. Brodie, 'Fox doth use its wiles to sell
Shakespeare', p. 7. Brown, 'All the way
with R & J', p. 45, gives different figures
(1,300 screens nationwide, followed by
2,000 in the following week).
Verzemnieks, 'Wherefore it's at, Romeo:
teen girls relate to screen's star-struck
lovers', n.p., gives the first week's
takings as $11.1 million. The IMDb gives
box-office takings for the first week as
$11.1 million and number of screens as
1,276 (see *Romeo + Juliet* entry at
<http://www.imdb.com>. Accessed 16
April 2009).

73. According to Brown, 'All the way with
R & J', p. 45.

74. Six weeks according to Jim Schembri,
'Luhrmann's law: why Baz did the Bard',
Age [Mebourne] 24 December 1996, n.p.
Three weeks according to Deborah
Jones, 'Arts & minds', *Weekend
Australian* 'Review' 11 January 1997,
p. 10.

75. Cochrane, 'Baz finds his place in the
sun', p. 9.

76. See Vicky Roach, 'Howfor art thou,
Romeo?', *Daily Telegraph* [Sydney] 3
January 1997, p. 29. The film's release
patterns are given in the *Romeo + Juliet*
entry on the IMDb: <http://www.imdb.
com>. Accessed 16 April 2009.

77. See Jane Read, 'Stars shine for Romeo and Juliet', *Adelaide Advertiser* 19 December 1996, p. 21.

78. See Stan James and Brady Haran, 'Aussie audiences' love affair with "Romeo"', *Adelaide Advertiser* 28 December 1996, p. 10.

79. A full list of *Romeo + Juliet*'s awards history is available in the film's entry on the IMDb: <http://www.imdb.com/>. Accessed 17 April 2009.

80. See round-up of US critics' response, no author, *Sydney Morning Herald*, 2 November 1996, p. 3. And Ebert, *Chicago Sun-Times*, n.p.; Desson Howe, 'This Romeo is bleeding', *Washington Post* 1 November 1996, n.p.; Janet Maslin, 'Soft! What light? It's flash, Romeo', *New York Times* 1 November 1996, n.p.; Amy Taubin 'Live fast, die young', *Village Voice* 12 November 1996, n.p.; and Mick La Salle, 'This "Romeo" is a true tragedy', *San Francisco Chronicle* 8 November 1996, p. C1.

81. See Danielle Wood, 'Fears movie makes suicide "sexy"', *Sunday Tasmanian* 2 March 1997, p.10; Claire Miller, 'Shakespeare tragedy sparks fears for youth', *Age* [Melbourne] 20 February 1997, p. A5; Jonathan Porter, 'Baz cut up at censor', *Daily Telegraph* [Sydney] 1 February 1997, p. 11; and Mordue, 'Romeo & Juliet "Appear thou in the likeness of a sigh"', p. 38.

82. In the Port Arthur massacre of 28 April 1996 a twenty-eight-year-old man on a mass killing spree shot thirty-five people and wounded twenty-one others in and around the historic site of the Port Arthur prison, a popular Tasmanian tourist attraction. See 'Port Arthur massacre (Australia)', *Wikipedia, The Free Encyclopedia*: <http://en.wikipedia.org/w/index.php?title=Port_Arthur_massacre_(Australia)&oldid=282303054>. Accessed 17 April 2009. Also Dale Paget, 'Luhrmann movie not strictly Shakespeare', *Canberra Times* 1 November 1996. p. 60; Michael Gawenda, 'Shakespeare by Baz is just as sweet', *Age* [Melbourne] 13 January 1997, p. A11.

83. Lucy Hamilton, 'Baz vs. the bardolaters, or why *William Shakespeare's Romeo + Juliet* deserves another look', *Literature/Film Quarterly* 28 (2), 2000, pp. 118–24. This article first appeared in *Metro* 118, 1999, pp. 12–17.

84. Hamilton, 'Baz vs. the bardolaters', p. 123.

85. For example, Crystal Downing, 'Misshapen chaos of well-seeming form: Baz Luhrmann's *Romeo + Juliet*', *Literature/Film Quarterly* 28 (2), 2000, pp. 125–31; Elsie Walker, 'Pop goes the Shakespeare: Baz Luhrmann's *William Shakespeare's Romeo + Juliet*, *Literature/Film Quarterly* 28 (2), 2000, pp. 132–9. See also Robert Kole, 'Shakespeare on film: Romeo and Juliet', *Shakespeare Bulletin*, summer 1997, pp. 33–5. Lehmann, 'Strictly Shakespeare?', cites a number of articles on the film by Shakespeare scholars.

86. Lehmann, 'Strictly Shakespeare?', p. 200, note 46.

87. Although *Romeo + Juliet* was not directly quoted, it gave rise to a vogue for

Shakespearian jeans commercials targeting young people, including one by H&M, viewable on YouTube: <http://www.youtube.com/watch?v= ZKdWFC9T9ps> (accessed 23 April 2009); and one with a *Midsummer Night's Dream* theme by Bartle Bogle Hegarty advertising agency for Levi's. 'Focus on Film: The Films of Baz Luhrmann' television programme on *William Shakespeare's Romeo + Juliet* was made for Channel 4 in 2000. In 2004 Channel 4 broadcast *My Shakespeare*, a programme in which Luhrmann mentored via video link a group of young non-actors from Harlesden in north London to produce their own version of Shakespeare's *Romeo and Juliet* (see Chapter 1, p. 33). The film was also credited with influencing street fashions (see Gaile Robinson, 'Wherefore this religious, violent style?', *San Francisco Chronicle* 21 November 1996, n.p.).

88. Gerard Whateley, 'Luhrmann on the love of his life', *Herald Sun* [Melbourne] 26 December 1996, p. 49.

4 – *Moulin Rouge!* (2001)

1. See Jim Schembri, 'Why Baz did the Bard', *Age* [Melbourne] 24 December 1996, n.p.; Julietta Jameson, 'Strictly Shakespeare', *Daily Telegraph* [Sydney] 9 November 1996, p. 38; Julietta Jameson, 'Star-cross'd and hip', *Weekend Courier-Mail* [Brisbane] 7 December 1996, p. 14. Unless indicated otherwise, all information relating to Baz Luhrmann and *Moulin Rouge!* is taken from interviews with the author, House of Iona, Sydney, 14 and 15 June 2005.

2. Lynden Barber, 'Big red', *Weekend Australian (Inquirer)* 17 March 2001, p. 22.

3. See David Hay, 'For Murdoch, it's strictly business', *Sydney Morning Herald* 9 November 1996, p. 5.

4. For details see Chapter 1, p. 25.

5. See Chapter 1, p. 25.

6. Craig Pearce, who co-scripted *Strictly Ballroom* and *Romeo + Juliet* with Luhrmann, talks about the experience of writing *Moulin Rouge!* in the Behind the Red Curtain bonus disc and in the special features on the *Moulin Rouge!* supplementary disc in the *Baz Luhrmann's Red Curtain Trilogy* boxed set.

7. See Paul Fischer, 'Strictly Baz!', *Beat* 23 May 2001, p. 16.

8. The IMDb gives $52.5 million as the estimated budget (see box office/ business for *Moulin Rouge!* at <http://www.imdb.com/>. Accessed 28 April 2009). Media reports suggested that the film's budget spiralled out of control, giving wildly different estimates of the amounts. Producer Martin Brown refuted the rumours (see 'Baz is off the lot, but still on the money', *Sun-Herald* [Sydney] 30 April 2000, p. 20). Luhrmann also put the record straight in Don Groves 'Luhrmann sings "Moulin" praises', *Variety* 16–22 April 2001, pp. 7, 46.

9. See Michael Bodey, 'Making a song & dance', *Daily Telegraph* [Sydney] 'Weekend' 2 December 2000, p. 6.

10. See Baz Luhrmann and Catherine Martin, 'Foreword', in *Moulin Rouge!*

A Film Directed By Baz Luhrmann (London: Pan Macmillan, 2001), n.p.

11. The Studio 54 analogy is made by Luhrmann in 'The making of *Moulin Rouge!*' on the *Moulin Rouge!* supplementary disc in the *Baz Luhrmann's Red Curtain Trilogy* boxed set. In the 1920s and 1930s Studio 54 was a theatre, and its opening production in 1927 was apparently *La Bohème* (see 'Studio 54' page on *Wikipedia, The Free Encyclopedia*: <http://en.wikipedia.org/w/index. php?title=Studio_54&oldid=286409352>. Accessed 1 May 2009).

12. *Moulin Rouge!* design folders viewed at Luhrmann personal archive, Sydney, June 2005.

13. Original archive footage can be seen in 'The making of *Moulin Rouge!*' on the *Moulin Rouge!* supplementary disc in the *Baz Luhrmann's Red Curtain Trilogy* boxed set. The influence of archive film on the CGI reconstruction of Montmartre is mentioned in 'Smoke and Mirrors' in the Design section of the supplementary disc.

14. The collaborative process of writing the script is described in David Michôd, 'Moulin Rouge: the script', *if MAG* 33, May 2001, pp. 036–7.

15. Material about the scriptwriting process is included in 'This story is about' on the *Moulin Rouge!* supplementary disc in the *Baz Luhrmann's Red Curtain Trilogy* boxed set. An interview with Craig Pearce about the *Moulin Rouge!* script is included in Red Curtain Cinema on the Behind the Red Curtain bonus disc in the boxed set. Script comparisons and extracts appear on the Special Edition

Moulin Rouge! DVD (not available on the Region 2 edition).

16. See Trivia section for *Moulin Rouge!* on the IMDb: <http://www.imdb.com/>. Accessed 1 May 2009.

17. Kidman, McGregor and the other actors were paid Equity rates, far less than their normal fees (see Bec Smith, 'Moulin Rouge', *if MAG* 33, May 2001, pp. 035, 039). McGregor had auditioned for *Romeo + Juliet*, but was considered too old for the part (see Colin Kennedy, 'Torch song trilogy', *Empire* 148, October 2002, p. 73).

18. 20th Century-Fox Australian production notes for *Moulin Rouge!*, p. 3.

19. See costume tests and workshop footage in the interview with Catherine Martin in the Design section of the *Moulin Rouge!* supplementary disc. Images of Gibson Girl hairstyles and dress viewed in Luhrmann personal archive, Sydney, May–June 2005.

20. See Peter N. Chumo II, 'Craig Pearce/*Moulin Rouge!*', *Creative Screenwriting* 37, May/June 2001, pp. 31–7, which includes annotated extracts from the screenplay.

21. See Don McAlpine in Rachael K. Bosley, 'Bohemian rhapsody', *American Cinematographer* 82 (6), June 2001, pp. 38–51.

22. See Chris Bassett, '… And sprinkle it with fairy dust', *if MAG* 35, July 2001, p. 034.

23. 20th Century-Fox Australian production notes for *Moulin Rouge!*, p. 4.

24. 20th Century-Fox Australian production notes for *Moulin Rouge!*, p. 4.

25. Red-room design discussed by Catherine Martin in the commentary on the *Moulin Rouge!* DVD.

26. See cinematography chapter in Luhrmann and Martin, *Moulin Rouge!*, p. 82. Toulouse-Lautrec used a particular hue of green to connote the absinthe that was a popular drink at the Moulin Rouge; this green tint was used in the film for the animated green fairy played by Kylie Minogue. See 'Smoke and Mirrors' in the Design section on the *Moulin Rouge!* supplementary disc.

27. See 'Oh la la! Behind the making of *Moulin Rouge!*', *HQ*, May 2001, p. 43.

28. See production design chapter in Luhrmann and Martin, *Moulin Rouge!*, pp. 78–81, which includes full-colour design illustrations.

29. See costume design chapter in Luhrmann and Martin, *Moulin Rouge!*, p. 84.

30. See costume design chapter in Luhrmann and Martin, *Moulin Rouge!*, p. 84. Design sketches for *Moulin Rouge!* costumes viewed at Luhrmann personal archive, Sydney, May–June 2005.

31. 20th Century-Fox Australian production notes for *Moulin Rouge!*, p. 5.

32. See costume design chapter in Luhrmann and Martin, *Moulin Rouge!*, p. 84.

33. See 'Back to the bohos' in Luhrmann and Martin, *Moulin Rouge!*, n.p., which features full-colour pictures of the costumes for the Moulin Rouge habitués. Toulouse-Lautrec himself was apparently fond of cross-dressing.

34. The costume design in the 'Spectacular Spectacular' finale of *Moulin Rouge!* is indebted to Bakst. Costume sketches viewed in Luhrmann personal archive, Sydney, May–June 2005.

35. See, for example, 'Oh la la! Behind the making of *Moulin Rouge!*', p. 43.

36. See visual effects chapter in Luhrmann and Martin, *Moulin Rouge!*, p. 90. At the time, this was one of the longest visual effects shots in cinema history, though it has now been surpassed.

37. See Chris Bassett, '… And sprinkle it with fairy dust', p. 032.

38. See Rachael Turk, 'Children of the digital revolution', *Metro* 129/130, spring 2001, p. 13.

39. Turk, 'Children of the digital revolution', p. 14.

40. For example, Umberto Eco, *Travels in Hyperreality* (New York: Harcourt Brace & Company, 1986); Jean Baudrillard, 'Simulacra and simulations', in Mark Poster (ed.), *Jean Baudrillard: Selected Writings* (Stanford: Stanford University Press, 1988).

41. The death scene is identified by Luhrmann in the commentary to the *Moulin Rouge!* DVD as a tribute to *Citizen Kane*'s celebrated special effects rooftop sequence.

42. For example in Luhrmann and Martin, *Moulin Rouge!*, p. 94.

43. See music production chapter in Luhrmann and Martin, *Moulin Rouge!*, p. 94. Much of the work on the music was done at Bazmark facilities at the House of Iona, Sydney.

44. The two who declined were Cat Stevens (Yusuf Islam) and Donna Summer, who objected to their songs being used in a story featuring sex outside marriage (see

Dino Scatena, 'The sweet sound of a melodic partnership', *Daily Telegraph* [Sydney] 17 May 2001, Supplements p. 9. Artists who performed for the film included Madonna, U2, Placido Domingo, David Bowie and Massive Attack.

45. A documentary 'The Musical Journey', showing Luhrmann and music supervisor Anton Monsted working with Craig Armstrong, is included in the special features on the *Moulin Rouge!* DVD in the *Baz Luhrmann's Red Curtain Trilogy* boxed set.

46. See Rudy Koppl, '*Moulin Rouge*', *Music from the Movies* 33, May 2002, p. 35.

47. See music production chapter in Luhrmann and Martin, *Moulin Rouge!*, p. 94.

48. See choreography chapter in Luhrmann and Martin, *Moulin Rouge!*, p.92.

49. See editing chapter in Luhrmann and Martin, *Moulin Rouge!*, p. 88.

50. Desson Howe, 'This Romeo is bleeding', *Washington Post* 1 November 1996, n.p.

51. See Mark Mordue, 'Romeo & Juliet "Appear thou in the likeness of a sigh ..." ', *Australian Style* January 1997, p. 35.

52. See José Arroyo, 'Kiss kiss bang bang', *Sight and Sound* 7 (3), March 1997, p. 9.

53. See Alexander Doty, *Making Things Perfectly Queer: Interpreting Mass Culture* (Minneapolis: University of Minnesota Press, 1993).

54. See Chapter 3, p. 78.

55. See Barbara Klinger's analysis of camp, 'Mass camp and the old Hollywood melodrama today', in *Melodrama and Meaning: History, Culture, and the Films of*

Douglas Sirk (Bloomington: Indiana University Press, 1994).

56. See Angela Ndalianis, *Neo-Baroque Aesthetics and Contemporary Entertainment* (Cambridge, MA: MIT Press, 2004), pp. 4–5.

57. Ndalianis, *Neo-Baroque Aesthetics*, pp. 9–10.

58. Ndalianis, *Neo-Baroque Aesthetics*, p. 14.

59. Ndalianis, *Neo-Baroque Aesthetics*, p. 17.

60. See, for example, Laura Mulvey, 'Notes on Sirk and melodrama', in *Visual and Other Pleasures* (London and New York: Palgrave Macmillan, 2009); Christine Gledhill (ed.), *Home Is Where the Heart Is: Studies in Melodrama and the Woman's Film* (London: BFI, 1987).

61. As feature film-making developed and close-ups became more common, silent cinema abandoned histrionic acting styles for more naturalistic perfor-mances. See Roberta E. Pearson, *Eloquent Gestures: The Transformation of Performance Style in the Griffith Biograph Films* (Berkeley: University of California Press, 1992). Histrionic acting survives in mainstream cinema in genres such as comedy, science fiction and horror.

62. See, for example, Geoffrey Nowell-Smith, 'Minnelli and melodrama', in Gledhill (ed.), *Home Is Where the Heart Is*.

63. Freud's reality principle is in opposition to the pleasure principle and is a function of the ego's role in learning to postpone gratification. For Freud, the reality and pleasure principles are constantly in tension with one another. See Sigmund Freud, 'Formulations on the two principles of mental function-ing', in James Strachey (ed.), *Standard*

Edition of Complete Psychological Works,
Vol. XII (London: Hogarth Press, 1961).

64. Ndalianis, *Neo-Baroque Aesthetics*, p. 5.

65. Reception theory, which focuses on the
transformation of media texts by
recipients, contributes to the idea of
consumers as active creators of meaning
in diverse contexts.

66. See Groves, 'Luhrmann sings "Moulin"
praises', p. 7.

67. *Moulin Rouge!* is dedicated to
Luhrmann's father Leonard.

68. See Barber, 'Big red', p. 22.

69. See Terry Oberg, 'Make or break',
Courier-Mail [Brisbane] 14 April 2001,
BAM section, p. 1. See also 'Baz is off the
lot, but still on the money', *Sun-Herald*
[Sydney] 30 April 2000, p. 20.

70. See producer Martin Brown in Bodey,
'Making a song & dance', p. 6.

71. See Barber, 'Big red', p. 22.

72. See Gerry Maddox, 'The red windmill is
turning fast and wide, with a lot toulouse',
Sydney Morning Herald 11 May 2001, p. 5,
which gives the marketing budget as
$2 million. Sophie Tedmanson, 'Painting
the towns red', *Australian* 19 April 2001,
p. 3, gives a rumoured figure for
marketing of $40 million.

73. See Groves, 'Luhrmann sings "Moulin"
praises', p. 46.

74. See Phillippa Hawker and Lawrie Zion,
'Moolah Rouge', *Age* 23 May 2001, p. 9.

75. See *'Moulin Rouge!* Music from Baz
Luhrmann's Film' on *Wikipedia, The Free
Encyclopedia*. Available at:
<http://en.wikipedia.org/w/index.
php?title=Moulin_Rouge!_Music_from_
Baz_Luhrmann%27s_Film&oldid=
288178537>. Accessed 14 May 2001.

76. See 'Lady Marmalade' on *Wikipedia, The
Free Encyclopedia*. Available at:
<http://en.wikipedia.org/w/index.
php?title=Lady_Marmalade&oldid=
289563646>. Accessed 14 May 2009.

77. See *'Moulin Rouge!'* on *Wikipedia, The
Free Encyclopedia*. Available at:
<http://en.wikipedia.org/w/index.
php?title=Moulin_Rouge!&oldid=
289581786>. Accessed 14 May 2001. See
also Gerry Maddox, 'Nicole, Ewan sing?
It's a can-can-do show', *Sydney Morning
Herald* 4 April 2001, Arts and
Entertainment section, p. 18. The 'Lady
Marmalade' music video is included in
the special features on the *Moulin Rouge!*
DVD in the *Baz Luhrmann's Red Curtain
Trilogy* boxed set.

78. The music video of 'One Day I'll Fly
Away' is included in the special features
on the Behind the Red Curtain DVD,
and 'Come What May' is included in the
special features on the *Moulin Rouge!*
DVD, both in the *Baz Luhrmann's Red
Curtain Trilogy* boxed set.

79. See Sasha Baskett, 'Kidman's cancan
breathes new life into the corset',
Courier-Mail [Brisbane] 29 May 2001,
p. 9; Ginia Bellafante, 'Film frock fest',
Age 9 May 2001, p. 4.

80. See Hawker and Zion, 'Moolah Rouge',
p. 9. The book came out in 2001: Baz
Luhrmann and Catherine Martin,
*Moulin Rouge!: A Film Directed by Baz
Luhrmann*, was published by Newmarket
Press in the USA, Pan Macmillan in the
UK and Allen & Unwin in Australia.

81. For example, 'Cabaret risque',
Australian 24 July 2000, p. 11;
Christopher Hudson, 'Portrait of a party

animal', *Sunday Mail* [Brisbane] 21 January 2001, p. 84.

82. See Bodey, 'Making a song & dance', p. 6; Barber, 'Big red', p. 22.

83. See the fifty-minute BBC television documentary 'Promoting *Moulin Rouge!*', produced and directed by Adrian Sibley in 2001, that followed the Cannes opening and Luhrmann's gruelling promotional tour of the USA.

84. See Maddox, 'The red windmill is turning fast', p. 5.

85. See 'Promoting *Moulin Rouge!*' (2001); also release dates for *Moulin Rouge!* on IMDb: <http://www.imdb.com/>. Accessed 15 May 2009. See also Groves, 'Luhrmann sings "Moulin" praises', p. 46.

86. For example, in Des Partridge, 'Classic approach to Nicole's role', *Courier-Mail* [Brisbane] 5 May 2001, p. 11; in 20th Century-Fox Australian production notes, p. 2; and in Smith, '*Moulin Rouge*', p. 034. See also Graham Fuller, 'Strictly red', *Sight and Sound* 11 (6), June 2001, pp. 14–16; Kennedy, 'Torch song trilogy', pp. 68–77.

87. See 'Promoting *Moulin Rouge!*' (2001); also Maddox, 'The red windmill is turning fast', p. 5.

88. See 'Australian box office', *Herald Sun* [Melbourne] 31 May 2001, Supplements section p. 59.

89. See 'Promoting *Moulin Rouge!*' (2001).

90. See Rachel Abramowitz, 'Baz goes global to drum up votes', *Sydney Morning Herald* 13 February 2002, p. 15.

91. See release dates and DVD details for *Moulin Rouge!* on IMDb:

<http://www.imdb.com/>. Accessed 19 May 2009.

92. See Abramowitz, 'Baz goes global', p. 15.

93. See Lawrie Zion, 'Kidman film sets box-office record', *Age* 26 May 2001, p. 3.

94. See awards information for *Moulin Rouge!* on IMDb: <http://www.imdb.com/>. Accessed 19 May 2009.

95. See Lawrie Zion, 'Moulin huge', *Age* 30 May 2001, Other section, p. 7; Lynden Barber, 'Moulin's US debut a sellout', *Australian* 23 May 2001, General news section, p. 17.

96. For example, J. Hoberman, 'Kitsch as kitsch can', *Village Voice* 29 May 2001, p. 119, described *Moulin Rouge!* as 'vulgar', 'truly awful' and 'tawdry'.

97. See Philip French, 'Review', *Observer* [London] 9 September 2001, p. 7; José Arroyo, '*Moulin Rouge* review', *Sight and Sound* 11 (9), September 2001, pp. 50–2; NJ [Nick James], '*Moulin Rouge*', *Sight and Sound* 11 (7), July 2001, p. 16; Adrian Martin, 'Review', *Age* 24 May 2001, Other section, p. 5; Edward Guthmann, 'Red hot', *San Francisco Chronicle* 1 June 2001, p. C1; Mark Naglazas, 'Sensual overload', *West Australian* 24 May 2001, Arts and entertainment section, p. 7; Jonathan Dawson, 'The fourth wall returns: *Moulin Rouge* and the imminent death of cinema'. Available online at: <http:www.sensesofcinema.com/contents/01/14/moulin_rouge.html>. Accessed 20 May 2009.

98. For example, Deirdre Macken, 'So superlatively superficial', *Australian Financial Review* 26 May 2001, General news section, p. 2.

99. Stephen Hunter, 'Musical heirs', *Washington Post* 20 May 2001, p. G1; Tim Lloyd, '"Moulin" has essence of theatre', *Advertiser* [Adelaide] 9 June 2001, p. 22.

100. See 'Our film industry comes of age', *Australian* 22 May 2001, General news section, p. 10; Lynden Barber, 'Get serious and think big', *Weekend Australian* 26–7 January 2002, Review section, p. 12; Nicole Lindsay, 'Fox film holds up industry', *Australian Financial Review* 16 November 2000, General news section, p. 8. For an account of changing production patterns in post-1990s Australian cinema, see Lisa French, 'Patterns of production and policy: the Australian film industry in the 1990s', in Ian Craven (ed.), *Australian Cinema in the 1990s* (Melbourne: Taylor & Francis, 2001).

101. See Garry Maddox and Nick O'Malley, 'Film industry sees rouge at tax ruling', *Age* 3 August 2001, Edition changes, p. 4; 'ATO firm on film ruling', *Canberra Times* 4 August 2001, General news section, p. 5; 'Don't give films the flick – they can be profitable', *Courier-Mail* [Brisbane] 8 August 2001, Business news section, p. 29.

102. For example, Marsha Kinder, 'Moulin Rouge', *Film Quarterly* 55 (3), 2002, pp. 52–9; and Kent Jones, 'Real artifice', *Film Comment* 37 (3), May/June 2001, pp. 22–5.

103. The NFT programme booklet can be seen in the interactive feature Red Curtain Cinema on the Behind the Red Curtain disc in the *Baz Luhrmann's Red Curtain Trilogy* boxed set. See also Fuller, 'Strictly red', p. 16.

104. See Geoffrey Macnab, *J. Arthur Rank and the British Film Industry* (London and New York: Routledge, 1993); Pam Cook, *I Know Where I'm Going!* (London: BFI, 2002).

105. See, however, a short discussion by Patricia Pisters, '"Touched by a cardboard sword": aesthetic creation and non-personal subjectivity in *Dancer in the Dark* & *Moulin Rouge*', in Joost de Bloois, Sjef Houppermans and Frans-Willem Korsten (eds), *Discern(e)ments: Deleuzian Aesthetics* (Amsterdam: Rodopi, 2004).

106. The best fan site is *Baz the Great!*, which was set up in 2002 and offers a wealth of information about all Luhrmann's film projects (see <http://www.bazthegreatsite.com/index.htm>. Accessed 20 May 2009). See also 'Spectacular! Spectacular! A *Moulin Rouge* Fansite' at: <http://two diamonddogs.tripod.com/links.html>, which provides links to *Moulin Rouge!* resources. Accessed 20 May 2009.

107. See Geoff King, *Indiewood, USA: Where Hollywood Meets Independent Cinema* (London: I. B. Tauris, 2008).

5 – *No. 5 The Film* (2004) and *Australia* (2008)

1. See Maggie Shiels, 'Baz's brilliant *La Boheme*', BBC News online, Entertainment section, 21 October 2002: <http://news.bbc.co.uk/1/hi/entertainment/reviews/2346351.stm>. Accessed 2 June 2009. (Unless indicated otherwise, information about Baz

Luhrmann and Catherine Martin is taken from interviews with the author, House of Iona, Sydney, 14, 15 and 16 June 2005.)

2. See 'Take five', *Vogue* (US), September 2004, pp. 717–21, 825–6. This feature also appeared in Australian *Vogue*, October 2004. See also Chapter 1, pp. 31–2.

3. See 'Take five', p. 717.

4. For further details about the fortunes of the *Alexander the Great* project see Chapter 1, pp. 31–2.

5. See 'Take five', p. 720.

6. See 'Take five', p. 720; and the twenty-five-minute documentary directed by Fabienne Isnard, *Le film du film Chanel No. 5* (2004), which aired on Channel 9 in Australia on 15 November 2004.

7. See *Le film du film Chanel No. 5*.

8. Photographs of Coco Chanel, and a list of her famous quotations, viewed at Luhrmann personal archive, Sydney, May–June 2005.

9. Celebrities and models associated with Chanel No. 5 included Suzy Parker, Carole Bouquet, Inès de la Fressange, Marilyn Monroe, Lauren Hutton and Jean Shrimpton (research viewed at Luhrmann personal archive, May–June 2005).

10. See 'Take five', p. 720. Other notable commercials were those directed by Ridley Scott in the late 1980s with Carole Bouquet; Luc Besson's 1999 ads starring Estella Warren; and Jean-Pierre Jeunet's 2009 commercial featuring Audrey Tautou, who played Coco Chanel in the film about the designer's early life, *Coco avant Chanel* (2009). See

Alison Kerr, '*Da Vinci Code* star Audrey Tautou the latest A-lister to promote Chanel's sweet smell of success', *Daily Record* [Glasgow] 9 June 2009. Available online at: <http://www.dailyrecord.co.uk/women/2009/06/09/audrey-tautou-the-latest-star-to-promote-chanel-s-sweet-smell-of-success-86908-21426831/>. Accessed 12 June 2009.

11. Advertisement featuring Deneuve viewed at Luhrmann personal archive, May–June 2005.

12. See 'Take five', p. 720.

13. Storyboards created for the commercial, viewed at Luhrmann personal archive in May–June 2005, referred to the romantic couple as 'Prince' and 'Princess', emphasising the fairy-tale aspects of the story.

14. See 'Take five', p. 720.

15. Photographs of Paris, the New York skyline and views of Manhattan seen from Brooklyn and Williamsburg viewed at Luhrmann personal archive, May–June 2005.

16. Scale models of the yellow cab and the Chanel rooftop sign, photograph of full-size rooftop set and set designs viewed at Luhrmann personal archive, May–June 2005. Animal Logic carried out the visual effects for *Moulin Rouge!* (see Chapter 4, pp. 92–3).

17. See 'Take five', p. 825.

18. See *Le film du film Chanel No. 5*.

19. See 'Take five', p. 825.

20. The film exists in two versions: one is two minutes long and the second, which includes one minute of end-credits, runs for three minutes. Television

versions of around thirty seconds were also made.

21. See 'Take five', pp. 825–6.

22. For details see Chapter 1, p. 32.

23. Promotional materials and *Le Figaro* advertisement viewed at Luhrmann personal archive, May–June 2005.

24. *Le film du film Chanel No. 5*, directed by Fabienne Isnard, viewed courtesy of Bazmark Inq.

25. The commercial's first UK broadcast was on Channel 4 at 9.20 pm on Saturday, 20 November 2004 during the first advertisement break in the screening of *Moulin Rouge!*.

26. See 'Take five', p. 826.

27. British screenwriter and playwright Ronald Harwood and Australian novelist and film director Richard Flanagan also collaborated on the script.

28. See 'Northern Territory' page in *Wikipedia, The Free Encyclopedia*: <http://en.wikipedia.org/w/index. php?title=Northern_Territory&oldid= 295975123>. Accessed 12 June 2009.

29. See 20th Century-Fox production notes for *Australia*, p. 11.

30. See *Australia*'s location supervisor Philip Roope in Bazmark's *Set to Screen* podcast 'Location Shooting II', aired 15 July 2008. Available at: <www.apple.com/podcasts/ settoscreen/sts_baz_08.xml>. Accessed 17 June 2009.

31. The history of the making of *Australia* is given on the *Australia*: a Baz Luhrmann Film website at: <http://www. australiamovie.net/about/film/>. Accessed 18 June 2009.

32. For example, Nina Caplan, 'Baz Luhrmann on *Australia*', *Time Out*

[London], 18–31 December 2008. Available online at: <http://www. timeout.com/film/features/show-feature/6456/baz-luhrmann-on-australia.html#mainNav>. Accessed 15 July 2009.

33. Angela Little performs under the name of Ophelia of the Spirits (see <http://www.opheliaofthespirits.com/>. Accessed 18 June 2009).

34. See Bazmark's *Set to Screen* podcast 'Music', aired 5 November 2008, Available at: <www.apple.com/ podcasts/settoscreen/sts_baz_08.xml>. Accessed 24 June 2009.

35. See Luhrmann interview about casting Brandon Walters on the *Kyle and Jackie O Show*, 2Day FM [Sydney] 24 April 2007. Available in Audio and Video section on *Australia*: a Baz Luhrmann Film website at: <http://www.australiamovie.net/ media/>. Accessed 19 June 2009. See also 20th Century-Fox production notes for *Australia*, p. 6.

36. See definitions of 'nullah' and 'nulla-nulla' [sic] in *Oxford English Dictionary*, available online at: <http://www.oed. com/>. Accessed 23 June 2009. Also see description of nullah nullah club at <http://www.nsw.nationaltrust.org.au/ ida/link_d2_nullah.html>. Accessed 23 June 2009.

37. See 'Krishna' page in *Wikipedia, The Free Encyclopedia*. Available at: <http://en.wikipedia.org/w/index. php?title=Krishna&oldid=297908251>. Accessed 23 June 2009.

38. See 'Australian Aboriginal English' page in *Wikipedia, The Free Encyclopedia*. Available at: <http://en.wikipedia.org/

w/index.php?title=Australian_
Aboriginal_English&oldid=282243959>.
Accessed 23 June 2009.

39. See Rainbow Serpent section on
'Australian Aboriginal mythology' page
in *Wikipedia, The Free Encyclopedia*.
Available at: <http://en.wikipedia.org/
w/index.php?title=Australian_
Aboriginal_mythology&oldid=
296558311>. Accessed 24 June 2009.

40. See digital booklet accompanying the
Australia soundtrack available from
iTunes, which includes Luhrmann's
notes about the music.

41. See soundtrack listing in credits
accompanying *Australia* review, *Sight
and Sound* 19 (2), February 2009,
pp. 48–9.

42. See David Hirschfelder in Bazmark's *Set
to Screen* podcast 'Music', accessed
24 June 2009.

43. See Luhrmann's notes about the music
in digital booklet accompanying the
iTunes *Australia* soundtrack.

44. First collage book for *Australia*,
featuring Nicole Kidman and Russell
Crowe, viewed at the House of Iona,
Sydney, June 2005.

45. See Bazmark's *Set to Screen* podcast
'Director of Photography', aired 30 July
2008. Available at: <www.apple.com/
podcasts/settoscreen/sts_baz_08.xml>.
Accessed 24 June 2009.

46. See Jack Egan, 'Mandy Walker:
Australia', *Variety* 31 December 2008.
Available online at: <http://www.
variety.com/index.asp?layout=
awardcentral&jump=contenders&id=
australia&articleid=VR1117997868>.
Accessed 24 June 2009.

47. See Egan, 'Mandy Walker'.

48. See *Australia* page on Animal Logic
website: <http://www.animallogic.
com/>. Accessed 26 June 2009.

49. See Heather Newgen, 'Exclusive:
Australia director Baz Luhrmann',
25 November 2008. Available online at:
<http://www.comingsoon.net/news/
movienews.php?id=50742>. Accessed
26 June 2009.

50. An interview with Catherine Martin
talking about Picture Australia can be
found in the Multimedia section of the
Australia: A Baz Luhrmann Film website.
Available at: <http://www.
australiamovie.net/media/>. Accessed
30 June 2009.

51. See 20th Century-Fox production notes
for *Australia*, pp. 11–12.

52. See 20th Century-Fox production notes,
p. 13.

53. See 20th Century-Fox production notes,
p. 14. See also Bazmark's *Set to Screen*
podcast 'Production Design', aired
6 May 2008. Available at:
<www.apple.com/podcasts/
settoscreen/sts_baz_08.xml>. Accessed
29 June 2009.

54. See Catherine Martin in Bazmark's *Set to
Screen* podcast 'Costume Design', aired
28 May 2008. Available at:
<www.apple.com/podcasts/
settoscreen/sts_baz_08.xml>. Accessed
29 June 2009.

55. The 'costume plot' exists alongside the
story-line and refers to the way the
costume interprets and comments on
the film's narrative and character
development. See also the costume
time-line for Sarah's character

illustrated in the *Set to Screen* podcast 'Costume Design'.

56. The revision of the heroine's priorities through contact with a mysterious other place is a feature of the story and costume plot in Powell and Pressburger's Gothic women's picture *I Know Where I'm Going!* (1945). See Pam Cook, *I Know Where I'm Going!* (London: BFI, 2002), pp. 57–64.

57. See 20th Century-Fox production notes, p. 15.

58. See Catherine Martin in the *Set to Screen* podcast 'Costume Design', which includes photographs and illustrations of Jackman's and other characters' costume designs.

59. The photographs of anthropologists Donald Thompson and Baldwin Spencer, who documented the lives of Australia's indigenous people in the 1920s and 1930s, were used as evidence. See 20th Century-Fox production notes, p. 16.

60. See Catherine Martin on the indigenous costume and body decoration in the *Set to Screen* podcast. The film-makers consulted indigenous body adornment expert Dr Louise Hamby at the Australian National University (see 20th Century-Fox production notes, p. 16).

61. See Catherine Martin quoted in 20th Century-Fox production notes, p. 16.

62. See 20th Century-Fox production notes, p. 12. See also 'The making of *Australia*' page on the *Australia*: A Baz Luhrmann Film website. Available at: <http://www.australiamovie.net/about/film/>. Accessed 30 June 2009.

63. *Australia* was said to be the most expensive Australian film ever made. See Ben Child, 'Australians fail to warm to Luhrmann's epic romance', *Guardian* online 2 December 2008, available at: <http://www.guardian.co.uk/film/2008/dec/02/baz-luhrmann-australia>. Accessed 30 June 2009.

64. Media coverage is available on the *Australia*: A Baz Luhrmann Film website at: <http://www.australiamovie.net/media/>. Accessed 30 June 2009.

65. The concept of de-familiarisation is similar to Brechtian distanciation or the 'making strange' of the Russian Formalists.

66. See Ross Gibson, *South of the West: Postcolonialism and the Narrative Construction of Australia* (Bloomington: Indiana University Press, 1992), p. 162.

67. See Felicity Collins and Therese Davis, *Australian Cinema After Mabo* (Cambridge and Melbourne: Cambridge University Press, 2004), pp. 12–13, 25–7.

68. *Terra nullius* is the idea that the land settled by British colonists was uninhabited and belonged to no one before they arrived.

69. See 'History wars' page in *Wikipedia, The Free Encyclopedia*. Available at: <http://en.wikipedia.org/w/index.php?title=History_wars&oldid=302713040>. Accessed 21 July 2009.

70. See Collins and Davis, *Australian Cinema After Mabo*, p. 13.

71. See 'Aussie battler' page in *Wikipedia, The Free Encyclopedia*. Available at: <http://en.wikipedia.org/w/index.php?title=Aussie_battler&oldid=296076543>. Accessed 23 July 2009.

72. See 'The Dreamtime' on the *Aboriginal Australia Art and Culture Centre* website. Available at: <http://aboriginalart.com.au/culture/dreamtime2.html>. Accessed 24 July 2009.

73. See 'Songlines' page in *Wikipedia, The Free Encyclopedia*. Available at: <http://en.wikipedia.org/w/index.php?title=Songlines&oldid=302684193>. Accessed 24 July 2009.

74. See Ellen Connolly, 'Hopes and hype at world premiere of Luhrmann's *Australia*', *Guardian* 18 November 2009. Available online at: <http://www.guardian.co.uk/film/2008/nov/18/australia-film-world-premiere>. Accessed 28 July 2009. Full list of release dates is on *Australia* page on IMDb: <http://www.imdb.com>.

75. See, for example, Richard Luscombe, 'Kidman's outback adventure gets happy ending after studio pressure', *Guardian* 10 November 2008. Available online at: <http://www.guardian.co.uk/film/2008/nov/10/australia-nicole-kidman-hugh-jackman-baz-luhrmann>. Accessed 28 July 2009.

76. See Steven Zeitchik, 'Baz Luhrmann, with a defense as full-throated as *Moulin Rouge*', *Hollywood Reporter* 19 December 2008. Available online at: <http://www.riskybusinessblog.com/baz_luhrmann/>. Accessed 3 August 2009.

77. See Frank Devine, 'Baz pulls it off with punters', *Australian* 5 December 2008. Available online at: <http://www.theaustralian.news.com.au/story/0,,24751715-31501,00.html>. Accessed 29 July 2009.

78. See Garry Maddox, 'Incentives spur camera action', *Sydney Morning Herald* 5 October 2007. Available online at: <http://www.smh.com.au/small-business/incentives-spur-camera-action-20090619-cpxa.html>. Accessed 29 July 2009. Also Christine Sams, 'Why you're footing the bill for Luhrmann's *Australia*', *Sydney Morning Herald* 14 December 2008. Available online at: <http://www.smh.com.au/news/entertainment/film/why-youre-footing-the-bill-for-luhrmanns-australia/2008/12/13/1228585174538.html>. Accessed 29 July 2009. Also Michaela Boland, ' "Australia" incentive stirs down under', *Variety* 30 January 2009. Available online at: <http://www.variety.com/article/VR1117999371.html?categoryid=1019&cs=1&query=Australia+incentive+stirs+down+under>. Accessed 29 July 2009. Details of the Producer Offset scheme available on the Screen Australia website: <http://www.screenaustralia.gov.au/producer_offset/default.asp>. Accessed 29 July 2009.

79. See Darren Davidson, 'Tourism Australia unveils Baz Luhrmann global ad campaign', *Brand Republic* 8 October 2008. Available online at: <http://www.brandrepublic.com/News/851788/Tourism-Australia-unveils-Baz-Luhrmann-global-ad-campaign/?DCMP=ILC-SEARCH>. Accessed 29 July 2009. Also *TravelMole* report 16 June 2008: 'Baz Luhrmann's *Australia* – the movie – creates a new marketing era for Australian tourism',

available online at <www.travelmole.
com>. Accessed 29 July 2009.

80. The commercials can be viewed on
YouTube: see 'Australia: Come
Walkabout' at <www.youtube.com>.
Accessed 29 July 2009.

81. See Sharri Markson, 'Oz ads a bloody
failure', *Sunday Telegraph* [Sydney]
14 December 2008. Available online at:
<http://www.dailytelegraph.com.au/
news/nsw-act/oz-ads-a-bloody-
failure/story-e6freuzi-1111118308391>.
Accessed 29 July 2009. Also Bonnie
Malkin, 'Advertising campaign based on
Nicole Kidman film fails to lift
Australian tourism', *Telegraph* [London]
online, 9 December 2008. Available at:
<http://www.telegraph.co.uk/news/
3688828/Advertising-campaign-based-
on-Nicole-Kidman-film-fails-to-lift-
Australian-tourism.html>. Accessed
29 July 2009.

82. See '"Come walkabout" tv ad wins
prestigious Clio award', *Scoop
Independent News* website 20 May 2009,
available at: <http://www.scoop.co.nz/
stories/BU0905/S00529.htm>.
Accessed 29 July 2009.

83. See 'The girl from Oz', *Age* 2 November
2008. Available online at:
<http://www.theage.com.au/news/
entertainment/film/the-girl-from-
oz/2008/10/30/1224956235619.
html>. Accessed 29 July 2009.
Also 'Nic's Australian story', *Sunday
Herald Sun* 2 November 2008.
Available online at: <http://www.news.
com.au/heraldsun/story/0,21985,
24589292-662,00.html>. Accessed
29 July 2009.

84. See Michael Bodey, 'Tidal wave of
marketing for Baz Luhrmann movie',
Australian Business section 4 September
2008. Available online at:
<http://www.theaustralian.news.com.
au/story/0,25197,24290123-
7582,00.html>. Accessed 29 July 2009.

85. Official website available at:
<http://www.australiamovie.com/
theatrical/>. Accessed 29 July 2009.

86. The results of the competition are not
known. If there was a winning project, it
did not appear on the first DVD version.

87. The *'Australia*: Meet the Filmmaker'
podcast is available free on iTunes.

88. See Mark Sweney, 'Film4 to show
"roadblock" ad breaks for Baz
Luhrmann's *Australia*', *Guardian* online
16 December 2008. Available at:
<http://www.guardian.co.uk/media/
2008/dec/15/film4-to-show-baz-
luhrmann-australia-ads>. Accessed
29 July 2009.

89. 'Strictly Baz: A Culture Show Special'
was broadcast in the UK on BBC2 at
10 pm on Tuesday, 9 December 2009.

90. Trailers, TV spots and featurette can be
viewed on the official website at:
<http://www.australiamovie.com/
theatrical/1>. Accessed 30 July 2009.

91. The quality newspaper the *Independent*
ran a competition tied in with
Australia's screening at the 2009
London Australian Film Festival and the
DVD/Blu-ray release (see 'Win a Canon
camera with your view of Australia',
Independent 9 February 2009. Available
online at: <http://www.independent.
co.uk/arts-entertainment/films/news/
win-a-canon-camera-with-your-view-

of-australia-1605022.html>. Accessed 30 July 2009). The *Sunday Times* issued a special supplement in association with Fox and Tourism Australia ('*Australia*: Epic Film, Epic Country', *Sunday Times* 7 December 2008). ITV's film slot 'ITV at the Movies' covered the London premiere in a six-minute featurette combining interviews with clips from the film (transmitted 10.30 pm, ITV2, 24 December 2008). Tabloid newspaper the *Sun* ran a competition tied in with the film's theatrical release (see 'Win an epic weekend away', *Sun* 22 December 2008. Available online at: <http://www.thesun.co.uk/sol/homepage/fun/competitions/article2051811.ece>. Accessed 30 July 2009).

92. See Kellie Hush, 'Get ready-to-wear Australia', *Age* 20 November 2008. Available online at: <http://www.theage.com.au/news/lifeandstyle/fashion/get-readytowear-australia/2008/11/19/1226770507083.html>. Accessed 30 July 2009.

93. See Sally Bennett, 'Baz Luhrmann's *Australia* set at ACMI exhibition', *Herald Sun* 10 December 2008. Available online at: <http://www.news.com.au/heraldsun/story/0,,24779333-5006023,00.html>. Accessed 30 July 2009.

94. 'Days of heaven', *Vogue* (US) July 2008, pp. 116–32. The feature can be viewed on the official website at: <http://www.australiamovie.com/theatrical/>. Accessed 30 July 2009. Leibovitz's video diary can be viewed in the Multimedia section of the *Australia*: A Baz Luhrmann Film website: <http://www.australiamovie.net/media/>. Accessed 30 July 2009.

95. See, for example, Jonathan Miles, 'You don't know Jackman', *Men's Journal* November 2008. Available online at: <http://www.mensjournal.com/jackman>. Accessed 30 July 2009.

96. See Eric Wilson, 'Socks to blouses, a film finds its look', *New York Times* 31 October 2008. Available online at: <http://www.nytimes.com/2008/11/02/movies/moviesspecial/02mart.html?_r=1>; 'The look of *Australia*' slide show available at: <http://www.nytimes.com/slideshow/2008/10/31/movies/20081102_MARTIN_SLIDESHOW_index.html?scp=1&sq=The%20'look'%20of%20Australia&st=cse>. Accessed 30 July 2009. Also Booth Moore, 'Film fashion: *Australia*'s costume vision', *LA Times* 4 December 2008. Available online at: <http://latimesblogs.latimes.com/alltherage/2008/12/film-fashion-au.html>. Accessed 30 July 2009. And Christopher Muther, 'Ensemble piece: *Australia* costume designer Catherine Martin stitches an epic tale together', *Boston Globe* 27 November 2008. Available online at: <http://www.boston.com/lifestyle/fashion/articles/2008/11/27/ensemble_piece/>. Accessed 30 July 2009.

97. See, for example, Susan King, 'Our big desire for epic films', *LA Times* 28 November 2008. Available online at: <http://articles.latimes.com/2008/nov/28/entertainment/et-epics28>. Accessed 30 July 2009.

98. See Matthew Benjamin and Miriam
     Steffans, ' "There's no hiding place –
     markets are in disarray": Murdoch',
     Sydney Morning Herald Business Day
     30 January 2009. Available online at:
     <http://business.smh.com.au/
     business/theres-no-hiding-place-
     markets-are-in-disarray-murdoch-
     20090129-7t1k.html?TB_iframe=
     true&height=800&width=1000>.
     Accessed 4 August 2009.

99. See Bodey, 'Tidal wave of marketing for
     Baz Luhrmann movie'. Also Michael
     Bodey, 'Abuzz about Baz in the bush',
     Australian 4 February 2009. Available
     online at: <http://www.theaustralian.
     news.com.au/story/0,25197,
     25004481-15803,00.html>. Accessed
     31 July 2009.

100. See 'Nic's Australian story', *Sunday
     Herald Sun* 2 November 2008; 'The girl
     from Oz', *Age* 2 November 2008.

101. See David Stratton, 'Baz Luhrmann's
     Australia is good, but not a master-
     piece', 18 November 2008. Available
     online at: <http://www.theaustralian.
     news.com.au/story/0,25197,24670334-
     601,00.html>. Accessed 31 July 2009.
     Jim Schembri, '*Australia* review: good,
     but no classic, and way, way too long',
     Canberra Times 18 November 2008.
     Available online at: <http://www.
     canberratimes.com.au/news/local/
     news/entertainment/australia-review-
     good-but-no-classic-and-way-way-
     too-long/1362949.aspx?storypage=1>.
     Accessed 31 July 2009. 'Mixed reviews
     for Baz's *Australia*', *ABC News* 18
     November 2008. Available online at:
     <http://www.abc.net.au/news/

     stories/2008/11/18/2423273.htm>.
     Accessed 31 July 2009.

102. See Andrew Bolt, 'Baz steals the
     president', *Herald Sun* 28 November
     2008. Available online at:
     <http://www.news.com.au/heraldsun/
     story/0,21985,24718189-
     500117,00.html>. Accessed 31 July
     2009. Paul Murray, 'Luhrmann's twists
     bend history out of shape', *West
     Australian* 4 December 2008. Available
     online at: <http://www.thewest.
     com.au/default.aspx?MenuID=
     9&ContentID=111546>. Accessed 31
     July 2009.

103. See Marcia Langton, 'Faraway Downs
     fantasy resonates close to home', *Age*
     23 November 2008. Available online at:
     <http://www.theage.com.au/news/
     entertainment/film/faraway-downs-
     fantasy-resonates-close-to-
     home/2008/11/23/1227375027931.
     html>. Accessed 3 August 2009;
     Germaine Greer, 'Baz Luhrmann's new
     film, *Australia*, takes too many liberties
     with history', *Guardian* 16 December
     2008. Available online (as 'Once upon
     a time in a land far, far away') at:
     <http://www.guardian.co.uk/film/
     2008/dec/16/baz-luhrmann-
     australia>. Accessed 3 August 2009;
     Marcia Langton, 'Aborigines have for
     too long been portrayed as victims',
     Guardian 23 December 2008. Available
     online at: <http://www.guardian.co.uk/
     commentisfree/2008/dec/23/australia-
     aborigines-race-issues-film> and (as
     'Why Greer is wrong on Australia') at:
     <http://www.theage.com.au/opinion/
     why-greer-is-wrong-on-australia-

20081222-73kk.html?page=-1>.
Accessed 3 August 2009.

104. See, for example, article and comments
on conservative website *American
Thinker*: Kidist Paulos Asrat, 'Australia:
whose land is it anyway?', 11 January
2009. Available at: <http://www.
americanthinker.com/2009/01/
australia_whose_land_is_it_any.html>.
Accessed 3 August 2009. And article
and comments on *Guardian* film blog:
David Thomson, 'Nicole Kidman is
queen of the flops', 8 December 2008.
Available at: <http://www.guardian.
co.uk/film/filmblog/2008/dec/08/
nicole-kidman-angelina-jolie>.
Accessed 3 August 2009.

105. See Roger Ebert, *'Australia'*, *Chicago
Sun-Times* 25 November 2008.
Available online at: <http://
rogerebert.suntimes.com/apps/
pbcs.dll/article?AID=/20081125/
REVIEWS/811259991>. Accessed
4 August 2009; Manohla Dargis,
'Australia (2008)', *New York Times*
26 November 2008. Available online at:
<http://movies.nytimes.com/2008/11/
26/movies/26aust.html>. Accessed
4 August 2009; Anne Thompson, 'Baz
Luhrmann's flair for the dramatic',
Variety 14 November 2008. Available
online at: <http://www.variety.com/
article/VR1117995925.html?
categoryid=2508&cs=1>. Accessed
4 August 2009.

106. See Todd McCarthy, *'Australia'*, *Variety*
19 November 2009. Available at:
<http://www.variety.com/review/
VE1117939080.html?categoryid=
31&cs=1>. Accessed 4 August 2009;

Kenneth Turan, *'Australia'*, *Los Angeles
Times* 26 November 2008. Available
online at: <http://articles.latimes.com/
2008/nov/26/entertainment/et-
australia26>. Accessed 4 August 2009;
Mick LaSalle, 'Movie review: one fair
lady meets Aussie cowboy', *San
Francisco Chronicle* 26 November 2008.
Available online at: <http://www.sfgate.
com/cgi-bin/article.cgi?f=/c/a/2008/
11/26/DDB714B4GG.DTL>. Accessed
4 August 2009; Sebastian Smee,
'Schlock on the barbie', *Boston Globe*
30 November 2008. Available at:
<http://www.boston.com/ae/movies/
articles/2008/11/30/schlock_on_the_
barbie/>. Accessed 4 August 2009.

107. See, for example, Jamie Lundborg,
'"Australia": four reasons to love the
embattled epic', *Entertainment Weekly*
8 December 2008. Available at:
<http://popwatch.ew.com/2008/12/
08/australia-hugh/>. Accessed
4 August 2009.

108. See Claire Harvey, 'Don't bet on
Australia', *Sunday Telegraph* [Sydney]
4 January 2009. Available at:
<http://www.dailytelegraph.com.au/
news/sunday-telegraph/dont-bet-on-
australia/story-e6frewto-
1111118468657>. Accessed 4 August
2009.

109. *Australia* won Satellite and Film Critics
Circle of Australia awards (see awards
history for Australia entry at IMDb:
<http://www.imdb.com/>. Accessed
4 August 2009).

110. See Michaela Boland, '"Australia" still
#1 down under', *Variety* 8 December
2008. Available at: <http://www.

variety.com/article/VR1117997048.
html?categoryid=1278&cs=1>. Accessed
4 August 2009. And Conor Bresnan,
'Around the world roundup: "Day"
remake opens quietly', *Box Office Mojo*
17 December 2008. Available at:
<http://boxofficemojo.com/news/
?id=2527&p=.htm>. Accessed 4 August
2009.

111. See Steven McElroy, ' "Earth Stood
Still" lands at top of box office', *New
York Times* 14 December 2008.
Available at: <http://www.nytimes.
com/2008/12/15/movies/15arts-
EARTHSTOODST_BRF.html>.
Accessed 4 August 2009.

112. See Ben Child, '*Australia* the
Thanksgiving turkey as *Four
Christmases* cleans up', *Guardian*
1 December 2008. Available at:
<http://www.guardian.co.uk/film/
2008/dec/01/four-christmases>; and
'Australians fail to warm to
Luhrmann's epic romance', *Guardian*
2 December 2008. Available at:
<http://www.guardian.co.uk/film/
2008/dec/02/baz-luhrmann-
australia>. Accessed 4 August 2009.

113. For example, Cosmo Landesman,
'*Australia*', *Sunday Times* 28 December
2008. Available at: <http://
entertainment.timesonline.co.uk/tol/
arts_and_entertainment/film/
article5403153.ece>. Accessed 4 August
2009. And Anne Barrowclough,
'Review: *Australia*, the movie', available
at: <http://entertainment.
timesonline.co.uk/tol/arts_and_
entertainment/film/article5178513.
ece>. Accessed 4 August 2009.

114. See David Thomson, 'Baz Luhrmann',
Guardian 12 December 2008. Available
at: <http://www.guardian.co.uk/film/
2008/dec/12/baz-luhrmann>. Accessed
4 August 2009. Philip Kemp,
'*Australia*', *Sight and Sound* 19 (2),
February 2009, pp. 48–9. Anthony
Quinn, '*Australia* (12A)', *Independent*
19 December 2008. Available at:
<http://www.independent.co.uk/
arts-entertainment/films/reviews/
australia-12a-1203514.html>. Accessed
4 August 2009. And Peter Bradshaw,
'*Australia*', *Guardian* 22 December
2008. Available at:
<http://www.guardian.co.uk/film/
2008/dec/22/baz-luhrmann-australia-
film>. Accessed 4 August 2009.

115. See Melanie Reid, 'Nicole Kidman
drifts about like a lost porcelain doll',
The Times 20 November 2008. Available
at: <http://www.timesonline.co.uk/
tol/comment/columnists/melanie_
reid/article5191828.ece>. Accessed
4 August 2009. Patrick Goldstein,
'Sorry, Nicole Kidman is no star', *Los
Angeles Times* 6 December 2008.
Available at: <http://articles.latimes.
com/2008/dec/06/entertainment/
et-bigpicture6>. Accessed 4 August
2009. And article and comments on
Guardian Film blog : David Thomson,
'Nicole Kidman is queen of the flops'.
For positive reviews see Manohla
Dargis, '*Australia* (2008)', and Elaine
Lipworth, 'Nicole Kidman: "I've been
through a lot in my life" ', *Independent* 5
December 2008. Available at:
<http://www.independent.co.uk/arts-
entertainment/films/features/

nicole-kidman-ive-been-through-a-lot-in-my-life-1051769.html>. Accessed 4 August 2009.

116. See Steven Zeitchik, '"Australia" director defends movie against critics', *Reuters* (UK) 19 December 2008. Available at: <http://www.reuters.com/article/entertainmentNews/idUSTRE4BI0I820081219>. Accessed 4 August 2009. And Glenn Milne, 'Film director Baz Luhrmann blasts Nicole Kidman critics', *Sunday Courier Mail* 24 January 2009. Available at: <http://www.news.com.au/couriermail/story/0,20797,24957742-5012980,00.html>. Accessed 4 August 2009.

117. See Michael Bodey, 'Abuzz about Baz in the bush'. *Australia* became the second-highest grossing film of all time at the Australian box office, surpassed only by *Crocodile Dundee* (1986) (see Michaela Boland, '"Australia" sets record down under', *Variety* 26 February 2009. Available at: <http://www.variety.com/article/VR1118000644.html?categoryid=19&cs=1> Accessed 4 August 2009).

118. See 'Baz Luhrmann's *Australia* to make a "small profit" for News Corporation', *Herald Sun* 6 February 2009. Available at: <http://www.news.com.au/business/story/0,27753,25015824-31037,00.html>. Accessed 4 August 2009.

119. See official movie website at: <http://www.australiamovie.com/>. Accessed 5 August 2009.

120. See Natasha Robinson, 'Baz Luhrmann's *Australia*'s takings are still growing steadily', *Australian* 4 April 2009. Available at: <http://www.theaustralian.news.com.au/story/0,,25286999-16947,00.html>. Accessed 5 August 2009.

121. Reported on the *Baz the Great!* fan website in the *Australia* DVD review, available at: <http://www.bazthegreatsite.com/australiamoviedvd.htm>. Accessed 5 August 2009.

122. Music videos available to view on the *Baz the Great!* fan website in the News Updates section, available at: <http://www.bazthegreatsite.com/newsupdates.htm>. Accessed 5 August 2009.

123. See Julian Lee, '*Australia* delivers publicity windfall', *Sydney Morning Herald Business Day* 18 June 2009. Available at: <http://business.smh.com.au/business/australia-delivers-publicity-windfall-20090617-chxf.html>. Accessed 5 August 2009.

124. See Melissa Singer, 'Baz or Hoges: who sells Australia best?', *Brisbane Times* 19 March 2009. Available at: <http://www.brisbane-times.com.au/news/travel/baz-or-hoges-who-sells-best/2009/03/19/1237054968025.html>. Accessed 5 August 2009.

125. See Zeitchik, '"Australia" director defends movie against critics'.

6 – DVD, the Internet and Nostalgia

1. See, for example, Barbara Klinger, *Beyond the Multiplex: Cinema, New*

Technologies, and the Home (Berkeley: University of California Press, 2006).

2. Klinger argues that there has been a huge rise in sales of home entertainment equipment over the last decade, with home cinema's penetration of the US market growing to 30 per cent in 2004 (Beyond the Multiplex, p. 23).

3. Hard figures are difficult to obtain. In her study of the impact of new technologies on Australian film culture, Deb Verhoeven argues that television and video, and increasingly DVD and the Internet, have had a significant impact on people's viewing habits, with the majority now experiencing films elsewhere than in cinemas. (See Verhoeven, 'Film and video', in Stuart Cunningham and Graeme Turner (eds), The Media and Communications in Australia (Netley: Allen & Unwin, 2002), pp. 168–9.)

4. See Verhoeven, 'Film and video', p. 171.

5. See Timothy Corrigan, 'The commerce of auteurism: a voice without authority', New German Critique 49, winter 1990, pp. 43–57.

6. Unless indicated otherwise, information about Baz Luhrmann is taken from interviews with the author at the House of Iona, 14 and 15 June 2005.

7. See also Chapter 1, p. 26.

8. In fact, the 'red room', which is a multipurpose space that houses Baz Luhrmann and Catherine Martin's memorabilia, including family photographs and newspaper clippings as well as trophies such as Oscars and BAFTAS.

9. See Svetlana Boym, The Future of Nostalgia (New York: Basic Books, 2001), pp. 49–55.

10. Boym, The Future of Nostalgia, pp. 345–55.

11. See M. Ackbar Abbas, Hong Kong: Culture and the Politics of Disappearance (Minneapolis: University of Minnesota Press, 1997); and Leela Gandhi, 'Review of Uncanny Australia', Meanjin, 57 (4), 1998. Both cited by Deb Verhoeven, 'Introduction: (pre) facing the nation', in Verhoeven (ed.), Twin Peeks: Australian and New Zealand Feature Films (Melbourne: Damned Publishing, 1999).

12. Details of the Advance Party project can be found at: <http://www.glasgowfilm.com/redroad/advance_party.html>. Accessed 18 August 2009.

13. Boym, The Future of Nostalgia, p. 349.

14. Boym, The Future of Nostalgia, p. 351.

15. Boym, The Future of Nostalgia, p. 350.

16. See, for example, Gareth Williams, Telling Tales: Fantasy and Fear in Contemporary Design (London: V&A Publishing, 2009).

17. See Tsvetan Todorov's much-debated analysis of the fantastic in The Fantastic: A Structural Approach to a Literary Genre (New York: Cornell University Press, 1975).

18. Sadly, this innovative website is no longer available. It was accessed at: <http://www.clubmoulinrouge.com/> at various times in 2004.

19. *Set to Screen* podcasts covering different aspects of *Australia*'s production process available at: <feed://www.apple.com/ podcasts/settoscreen/sts_baz_o8.xml>. Accessed 19 August 2009.

20. See Toby Miller, Nitin Govil, John McMurria and Richard Maxwell, *Global Hollywood* (London: BFI, 2001).

BIBLIOGRAPHY

The bibliography lists books and articles in books and journals cited in the text. References to press and online materials appear in the chapter notes.

Abbas, M. Ackbar. *Hong Kong: Culture and the Politics of Disappearance* (Minneapolis: University of Minnesota Press, 1997).

Adamek, Pauline. 'Baz Luhrmann's *William Shakespeare's Romeo and Juliet*', *Cinema Papers* 14, February 1997.

'AFI conversations on film: Jill Bilcock and Roger Savage on the making of Baz Luhrmann's *Romeo + Juliet*', *Metro* 113/114, 1998.

Arroyo, José. 'Kiss kiss bang bang', *Sight and Sound* 7 (3), March 1997.

Arroyo, José. 'Moulin Rouge review', *Sight and Sound* 11 (9), September 2001.

Bassett, Chris. '... And sprinkle it with fairy dust', *if MAG* 35, July 2001.

Baudrillard, Jean. 'Simulacra and simulations', in Mark Poster (ed.), *Jean Baudrillard: Selected Writings* (Stanford: Stanford University Press, 1988).

Bauer, Erik. 'Re-revealing Shakespeare: an interview with Baz Luhrmann', *Creative Screenwriting* 5 (2), 1998.

Bondanella, Peter. *The Cinema of Federico Fellini* (Princeton, NJ: Princeton University Press, 1992).

Bosley, Rachael K. 'Bohemian rhapsody', *American Cinematographer* 82 (6), June 2001.

Boym, Svetlana. *The Future of Nostalgia* (New York: Basic Books, 2001).

Champagne, John. 'Dancing queen? Feminist and gay male spectator-ship in three recent films from Australia', *Film Criticism* 21 (3), Spring 1997.

Chumo II, Peter N. 'Craig Pearce/*Moulin Rouge!*', *Creative Screenwriting* 37, May/June 2001.

Collins, Felicity and Davis, Therese. *Australian Cinema After Mabo* (Cambridge and Melbourne: Cambridge University Press, 2004).

Cook, Pam. *I Know Where I'm Going!* (London: BFI, 2002).

Cook, Pam. 'Rethinking nostalgia: *In the Mood for Love* and *Far From Heaven*', in *Screening the Past: Memory and Nostalgia in Cinema* (Oxford and New York: Routledge, 2005).

Corrigan, Timothy. 'The commerce of auteurism: a voice without authority', *New German Critique* 49, Winter 1990, pp. 43–57.

Donaldson, Peter S. ' "In fair Verona": media, spectacle and performance in *William Shakespeare's Romeo + Juliet*', in Richard Burt (ed.), *Shakespeare After Mass Media* (New York and London: Palgrave Macmillan, 2002).

Doty, Alexander. *Making Things Perfectly Queer: Interpreting Mass Culture* (Minneapolis, University of Minnesota Press, 1993).

Downing, Crystal. 'Misshapen chaos of well-seeming form: Baz Luhrmann's *Romeo + Juliet*', *Literature/Film Quarterly* 28 (2), 2000.

Dyer, Richard. *Pastiche: Knowing Imitation* (Oxford and New York: Routledge, 2006).

Eco, Umberto. *Travels in Hyperreality* (New York: Harcourt Brace & Company, 1986).

French, Lisa. 'Patterns of production and policy: the Australian film industry in the 1990s', in Ian Craven (ed.), *Australian Cinema in the 1990s* (Melbourne: Taylor & Francis, 2001).

Freud, Sigmund. 'Formulations on the two principles of mental functioning', in James Strachey (ed.), *Standard Edition of Complete Psychological Works, Vol. XII* (London: Hogarth Press, 1961).

Fuller, Graham. 'Strictly red', *Sight and Sound* 11 (6), June 2001.

Gandhi, Leela. 'Review of Uncanny Australia', *Meanjin* 57 (4), 1998.

Gibson, Ross. 'Yondering: a reading of *Mad Max Beyond Thunderdome*', in *South of the West: Postcolonialism and the Narrative Construction of Australia* (Bloomington: Indiana University Press, 1992).

Gledhill, Christine (ed.). *Home Is Where the Heart Is: Studies in Melodrama and the Woman's Film* (London: BFI, 1987).

Guback, Thomas H. 'Hollywood's international market', in Tino Balio (ed.), *The American Film Industry* (Madison: University of Wisconsin Press, 1985).

Gunning, Tom. 'The cinema of attractions: early film, its spectator and the avant-garde', in Thomas Elsaesser and Adam Barker (eds), *Early Cinema: Space, Frame, Narrative* (London: BFI, 1990).

Gunning, Tom. 'An aesthetic of astonishment: early film and the [in]credulous spectator', in Linda Williams (ed.), *Viewing Positions: Ways of Seeing Film* (New Brunswick, NJ: Rutgers University Press, 1995).

Hamilton, Lucy. 'Baz vs the bardolaters, or why *William Shakespeare's Romeo + Juliet* deserves another look', *Literature/Film Quarterly* 28 (2), 2000.

Harden, Fred. 'Characterizing Mr Storm … and other stories', *Cinema Papers* 14, February 1997.

Hoorn, Jeanette. 'Michael Powell's *They're a Weird Mob*: dissolving the "undigested fragments" in the Australian body politic', *Continuum: Journal of Media and Cultural Studies*, 17 (2), 2003.

James, Nick. '*Moulin Rouge*', *Sight and Sound* 11 (7), July 2001.

Jameson, Fredric. 'Postmodernism, or, the cultural logic of late capitalism', in Thomas Docherty (ed.), *Postmodernism: A Reader* (New York: Columbia University Press, 1993).

Jones, Kent. 'Real artifice', *Film Comment* 37 (3), May/June 2001.

Kemp, Philip. '*Australia* review', *Sight and Sound* 19 (2), February 2009.

Kennedy, Colin. 'Torch song trilogy', *Empire* 148, October 2002.

Kinder, Marsha. '*Moulin Rouge*', *Film Quarterly* 55 (3), 2002.

King, Geoff. *Indiewood USA: Where Hollywood Meets Independent Cinema* (London: I. B. Tauris, 2008).

Klinger, Barbara. 'Mass camp and the old Hollywood melodrama today', in *Melodrama and Meaning: History, Culture, and the Films of Douglas Sirk* (Bloomington: Indiana University Press, 1994).

Klinger, Barbara. *Beyond the Multiplex: Cinema, New Technologies, and the Home* (Berkeley: University of California Press, 2006).

Kole, Robert. 'Shakespeare on film: *Romeo and Juliet*', *Shakespeare Bulletin*, Summer 1997.

Koppl, Rudy. '*Moulin Rouge*', *Music from the Movies* 33, May 2002.

Lehmann, Courtney. 'Strictly Shakespeare? Dead letters, ghostly fathers, and the cultural pathology of authorship in Baz Luhrmann's "William Shakespeare's Romeo + Juliet"', *Shakespeare Quarterly* 52 (2), Summer 2001.

Luhrmann, Baz and Pearce, Craig. *Strictly Ballroom* (Strawberry Hills, NSW: Currency Press, 1992).

Luhrmann, Baz and Martin, Catherine. 'Foreword', in *Moulin Rouge! A Film Directed By Baz Luhrmann* (London: Pan Macmillan, 2001).

Macnab, Geoffrey. *J. Arthur Rank and the British Film Industry* (London and New York: Routledge, 1993).

Maltby, Richard. 'Nobody knows everything: post-classical historiographies and consolidated entertainment', in Neale and Smith (eds), *Contemporary Hollywood Cinema*.

McFarlane, Brian. '*Strictly Ballroom*: old stories, new images', *mETAphor: Journal of the Australian English Teachers' Association* 3, July 2000.

Michôd, David. '*Moulin Rouge*: the script', *if MAG* 33, May 2001.

Miller, Toby, Govil, Nitin, McMurria, John and Maxwell, Richard. *Global Hollywood*, (London: BFI, 2001).

Mulvey, Laura. 'Notes on Sirk and melodrama', in *Visual and Other Pleasures* (London and New York: Palgrave Macmillan, 2009).

Ndalianis, Angela. *Neo-Baroque Aesthetics and Contemporary Entertainment* (Cambridge, MA: MIT Press, 2004).

Neale, Steve and Smith, Murray (eds). *Contemporary Hollywood Cinema* (London and New York: Routledge, 1998).

Nowell-Smith, Geoffrey. 'Minnelli and melodrama', in Gledhill (ed.), *Home Is Where the Heart Is*.

'Oh la la! Behind the making of *Moulin Rouge!*', *HQ*, May 2001.

O'Regan, Tom. *Australian National Cinema* (London and New York: Routledge, 1996).

Pearson, Roberta E. *Eloquent Gestures: The Transformation of Performance Style in the Griffith Biograph Films* (Berkeley: University of California Press, 1992).

Pisters, Patricia. '"Touched by a cardboard sword": aesthetic creation and non-personal subjectivity in *Dancer in the Dark* & *Moulin Rouge*', in Joost de Bloois, Sjef Houppermans and Frans-Willem Korsten (eds), *Discern(e)ments: Deleuzian Aesthetics* (Amsterdam: Rodopi, 2004).

Quinn, Karl. 'Drag, dags and the suburban surreal', *Metro* 100, Summer 1995/6.

Schamus, James. 'To the rear of the back end: the economics of independent cinema', in Neale and Smith (eds), *Contemporary Hollywood Cinema*.

Smith, Bec. '*Moulin Rouge*', *if MAG* 33, May 2001.

Stanivukovic, Goran V. '"Mounting above the truthe": on hyperbole in English renaissance literature', *Forum for Modern Language Studies* 43 (1), 2007.

Stratton, Jon. *Race Daze: Australia in Identity Crisis* (Sydney: Pluto Press, 1998).

Swartz, David. *Culture and Power: The Sociology of Pierre Bourdieu* (Chicago: University of Chicago Press, 1997).

Todorov, Tsvetan. *The Fantastic: A Structural Approach to a Literary Genre* (New York: Cornell University Press, 1975).

Turk, Rachael. 'Children of the digital revolution', *Metro* 129/130, Spring 2001.

Turner, Graeme. *Making It National: Nationalism and Australian Popular Culture* (Sydney: Allen & Unwin, 1994).

Verhoeven, Deb. 'Introduction: (pre) facing the nation', in Verhoeven (ed.), *Twin Peeks*.

Verhoeven, Deb (ed.). *Twin Peeks: Australian and New Zealand Feature Films* (Melbourne: Damned Publishing [Australian Catalogue Co.], 1999).

Verhoeven, Deb. 'Film and video', in Stuart Cunningham and Graeme Turner (eds), *The Media and Communications in Australia* (Netley: Allen & Unwin, 2002).

Walker, Elsie. 'Pop goes the Shakespeare: Baz Luhrmann's *William Shakespeare's Romeo + Juliet*', *Literature/Film Quarterly* 28 (2), 2000.

Wayne, Michael. 'Working Title Mark II: a critique of the atlanticist paradigm for British cinema', *International Journal of Media and Cultural Politics* 2 (1), January 2006.

Welsh, Jim. 'Postmodern Shakespeare: Strictly Romeo', *Literature/Film Quarterly* 25 (2), April 1997.

Williams, Gareth. *Telling Tales: Fantasy and Fear in Contemporary Design* (London: V&A Publishing, 2009).

William Shakespeare's Romeo & Juliet: The Contemporary Film, The Classic Play (New York: Bantam Doubleday Dell, 1996).

Worthen, W. B. 'Drama, performativity, and performance', *PMLA* 113, October 1998.

Wyatt, Justin. *High Concept: Movies and Marketing in Hollywood* (Austin: University of Texas Press, 1994).

Wyatt, Justin. 'The formation of the "major independent": Miramax, New Line and the new Hollywood', in Neale and Smith (eds), *Contemporary Hollywood Cinema*.

THE WORKS

Feature films

Strictly Ballroom (1992)
Director: Baz Luhrmann
Screenplay: Baz Luhrmann, Craig Pearce
Production company: M&A Film
    Corporation
Producer: Tristram Miall
Production design: Catherine Martin,
    Martin Brown
Costumes: Angus Strathie
Cinematography: Steve Mason
Music: David Hirschfelder
Editing: Jill Bilcock
Cast: Paul Mercurio, Tara Morice, Bill
    Hunter, Pat Thomson, Barry Otto,
    Antonio Vargas, Armonia Benedito
Running time: 94 minutes
Colour

William Shakespeare's Romeo + Juliet (1996)
Director, producer: Baz Luhrmann
Screenplay: Baz Luhrmann, Craig Pearce
Production company: 20th Century-
    Fox
Producer: Martin Brown, Gabriella
    Martinelli
Costumes: Kym Barrett
Production design: Catherine Martin
Cinematography: Donald M. McAlpine
Music: Nellee Hooper

Editor: Jill Bilcock
Cast: Leonardo DiCaprio, Claire
    Danes, John Leguizamo, Harold
    Perrineau, Pete Postlethwaite,
    Miriam Margolyes
Running time: 120 minutes
Colour

Moulin Rouge! (2001)
Director, producer: Baz Luhrmann
Screenplay: Baz Luhrmann, Craig Pearce
Production companies: 20th Century-
    Fox, Bazmark
Producer: Fred Baron, Martin Brown
Costumes: Catherine Martin, Angus
    Strathie
Production design: Catherine Martin
Cinematography: Donald M. McAlpine
Music: Craig Armstrong
Editor: Jill Bilcock
Cast: Nicole Kidman, Ewan McGregor,
    John Leguizamo, Jim Broadbent,
    Richard Roxburgh, Jacek Koman
Running time: 127 minutes
Colour

Australia (2008)
Director, producer: Baz Luhrmann
Screenplay: Baz Luhrmann, Stuart
    Beattie, Ronald Harwood, Richard
    Flanagan

Production companies: 20th Century-
  Fox, Dune Entertainment, Bazmark
Producers: G. Mac Brown, Catherine
  Knapman
Costumes: Catherine Martin
Production design: Catherine Martin,
  Ian Gracie
Cinematography: Mandy Walker
Music: David Hirschfelder
Editors: Dody Dorn, Michael McCusker
Cast: Nicole Kidman, Hugh Jackman,
  Bryan Brown, David Wenham, David
  Gulpilil, Brandon Walters, Jacek
  Koman, David Ngoombujarra, Jack
  Thompson
Running time: 165 minutes
Colour

Commercials

No. 5 The Film (2004) (Advertising film
  for Chanel No. 5 perfume)
Director, producer, writer: Baz
  Luhrmann
Production companies: Revolver Film,
  Bazmark
Executive producer: Anton Monsted
Costumes: Karl Lagerfeld, Catherine
  Martin
Production design: Catherine Martin
Cinematography: Mandy Walker
Music ('Clair de lune' by Claude
  Debussy) arranged by Craig
  Armstrong
Editor: Daniel Schwarze
Cast: Nicole Kidman, Rodrigo Santoro
Running time: 3 minutes
Colour

Come Walkabout (2008) (Two
  advertising films, set in New York
  and Shanghai, for Tourism
  Australia)
Creative director: Baz Luhrmann
Production companies: Bazmark,
  Revolver Film
Director: Bruce Hunt
Producer: Michael Ritchie
Costumes: Eliza Godman
Production design: Karen Murphy
Cinematography: Mandy Walker
Music: Elliot Wheeler
Editor: Drew Thompson
Cast: Brandon Walters
Running time: 1 minute 30 seconds
Colour

Music videos/clips

'Beat Me Daddy, Eight to the Bar'
  (1987)
Director: Baz Luhrmann
Performed by Ignatius Jones, Pardon
  Me Boys

'Love Is in the Air' (1992)
Producer: M&A
Director: Baz Luhrmann
Performed by John Paul Young

'Time After Time' (1992)
Producer: M&A
Director: Baz Luhrmann

'Young Hearts Run Free' (1996)
Director: Baz Luhrmann
Performed by Harold Perrineau

'Kissing You' (1996)
Director: Baz Luhrmann
Performed by Des'ree

'Now Until the Break of Day' (1997)
Director: Baz Luhrmann
Performed by Christine Anu,
    David Hobson, Royce Doherty,
    Café at the Gates of Salvation
    gospel choir

'Lady Marmalade' (2001)
Director: Baz Luhrmann
Performed by Christina Aguilera, Lil'
    Kim, Mýa, Pink

'One Day I'll Fly Away' (2001)
Director: Baz Luhrmann
Performed by Nicole Kidman

'Come What May' (2001)
Director: Baz Luhrmann
Performed by Nicole Kidman, Ewan
    McGregor

'Waltzing Matilda' (2008)
Producer: Bazmark
Performed by Ophelia of the Spirits

'By the Boab Tree' (2009)
Producer: Bazmark
Performed by Ophelia of the Spirits

Main theatre productions

Strictly Ballroom (1984). 30-minute
    stage play
Co-deviser, writer, performer,
    director: Baz Luhrmann

Strictly Ballroom (1986). 50-minute
    stage play
Co-deviser, writer, performer,
    director: Baz Luhrmann

Crocodile Creek (1986). Community
    theatre musical production
Co-deviser, director: Baz Luhrmann

Lake Lost (1988). Experimental opera
    for Australian Opera
Co-deviser, director: Baz Luhrmann
Costumes: Catherine Martin
Sets: Angus Strathie
Music: Felix Meagher

Haircut (1988). Reworking of musical
    Hair staged by Six Years Old theatre
    company
Co-deviser, director: Baz Luhrmann

Strictly Ballroom (1988). Revised stage
    play
Director: Baz Luhrmann
Screenplay: Baz Luhrmann, Craig
    Pearce

Dance Hall (1989). 1940s-themed
    musical event for Sydney Festival
Co-deviser, director: Baz Luhrmann
Costumes and sets: Catherine Martin

La Bohème (1990). Opera for
    Australian Opera staged at Sydney
    Opera House
Director: Baz Luhrmann
Costumes and sets: Catherine Martin

A Midsummer Night's Dream (1993).
Hindu version of Benjamin Britten's
opera, set in colonial India, for
Australian Opera
Director: Baz Luhrmann
Sets and costumes: Catherine Martin.

La Bohème (2002). Broadway
production
Director: Baz Luhrmann
Costumes and sets: Catherine Martin

Main DVD editions

William Shakespeare's Romeo + Juliet
special edition DVD (2002).
Designer: Bazmark
Producer: Baz Luhrmann
Issued by Fox Home Entertainment

Moulin Rouge! two-disc DVD (2002).
Designer: Bazmark
Producer: Baz Luhrmann
Issued by Fox Home Entertainment

Baz Luhrmann's Red Curtain Trilogy
four-disc boxed set (2002, regions 1
and 4 only).
Designer: Bazmark
Producer: Baz Luhrmann
Issued by Fox Home Entertainment

William Shakespeare's Romeo + Juliet
tenth anniversary music edition
(2007).
Designer: Bazmark
Issued by Fox Home Entertainment

Music

First *William Shakespeare's Romeo +
Juliet* soundtrack CD (1996)
Co-producer: Baz Luhrmann

Second *Romeo + Juliet* soundtrack CD
with orchestral score (1997)
Producer: Bazmark
Co-producer: Baz Luhrmann

'Something for Everybody' album CD
(1998)
Producer: Bazmark/Baz Luhrmann

'Everybody's Free (To Wear Sunscreen)'
spoken-word single CD (1999)
Producer: Baz Luhrmann

First *Moulin Rouge!* soundtrack CD
(2001)
Producer: BLAM
Co-producer: Baz Luhrmann

Second *Moulin Rouge!* soundtrack CD
with added material (2002)
Producer: BLAM
Co-producer: Baz Luhrmann

Australia soundtrack album published
on iTunes, with digital booklet
(2009)
Producer: Bazmark

Live events

Australian Labor Party televised re-
election campaign launch (1993)
Deviser/producer: Baz Luhrmann

Australian fashion designer Collette
   Dinnigan's Autumn/Winter
   collection staged at the Louvre, Paris
Director: Catherine Martin
Producer: Bazmark

Events celebrating opening of Fox
   Australia new studio development
   (1998)
Deviser/producer: Baz Luhrmann
Producer: Bazmark

Opening musical number for 81st
   Academy Awards (2009)
Director/producer: Baz Luhrmann

Other

Kids of the Cross (1981)
Television docu-drama
Deviser, co-director, performer: Baz
   Luhrmann
Australian *Vogue* (January 1994)
Guest editor with Catherine Martin and
   Bill Marron
Series of ten *Set to Screen* podcasts in
   conjunction with Apple about the
   making of *Australia*.
   April–November 2008
Producer: Bazmark
Director/performer: Baz Luhrmann

INDEX

Films listed by title are by Baz Luhrmann unless stated otherwise. Page numbers in **bold** indicate detailed analysis; those in *italics* denote illustrations. *n* = endnote.